U.S. Foreign Policy and the Other

U.S. Foreign Policy and the Other

Edited by
Michael Patrick Cullinane and David Ryan

berghahn
NEW YORK · OXFORD
www.berghahnbooks.com

First edition published in 2015 by

Berghahn Books

www.berghahnbooks.com

Library of Congress Cataloging-in-Publication Data

U.S. foreign policy and the other / edited by Michael Patrick Cullinane and David
Ryan.
        p. cm.
    Includes bibliographical references and index.
    ISBN 978-1-78238-439-7 (hardback : alk. paper) — ISBN 978-1-78533-350-7
    (paperback) — ISBN 978-1-78238-440-3 (ebook)
    1. United States—Foreign relations—Social aspects. 2. Other (Philosophy)
I. Cullinane, Michael Patrick, 1979– author, editor of compilation. II. Ryan,
David, 1965– author, editor of compilation.
    E183.7.U815 2014
    327.73—dc23

                                                                2014018764

British Library Cataloguing in Publication Data

A catalogue record for this book is available from the British Library

ISBN: 978-1-78238-439-7 hardback
ISBN: 978-1-78533-350-7 paperback
ISBN: 978-1-78238-440-3 ebook

Contents

Introduction

Michael Patrick Cullinane and David Ryan

After World War II, U.S. identity faced severe dilemmas. Its constructed image—the power, the arsenal for democracy, representing liberty, self-determination, and economic liberalism—found itself closely allied with and cooperating with a range of European colonial empires reluctant to cede power in Asia and Africa. Moreover, Washington was quick to cultivate a dualistic image of the world, positing two ways of life that represented a defining choice in world history.

That construction was advanced in the Truman Doctrine of 1947 and elided the ties with European colonialism as it focused on the new other, the Soviet Union. The Cold War constructions pervaded U.S. foreign policy until the early 1990s, with significant disruption in the early 1970s during the era of détente and multipolarity brought on by the recovery of Europe and Japan and the consolidation of Chinese power. The polycentric world was constantly challenged by peripheral powers, nationalist movements, and revolutionaries that did not always move in tune with a superpower, but in pursuit of their own local and indigenous agendas.[1] Even as superpower tensions rose again in the late 1970s and then when Reagan entered the White House, the multipolar world remained, but Reagan's discourse and foreign policy agendas worked to ignore the changed context.[2]

This discourse and Manichaean outlook recurred frequently in the history of U.S. foreign policy. Eisenhower's National Security Council considered the dilemma on the eve of Africa's decolonization in 1957. The resulting policy document (NSC 5719) illustrated the conundrum:

> Premature independence would be as harmful to our interests in Africa as would be a continuation of nineteenth century colonialism, and we must tailor our policies to the capabilities and needs of each particular area as well as to our over-all relations with the metropolitan power concerned. It should be noted that all the metropolitan powers are associated with us in the NATO alliance or in military base agreements.[3]

Notes for this chapter begin on page 13.

The document's policy guidance section suggested that Washington support the principle of self-determination; however, it stressed that such a reality incurred associated responsibilities. It noted care should be taken to "avoid U.S. identification with those policies of the metropolitan powers, which are stagnant or repressive, and, to the extent practicable, seek effective means of influencing the metropolitan powers to abandon or modify such policies." And, for good measure, "emphasize through all appropriate media the colonial policies of the Soviet Union and particularly the fact that the Soviet colonial empire has continued to expand throughout the period when Western colonialism has been contracting."[4]

Such *alterity* has frequently played a defining role in the manufacturing of U.S. foreign policy. As a term, originated in the early 1970s, alterity refers to the construction of an "other" in juxtaposition to the "self." It is vitally important to reiterate that the "other" that is described, defined, and articulated by the various policy makers rests on a discourse that is constructed largely within U.S. culture and its ideological sphere of influence. Those depictions do not actually describe the detailed, multilayered, textured features of the cultures under consideration, cultures that are situated in both time and space and made up of a multiplicity of different influences, stories, myths, flavors, images, and so forth. The importance of the discourse of alterity is its ability to simplify and to remove the culture of its complexity, its position in historical time, place, and geographical location. So in our cases the constructions of alterity largely emanating in U.S. political and cultural discourse do not seek, as perhaps an anthropologist might, the detail and insight into other cultures, but create a simplified depiction of the Indian, the European, the Nazi, and the Communist, and of Islam. They are discourses that resonate in U.S. culture because they not only attempt to depict the other, from afar and above, but also to sharpen U.S. identity through its difference and its long-held notions of exceptionalism. It works most effectively in stark depictions of a "threat" that can solidify the meaning of U.S. identity, juxtaposing the "self" against an enemy "other." For instance, the United States identified itself in contrast to the Communist threat. The poignancy of Martin Luther King, Jr.'s rhetoric on freedom during the Vietnam War and within the context of the U.S. Civil Rights movement undermined the Cold War constructions of U.S. identity; yet without any trace of irony or historical context President Reagan deployed the language of freedom in opposition to the evil Soviet empire. There is thus a "social space" of who is included and excluded in such identity politics and a notion of superiority and inferiority running through such discourse.[5]

It is essential to remember that Edward Said's *Orientalism,* and later his *Culture and Imperialism,* did not try to depict the other; instead they set about deconstructing the Western discourse on the Orient or more correctly the West's construction of the Orient. It is, according to Arshin Adib-Moghaddam's reading of Said, "the product of ideological fiction with no real linkage to the cultures and peoples it claims to explain." Or as Said emphasized, over and over again in response to criticism, the "line separating Occident from Orient ... is less a fact of nature than it is a fact of human production" that lies in what he calls "imaginative geography." This imaginative geography is removed and distinct from the actual culture set in time and place, whether the Middle East, the Sandinistas and the Nicaraguans, the Soviets of the 1940s, or the Nazis of the 1930s, and extends back to the discourse on the "savage" within and outside colonial, antebellum, and Gilded Age America. The discourse relates to the epistemology and construction of knowledge that is closely related to the powers of production both cultural and material, rather than the ontology of the culture, people, or "threat" under consideration.[6]

In part, these discourses have informed the implementation of foreign policies. The importance of discourse rests in the symbolic patterns "that reflect and form societal ideals and views of the international environment."[7] Certainly the attitudes of key protagonists and authors of strategy papers have succumbed to what Edward Said popularized as orientalism. For instance, the Monroe Doctrine and its influence on subsequent U.S. foreign policy are characterized by elements of orientalism. It set up tendencies of thought, a familiar mind-set, intellectual paths along which subsequent politicians and generations would feel comfortable as they confronted a bewildering and incoherent world. This dualistic tendency exists at the conceptual level. Two abstract spheres of influence, entities and identities that are not necessarily the repository of the characteristics ascribed to them, have been created in speech and subsequent discourse. The notions of "new" and "old" worlds are concepts deployed for political purposes rather than effective descriptions of the Americas and Europe. Too much empirical detail and historical specificity belie such conceptual identities. Said's initial objection was that, as a system of thought, orientalism approached a diverse and heterogeneous world, fixed it in time, and ascribed to political entities enduring essences that cannot be substantiated in history. Furthermore, Said suggests the tendency to regard the other from afar and from above is evident in the doctrine and the discourse. Foreign policy scholar Michael Hunt has demonstrated in *Ideology and U.S. Foreign Policy* that the projection of U.S. identity and the paternalism of its foreign policies extended throughout its history.[8] Despite the deconstruction of orientalism and its application to U.S. foreign policy, one also frequently sees it at work, advanced by various presidents and political commentators to elicit a certain cultural effect.[9] President Monroe drew a mental geography of two worlds divided in space by the Atlantic Ocean and concurrently on the differences between republicanism and various forms of authoritarianism or monarchy. Such an approach resonated through the future to the present.

Let's start in the near present. Soon after 9/11 the Bush administration engaged in a series of speeches that conflated various "others" into a singular "other." Al Qaeda, the Taliban, and soon after, Saddam Hussein, were joined together in the terrifying and comforting phrase advanced at West Point in June 2002: "the terrorists and the tyrants."[10] The first conflation provided comfort and definition that paved the way to Afghanistan; the second represented what John Dower has called "strategic imbecility."[11] President Bush was predisposed to view the challenges the United States faced before 9/11 in such dualistic terms.[12]

One hundred eighty years before the terrorist attacks of 9/11 and President Bush's response—in 1821—John Quincy Adams warned Americans not to search abroad for monsters to destroy, yet such figures have frequently inhabited the discourses of U.S. foreign policy.[13] The existence of an alter ego or other has been vital to U.S. social cohesion and domestic mobilization despite publics that are sometimes reluctant to engage in the world. It is not peculiar to the United States. Edward Said writes, "throughout the exchange between Europeans and their 'others' that began systematically half a millennium ago, the one idea that has scarcely varied is that there is an 'us' and a 'them,' each quite settled, clear, unassailably self-evident."[14] Such dichotomies run through U.S. diplomacy from the Monroe Doctrine, creating conceptual dualities in the old and the new world, in the Truman Doctrine, positing the existence of two ways of life, which was often welcomed because it made U.S. culture more cohesive.

The Cold War sustained that conceptual divide and enhanced that world view, even though actualities were always far more complex, but such complications and contingency do not have the same appeal. The boldness of an overarching depiction or thesis that can explain the broad geopolitical situation, marrying as it does an intellectual concept with a spatial image, is enticing. After the Cold War, the two articles that invoked the most comment on foreign policy were Francis Fukuyama's "End of History" thesis and Samuel Huntington's "Clash of Civilizations." Fukuyama's thesis lacked discussion of the other, which had been transcended with the end of the Cold War.[15] Though widely criticized, Huntington provided a reference point for many Americans as they searched for the overarching meaning of 9/11. The formula was echoed in President Bush's rhetoric when he explained, "either you are with us, or you are with the terrorists."[16] The admonition obscured the arguments on war in Afghanistan but also found multiple echoes throughout U.S. culture.

As Said suggested, "the basic paradigm of West versus the rest (the cold war opposition reformulated) remained untouched, and this is what has persisted, often insidiously and implicitly, in discussion since the terrible events of 9/11."[17]

More examples from other periods are not hard to find. The Inquiry documents produced at the closing of World War I as the Wilson administration considered its position in the world are similarly revealing. One document, number 137, written by Leon Dominian on the "Mohammedan World," is illustrative of the kinds of depictions studied more systematically by Douglas Little, Melani McAlister, Edward Said, Michael Hunt, James William Park, Arshin Adib-Moghaddam, and in the literature on race and U.S. foreign policy.[18] Dominian represented the Mohammaden world as geographically arching from the northwest of Africa to "China and the Dutch East Indies … A chafing of the Mohammaden spirit," he reported, was "observable everywhere." They resented the foreign powers and their ways were incompatible "with the spirit of modern progress." In sum, "[h]e is generally bigoted and inclined to be violent in word and deed against non-Mohammedans."[19] This tone prevails through the seventy-two-page report.

The language of racial hierarchies, civilization, and barbarism were no longer culturally acceptable in public discourse later in the twentieth century; instead, the discourse on development, modernity, and tradition replaced the old forms of depiction, though the hierarchy was frequently the same.[20] One could skip several decades and still detect the sentiment in such strategic papers as NSC 5801, "Long Range U.S. Policy toward the Near East." This top secret document opined that the "area's indigenous institutions and religions lack vigor (partly as a result of the impact of nearly 200 years of Western culture), and native resistance to Communism *per se* has, therefore, been disappointing. Furthermore, Communist police-state methods seem no worse than similar methods employed by Near East regimes, including some of those supported by the United States." Despite conclusions similar to those in the Inquiry document that the United States enjoyed some respect in the region generated through its presence in educational institutions, its "philanthropic … efforts," the respect for its military power, "our own revolutionary tradition and our identification with the principle of self-determination," U.S. wealth, and the country's science and technology, NSC 5801 concludes that "there are no basic impediments of personality, background or culture to the establishment and maintenance of close personal friendships between the peoples of the Near East and Americans." Yet it did identify certain political problems; the Israeli-Palestinian conflict, as well as the "continuing and necessary association of the United States in the Western European Alliance makes it impossible for us to avoid some identification with the powers which formerly had, and still have, 'colonial' interests in the areas."[21]

McAlister argues for scholars to move beyond orientalism. The primary problem is that orientalism "fundamentally depends on the presumption that the 'us' of the West is, or is perceived to be, a homogenous entity." Yet the diversity within the nation and the narratives of nationalism have always been more diverse than Said acknowledges.[22] Certainly, McAlister's work centered on the politics of cultural production captures some of the ambivalence of the fear, loathing, attraction, and desire that is going on in U.S. depictions of the Arab world but also in various Arab views of the United States. In that sense it feeds into the not-so-recent turn in American Studies.[23] Said believed that his work merely represented the essences that existed in cultures in time and space.[24] The difference relates to the degree of fluidity and identity within the cultures. It is important to emphasize here that such claims are dealing with dominating discourses that shape and influence structures of thought or "truth regimes," but that they frequently have a very loose relationship with the subjects with which they deal. In that regard, while the internal analysis of the Monroe, Truman, Reagan, or Bush presidencies was no doubt far more informed on particulars and actualities, the overarching discourse that they employed created truth regimes that affected the public discourse and understanding, which in turn affected domestic debate and expectations and informed the questions of credibility surrounding their administrations.

There is still the importance of the rhetorical depiction and the return to the simpler view of the other as somewhat homogenous. Fabian Hilfrich's reading of the American visions of the Asian periphery is instructive on this. He compares the visions of Vietnam in the mid 1960s with the U.S. acquisition of the Philippines in 1898 to conclude that the Cold War, though important, did not solely determine American views. The rhetorical construct that became the domino theory was important because it was built on a geographical premise coupled with a psychological injunction that moved from the local to the regional and on to the universal. So, the movement in thought is one that passed through concentric circles, none of which related to the importance of the country in question, but rather related more to the U.S. vision of itself. That is, the fear of losing Vietnam (through the narratives of geography, credibility, commitment, and U.S. leadership) pass through the concentric circles to the regional concerns with Southeast Asia and the Pacific, through the logic of the domino theory; "in the outer circle, the psychological domino theory extended the significance of a defeat in South Vietnam to the world, for it spelled the loss of confidence in the United States and, by encouraging the enemies of the United States, the onset of a wider war."[25] Thus ultimately, the construction suggested that their worldview "remained anchored in the mon- umental conflict between barbarism and civilization, much as the domino theory relied on the binary opposition of democracy and communism."[26]

While Said's approach to orientalism has been criticized for its exclu- sion of the voices of the other, in his attempt to demonstrate and decon- struct the series of western homogenizing constructions, Heller contends that Said also essentializes the West. It is not only essentialized but simul- taneously is presented as having the power and the ability to define the other. Similarly, Christopher Browning and Marko Lehti contend, "whilst the West is constructed as an unproblematic unified acting subject, the outside (the Orient) is presented as largely passive and reactive, as unable to (in turn) act back and assert constitutive power of its own."[27] Andrew Rotter argues that this is quite problematic for diplomatic historians: "Said most emphatically subverts what historians try to do by confounding the idea of the subject. In *Orientalism,* the 'Orient' exists only as a useful cre- ation of the West, a projection of Western desire and fear, a subject without its own identity. There is no who there."[28]

Indeed, Said insists on the relationship between ideas and power. The Orient was orientalized precisely because it could be, especially in the nineteenth century, "through varying degrees of complex hegemony"; it "submitted to being—made Oriental." Said is quick to argue that there is very little consent to be found in Flaubert's encounter with the Egyptian courtesan who "never spoke of herself; she never represented her emo- tions, presence, or history. He spoke for and represented her." Said wanted to argue that Flaubert's relationship was not an isolated case; "[i]t fairly stands for the pattern of relative strength between East and West, and the discourse about the Orient that it enabled."[29] Said, however, was insistent that his essences were just that: essences. He argued that "men make their own history" and that what they produce are just that: constructions. The constructions exist in time and space, even though those depicted in the constructions are represented as existing in a timeless zone; viewed from above and afar they are considered unchanging. Said's argument is very different from the constructions and depictions that he studies. He con- cludes that it is precisely the "sense of fixed identities battling across a per- manent divide that my book quite specifically abjures, but which it para- doxically presupposes and depends on."[30] When *Orientalism* is considered within the range of Said's work, the functions of "talking back" and the deconstructions of moments in the West are recurrent.[31] The parameters of time and space are important. What must be separated in further research, in this regard, are the concepts of audience and the politics of cultural pro- duction.[32] What audiences are at the receiving end of the so-called process of talking back? What cultural resonance do their voices achieve, in what spaces, and at what times? One could even think about voices of dissent within a particular space in the West and question the access to media and its sphere of influence.

It is not only this ability to talk back to the West, but also to contribute to the construction of the West that Browning and Lehti advance as one of the contributions that they make to our understanding of the West. Working through the writings of David Campbell and Lene Hansen that recognized that the construction of identity was drawn from a dialogue, and that the strength of those differences relied on the interlocution, they claim that the other is given agency, not only in terms of self-representation but in this case in their contributions to the construction of the West.[33]

What we want to argue here is that these positions are not mutually exclusive. Drawing on the methodologies advanced by Gerd Baumann and Andre Gingrich—from the *Grammars of Identity/Alterity*—the hierarchical structure of alterity is a useful lens through which to view the U.S. dilemma on colonialism and decolonization and its concurrent attempts to bolster the construction and identity of communities such as the nation and the West. Baumann, an anthropologist, suggests that greater insight is derived from moving away from the binary constructions of identity in favor of "philosophically 'weak' interpretations of the concept of identity," which facilitates the ability to "differentiate between different modalities of selfing/othering." Baumann starts by rejecting the contention that Said engaged in a binary methodology; rather, he watches it at work among the Westerners he studied. But Bauman also argues that the binary opposition is constantly subject to reversal. It lies in "Said's recognition that Westerners not only denigrated that which they called 'oriental,' but also desired it." They desired it because in their constructions the Orient, despite its (considered) strangeness and inferiority, was also ascribed with traits that were lost in the West. This grammar of alterity is interwoven with E.E. Evans-Pritchard's "ordered anarchy," which advances a hierarchy of othering and identity. In the early Cold War, for instance, the European colonial powers represented something other than what the United States saw itself as (and constructed itself as), yet within the context of the Cold War they pulled together to resist the Soviet threat. The pulling together necessitated the exaggeration of the Soviet threat. The identity of the West worked at one level on the Cold War question and was simultaneously problematic on the question of decolonization. Yet, given the promises of the Atlantic Charter it was presumed that in time, these transatlantic differences on colonialism and self-determination would be removed. Baumann contends:

> The intellectual beauty of this segmentary grammar of identity / alterity lies in its contextual awareness. The Other may be my foe in a context placed at a

lower level of segmentation, but may simultaneously be my ally in a context placed at a higher level of segmentation. Identity and alterity are thus a matter of context, and contexts are ranked according to classificatory levels. Fusion and fission, identity and difference are not matters of absolute criteria in this grammar, but functions of recognizing the appropriate segmentary level. In the segmentary grammar, people can thus selve themselves, and can other others according to context, that is, according to the structural level of the conflict or contest, coalition or cooperation that is at stake at any one given moment.[34]

The period of transition, the construction of the new West after WWII, and the coincidence of decolonization threw these identities into juxtaposition and they were indeed considered strategically in a hierarchical form. The U.S. privileging of an integrated Europe and the transatlantic relationship incurred costs to its own reputation and long-term identity, especially among various nationalists throughout the colonial world. Its ambivalence on decolonization ultimately meant that the West was certainly constructed not only through internal transatlantic hagiography but also by external criticism.[35]

It should be no surprise that the advocates for the new West propagated their identity in such seminal documents as the Atlantic Charter, and other wartime iconic documents, like the Truman Doctrine, NSC 68, Winston Churchill's Iron Curtain speech, or even Henry Luce's article on the "American Century." The power to narrate and to propagate abstract ideas cannot be underestimated. Cultural and ideological inclinations among audiences that adhered to these discourses undoubtedly understood the intentions of these messages. The power of the discourse was unassailable. Yet the content of these documents could also be read as signs of weakness, delivered on occasion to patch over internal inconsistencies and divisions. The power to effectively talk-back to the hegemonic propensity of the United States and the colonial and metropolitan centers in Europe only eventuated with the adherence of the postcolonial discourse and the breakdown of the Western-centered narratives, and only gained momentum between the end of the Vietnam War and the 1980s, before becoming more widespread.

The contributing chapters of this book examine the tendency to construct such discourses of selves and others and explain how these are transmitted to U.S. foreign policy since the colonization of North America. The complex evolution of an American identity through alterity is made evident in the first chapter by Walter L. Hixson, who explores the settler-colonialist disposition toward Native American Indians. The viciousness of Indian genocide, Hixson argues, is a product of a stark othering accomplished by conceiving Native Americans in contradictory physiological and civilizational tropes. The Native American as a savage barbarian was the prevailing view of colonialists, and not just in the seventeenth century, but long into the nineteenth, thus making this discourse of alterity the most enduring in North American history. The Indian wars (1675–1763) though fought intermittently, were not instigated for discontinuous reasons, but always for the control of North America, and while these wars were essentially prompted by European rivalry, they were consistently waged by Anglo-American colonialists determined to eradicate the Native American other. The regularity of war and the resolve to have an all-white-settler frontier, Hixson argues, were characteristics ingrained into the Anglo-American colonial self, and through repetition it was embossed into the minds of later generations of Americans.

The colonialists, however, were also others, as Jack P. Greene explains in chapter 2. He portrays the multilayered conception of otherness in colonial discourse by grappling with American identity from the vantages of Britain and North America. Though many colonialists identified themselves as British—not merely by heritage, but by seeking recognition from the mother country in political and cultural affirmations—their peripheral place geographically and their proximity to universally acknowledged others, namely, Native Americans, resulted in the refusal by the British metropole to recognize its colonialists as entirely British. As this sense of distancing intensified, Greene argues, a new comprehension of the colonial "self" emerged, this one reactionary and resistant to affiliation with the metropole, a differentiation most evident in the discourse of the American Revolution, which gave colonialists an identity no longer dependent on cultural ties to Europe.

In the early years of the American republic, such internal and external others persisted to affect U.S. foreign policies. Europe continued to act as an American foil best exemplified by the Monroe Doctrine, Marco Mariano points out. Chapter 3 examines this seminal foreign policy—the doctrine to precede all future doctrines—that pronounced European colonization the ideological other to the growing democracies of the Western hemisphere. Mariano also argues that the Monroe Doctrine conceived an internal other in the Americas south of the U.S. border. The discourse of the doctrine was rooted in developing Latin and South American others in the image of the United States. Beyond space, Mariano explores the temporal reach of the doctrine and its underlying ability to bifurcate in the twentieth century. The Roosevelt corollary, the new world/old world isolationism of the 1920s, the Truman Doctrine, and the Manichaean nature of the Cold War are styled, Mariano writes, from the Monroe Doctrine.

The geographical discourses of war, the frontier, and the notion of the West are complimented by Kristin Hoganson's view of the self/other discourse inherent in the cultural geographies of pleasure. Consumerism in the nineteenth and early twentieth century was obsessed with the foreign. The indulgence in obscure and alien artifacts, while certainly an appreciation of otherness, was no less covetous and capable of making a distinction between self and other. Chapter 4 focuses on the American appetite for collectable otherness as a cultural appreciation of the self. Hoganson argues that the fad for foreign imports, particularly Oriental rugs, overseas couture, exotic foods, and quirky knickknacks brought pleasure to their consumers through a reinforced sense of self-worth. This blurring of self and other in consumer geographies nicely foreshadows the domestic debates about American-ness occurring in the same period examined by Michael Patrick Cullinane in the "great debate" about overseas colonial acquisition. The U.S. foreign policy articulated by self-proclaimed imperialists led to the acquisition and government of the Philippines, Puerto Rico, Guam, and Cuba, a program opposed by self-proclaimed anti-imperialists. The dualistic name of these activists only highlights the deeper- seated arguments both groups held regarding American identity. The "great debate" at the turn of the century led Americans to take up the perennial questions, "who is a U.S. citizen," and "where exactly are the nation's borders," raising the potential for these differences among the domestic community to create yet another identity: the un-American American.

Internal debates among Americans in the early twentieth century were subsequently internationalized in the peace following World War I. Wilsonianism—the conception of global harmony by extending democracy, self-determination, and free trade—was a foreign policy seemingly without others. Advocacy for covenants of peace, as President Wilson saw them, was applicable universally. Lloyd Ambrosius, however, illustrates in chapter 6 just how segregationist Wilson's philosophy was. Wilsonian self-determination constructed a global system of stratification based on race and nineteenth-century preconceptions of civilization. Outwardly, Wilson's Fourteen Points declared universal liberties for all and equality among nations, but as Ambrosius shows, the mandate system copperfastened a sense of otherness based on common imperial geographies with lasting implications for the American Century.

The bifurcation of the world into us and them after World War I was problematic when it came to waging war again in the 1940s. From the vantage of the twenty-first century it is hard to imagine Hitler and the Nazis as anything but a quintessential other. Fascism by 1945 had come to be seen as the world's greatest evil, but Nazi Germany was considered in a very different sense during the interwar years. The ubiquitous view of Nazis as evil did not exist before the war, Michaela Hoenicke Moore writes. American policy makers, American soldiers, and even the general public could see themselves in the Nazis, complicating the war and the rationale for fighting. Hoenicke Moore explains how the Roosevelt administration—to varying degrees of success—transformed the image of Germany from a kindred nation to that of the other in order to effectively execute the war.

In the aftermath of World War II the United States sought to decolonize European empires based on the doctrine of the Atlantic Charter, a document that promoted ideals remarkably similar to Wilsonianism, but the establishment of a Jewish state in Palestine ran contrary to these ideals as it stripped Palestinian Arabs of their right to self-determination. The creation of Israel has been the subject of substantial scholarly writing, much of which takes up the view that Palestinians were conceived of in a way consistent with Said's orientalism. Instead of recounting this well-trodden trope, Geraldine Kidd surveys the manufacturing of such alterity by one individual: Eleanor Roosevelt. Though more traditionally known as an activist for human rights and for the plight of the Third World, Kidd exposes Roosevelt's perception of the Palestinian Arabs as others, incapable of development. This outlook is an account of how a sense of otherness is arrived at via oft-repeated racial stereotypes, personal contact with foreign people, and the inherent imperial spirit of liberal internationalism. Regardless of Roosevelt's empathy with many in the Third World, and the appeals of Palestinian Arabs for her to see their liberation as a cause similar to her crusade for human rights, she remained intractably devoted to the Israeli state.

David Ryan examines the persistent use of othering during the Cold War and after. The attractions of orientalism among U.S. foreign policy makers led to constructed images of American opponents as others and created various essences that had little relation to the more complex and particularistic reality. Ryan explores four such examples ranging from the Truman Doctrine and the construction of the West, to the Reagan doctrine as applied in Nicaragua, through to the post–Cold War thesis on the Clash of Civilizations and the rhetoric employed by George W. Bush after 9/11. U.S. policy makers found that in some instances such depictions facilitated domestic and congressional mobilization, yet these perspectives also vitiated the application of U.S. policy and force. The Cold War as a Manichaean construct of U.S.-styled democracy as the "good" ideology versus Soviet communism as the "evil" ideology played out around the world. In no place was this construct more complicated than in Vietnam, where U.S. intervention was waged—at least outwardly by American politicians—to save millions of Southeast Asians from despotism. Liam Kennedy writes that photography played a significant role in creating and dispelling the imagery of otherness. The representations of the Vietnamese captured by the lens of Philip Jones Griffiths, a Welsh photojournalist who saw the war as a brutal mixing pot, are dissected for the purpose of understanding the complexities of visual portrayals of identity. Griffiths sympathized with the Vietnamese people and attempted to illustrate them in less abstract and symbolic ways, and more as complex humans. His ultimate purpose, Kennedy argues, is to eliminate the distance between American and Vietnamese, to eliminate the sense of otherness, and move beyond the ideological frame of the war.

The final chapter engages the contemporary discourse on Islamism. Adib-Moghaddam examines the uses of the post-9/11 Islamophobia as a means for promoting the war on terror and explains how such otherness is manifested in a Foucauldian "bio-power." The otherness is best exemplified in the torture techniques used in the Abu Ghraib and Guantanamo Bay prisons. This reminds us of the persistence of the other in U.S. foreign policy, which we need only look to the daily newspapers to find.

Notes

1. Odd Arne Westad, *The Global Cold War: Third World Interventions and the Making of Our Times* (Cambridge: Cambridge University Press, 2005).
2. Walter LaFeber, *America, Russia, and the Cold War 1945-1990* (New York: McGraw-Hill, 1991), 302.
3. National Security Council, "U.S. Policy toward Africa South of the Sahara Prior to Calendar Year 1960, NSC 5719, July 31, 1957," Record Group 273, National Archives and Record Administration (hereafter cited as NARA).
4. Ibid.
5. David Campbell, *Writing Security: United States Foreign Policy and the Politics of Identity* (Minneapolis: University of Minnesota Press, 1992), 85–86; X [George Kennan], "The Sources of Soviet Conduct," *Foreign Affairs* 25 (July 1947).
6. Edward W. Said, *Orientalism: Western Conceptions of the Orient* (London: Penguin, 1995); idem, *Culture and Imperialism* (London: Chatto and Windus, 1993); Arshin Adib-Moghaddam, *A Metahistory of the Clash of Civilisations: Us and Them Beyond Orientalism* (London: Hurst, 2011), 13; Edward W. Said, "Orientalism Reconsidered," in his *Reflections on Exile and Other Literary and Cultural Essays* (London: Granta, 2000), 1999.
7. Fabian Hilfrich, "Visions of the Asian Periphery: Vietnam (1964-1968) and the Philippines (1898-1900)," in *America, the Vietnam War, and the World,* ed. Andreas W. Daum, Lloyd C. Gardner, and Wilfried Mausbach (Cambridge: Cambridge University Press, 2003), 44. See also Michel Foucault, *The Archaeology of Knowledge* (London: Routledge, 1989); David Campbell, *Writing Security: United States Foreign Policy and the Politics of Identity* (Minneapolis: University of Minnesota Press, 1992); David Ryan, *US Foreign Policy in World History* (London: Routledge, 2000); Frank Ninkovich, "Interests and Discourse in Diplomatic History," *Diplomatic History* 13, no. 2 (2007); Arshin Adib-Moghaddam, *A Metahistory of the Clash of Civilisations.*

8. Edward Said, _Orientalism_ (London: Penguin, 1995), 333; Michael H. Hunt, _Ideology and U.S. Foreign Policy_ (New Haven: Yale University Press, 1987); David Ryan, _US Foreign Policy in World History_ (London: Routledge, 2000), 1–54.

9. Melani McAlister, _Epic Encounters: Culture, Media, and U.S. Interests in the Middle East, 1945-2000_ (Berkeley: University of California Press, 2001); Matthew Frye Jacobson, "Post-Orientalism," _American Quarterly_ 54, no. 2 (June 2002), 307–15; Gyan Prakash, "Orientalism Now," _History and Theory_ 34, no. 3 (October 1995), 199–212; Edmund Burke III, "Orientalism and World History: Representing Middle Eastern Nationalism and Islamism in the Twentieth Century," _Theory and Society_ 27, no. 4 (August 1998), 489–507; Fred Halliday, _Islam and the Myth of Confrontation_ (London: I.B. Tauris, 1996), 199–200; Fred Halliday, _Two Hours that Shook the World: September 11, 2001: Causes and Consequences_ (London: Saqi Books, 2002); Kail Ellis, "Review of _American Orientalism_ by Douglas Little," _H-Net Reviews_, H-Levant (March 2004); Andrew J. Rotter, "Saidism without Said: _Orientalism_ and U.S. Diplomatic History," _The American Historical Review_ 105, no. 4 (September 2006); Edward Said, "Orientalism Reconsidered," _Cultural Critique_ 1 (Autumn 1985), 89–107.

10. Barack Obama worked hard with his Afghan allies to redraw distinctions between al Qaeda and the Taliban, offering various incentives to the latter to talk with Kabul, after the necessary delineations of war and U.S. military encounters of eight years failed.

11. John W. Dower, _Cultures of War: Pearl Harbor/Hiroshima/9-11/Iraq_ (New York: W. W. Norton, 2010), xxiv.

12. David Ryan, _Frustrated Empire: US Foreign Policy, 9/11 to Iraq_ (London: Pluto, 2007).

13. Ibid., 24.

14. Edward W. Said, _Culture and Imperialism_ (London: Chatto and Windus, 1993), xxviii.

15. Francis Fukuyama, _The End of History and the Last Man_ (London: Penguin, 1992); Samuel P. Huntington, "Clash of Civilizations," _Foreign Affairs_ 72, no. 3 (Summer 1993); Samuel Huntington, _The Clash of Civilizations and the Remaking of World Order_ (New York: Simon and Schuster, 1996).

16. President George Bush, "Address to a Joint Session of Congress and the American People," 20 September 2001 (http://www.whitehouse.gov/news/releases/2001/09/20010920-8.html).

17. Edward Said, "The Clash of Ignorance," in _After 9/11: Solutions for a Saner World_, ed. Don Hazen et al. (San Francisco: AlterNet, 2001), 84.

18. Douglas Little, _American Orientalism: The United States and the Middle East since 1945_ (London: I.B. Tauris, 2002); McAlister, _Epic Encounters_; Said, _Orientalism_; Said, _The World, The Text, and The Critic_ (London: Vintage, 1983); Said, _Covering Islam: How the Media and the Experts Determine How We See the Rest of the World_ (London: Vintage, 1997); Hunt, _Ideology and U.S. Foreign Policy_; James William Park, _Latin American Development: A History of Perspectives in the United States 1870-1965_ (Baton Rouge: Louisiana State University Press, 1995); Adib-Moghaddam, _A Metahistory of the Clash of Civilisations_.

19. Leon Dominian, "The Mohammedan World, May 20, 1918," Inquiry Document 137, M1107, roll 10, NARA.

20. Hunt, _Ideology and U.S. Foreign Policy_, 161–62.

21. National Security Council, "Long-Range U.S. Policy toward the Near East, NSC 5801, January 10, 1958," RG 273, NARA.

22. McAlister, _Epic Encounters_, 11.

23. John Carlos Rowe, "Edward Said and American Studies," _American Quarterly_ 56, no. 1 (March 2004), 33–47.

24. It is important to note that while Said identified certain homogenous constructions, he did not believe in them himself. His work on Western and Arab cultures and contexts in time and place was extensive and important because it simultaneously worked against the powerful cultural images or mental maps. Said argues:

My position is that in the case of an essential Islam or Orient, these images are no more than images, and are upheld as such both by the community of the Muslim faithful and (the correspondence is significant) by the community of Orientalists. My objection to what I have called Orientalism is not that it is just the antiquarian study of Oriental languages, societies, and peoples, but that as a system of thought it approaches a heterogeneous, dynamic, and complex human reality from an uncritically essentialist standpoint; this suggests both an enduring Oriental reality and an opposing but no less enduring Western essence, which observes the Orient from afar and so to speak, from above. This false position hides historical change. Even more important ... it hides the interests of the Orientalist.

Said, *Orientalism*, 333–34; Ryan, *US Foreign Policy in World History*, 27.

25. Hilfrich, "Visions of the Asian Periphery," 53–54.
26. Ibid., 57.
27. Christopher S. Browning and Marko Lehti, "The West: Contested, Narrated and Clustered," *The Struggle for the West: A Divided and Contested Legacy*, ed. Christopher S. Browning and Marko Lehti (London: Routledge, 2010), 26.
28. Rotter, "Saidism without Said."
29. Said, *Orientalism*, 5–6.
30. Ibid., 5, 336.
31. Johannes Fabian, *Time and the Other: How Anthropology Makes Its Object* (New York: Columbia University Press, 1983); Johannes Fabian, *Memory against Culture: Arguments and Reminders* (Durham, NC: Duke University Press, 2007).
32. Pierre Bourdieu, *The Field of Cultural Production* (Cambridge: Polity, 1993).
33. Browning and Lehti, *The Struggle for the West*, 26.
34. Gerd Baumann, "Grammars of Identity/Alterity: A Structural Approach," in *Grammars of Identity/Alterity: A Structural Approach*, ed. Gerd Baumann and André Gingrich (New York: Berghahn Books, 2004), 18–23.
35. David Ryan and Victor Pungong, *The United States and Decolonization: Power and Freedom* (London: Macmillan, 2000).

Chapter 1

"No Savage Shall Inherit the Land"
The Indian Enemy Other, Indiscriminate Warfare,
and American National Identity, 1607–1783

Walter L. Hixson

American conceptions of the other are inherent in the binary world view of expansive European modernity in which civilization encountered savagery.[1] On the North American frontier, identification of the Indian as an enemy other fueled indiscriminate warfare, establishing a pattern of behavior that would play out continuously in subsequent American history.[2] As the primary and quintessential American other, Indians proved central to forging national identity—not merely through their existence but rather through their resistance and removal.

The interrelationship between perceptions of the Indian other and the continuous campaigns of often-indiscriminate warfare waged against the indigenous population from the beginning of Euro-American settlement through the American Revolutionary War deserves consideration because the extirpative violence against Indians went a long way toward defining American national identity. In the same sense that Frantz Fanon argued that "Europe is literally the creation of the Third World"—that is, that the colonization process forged European identity—the indigenous Indian other forged American national identity. "It is in fact the conquest of America that heralds and establishes our present identity," Tzvetan Todorov notes. "The very identity and meaning implied in the name *America* as the national identity of the United States," Kevin Bruyneel observes, "was in no small part constituted through this nation's real and imagined relationship with indigenous people."[3]

I am struck by both the intensity and the continuity over the *longue dureé* of early American extirpative warfare and the implications of that

Notes for this chapter begin on page 37.

violence on the formation of national identity.[4] Borderland violence had a traumatic and enduring impact; one that I am suggesting has carried over and pervades all of American history. I thus concur with Malani Johar Schueller and Edward Watts on the need for "reexamination of how the nation's sense of itself was constructed through longer processes of multiracial conflict and Western imperialism and colonization going back ... to the very beginnings of Anglophone colonization."[5] The following narrative incorporates aspects of postcolonial analysis[6] in seeking to understand the impact of American settler colonialism[7] not only on the colonized indigenous other but also on the colonizing Euro-American. As Aimé Césaire points out, "Colonization works to *de-civilize* the colonizer, to brutalize him in the true sense of the word, to degrade him, to awaken him to buried instincts, to covetousness, violence, race hatred, and moral relativism." Césaire calls this phenomenon "the boomerang effect of colonization."[8]

Postcolonial studies, along with several stimulating recent works on Amerindian history, offer analysis that goes beyond binaries of self and other, white and red, victim and conquest. "Postcolonial studies," as Ania Loomba explains, "have been preoccupied with issues of hybridity, creoloization, and mestizaje—with the in-betweenness, diasporas, mobility and crossovers of ideas and identities generated by colonialism."[9] The American Indian histories, meanwhile, emphasize indigenous agency rather than a simplified narrative of victimization that would reinscribe the mind-set of colonization itself.[10] That said, there is some risk that such accounts can become essentialist in their own right, that in their desire to transcend an earlier binary narrative they obscure the very history of colonial domination that they attempt to contextualize. While there is no end of complexity in early American history, the identification and destruction of the Indian other nonetheless forged a powerful continuity and left a deep and lasting imprint on national identity.

Early English Colonization

Prior to the arrival of Europeans the land that they would call the new world was of course not new at all but rather a "thriving, stunningly diverse place, a tumult of languages, trade, and culture, a region where millions of people loved and hated and worshipped as people do everywhere."[11] Only 160 or so years later, by the middle of the seventeenth century, European diseases devastated Indian populations that had acquired no immunities, killing as much as 90 percent of the indigenous population. But this period, and the generations that followed, would also be characterized by violent Indian removal, a process that occurred in concert with the formation of early American national identity. It may thus be useful to "track the violence embedded in the articulations of national identity and territoriality" in U.S. history.[12]

Fueled by the discourses associated with early-modern capitalism, Christianity, and racial formation, European settler colonialists drove Indians from the land over the *longue dureé* of early American history. As private property and individual landholding became foundational under modernity, Europeans violently displaced Indians for personal gain. Christian texts, such as the admonition in Genesis 1:28 to "subdue the earth and have dominion over every living thing that moves on the earth," undergirded conquest of both the human and environmental other. Indians, then, like the land itself, became blank spaces on the colonial map, there to be conquered. Racial modernity—especially with the unfolding of the African slave trade, the largest forced migration in human history— reinforced violent repression and dispossession. "Convinced that Europe was synonymous with civilization," Colin Calloway notes, "colonizing Europeans failed to see anything of value in Indian civilization."[13]

The European colonial assault on the Americas encompassed a continuous history of extirpative war sanctioned by the "savagery" of the Indian other. Although Protestant Europeans denounced cruelties associated with the conquistadores, settler colonialism proved no less destructive of Indian cultures. Fueled by the modernist discourses of individual opportunity, "the pilgrim's progress," and the inevitable triumph of a superior people, Euro-American settlers repeatedly resorted to indiscriminate warfare to drive out or destroy their "savage neighbors."[14]

Perplexed and repulsed by the concept of private property, Indians often proved willing to share space but not to remove from it in deference to European settler colonialism. Indians used and changed the land for their own purposes but they refused to see the land as something to be carved up and claimed by the individual. The Euro-Americans, however, could see it in no other way. To the Euro-Americans under modernity, a sovereign people, under God, were on a mission to take command over nature, including the savage Indians. This process entailed demarcation and control of space; establishment of boundaries, maps, surveys, treaties, and seizures; and the commodification of the land. Individual Euro-American settlers, as British authorities as well as the Indians would discover, would not be restrained in their borderland expansion. Although settler colonialists would perfect the art of taking Indian lands through unequal treaties and other modernist legal means, extirpative warfare inhered in the emergent American identity.[15]

Amerindians engaged in violence as well as trade and diplomacy as they evolved complex strategies of homeland defense. Highly gendered, Indian violence typically focused on the individual attainment of the masculine warrior through demonstration of his bravery in the field. Most indigenous groups had strong warrior traditions dating back for centuries. Warfare characteristically was short and seasonal but often cruel and vicious. Indians had fought each other for centuries; they regularly aligned with Euro-Americans to kill other Indians; they attacked by surprise, killed, took scalps, tortured their captives often excruciatingly, and sometimes posed the corpses of dead women, children, and babies to taunt and to terrorize. Native Americans rarely sought to annihilate their enemies, to wipe them from the face of the earth; they typically did not demand unconditional surrender or utter destruction of their foes. They sometimes engaged in rape but apparently less often than did the Euro-Americans.

The cultural practice of adopting captives distinguished most Amerindian tribes from the Euro-American way of war. Indians took into their societies captives—both Indian and white—to replace those who had been lost. For many North American Indian tribes, ravaged by disease, war and captive taking provided the only means to rebuild their numbers. Rather than wage indiscriminate warfare, Indians typically preferred to take captives rather than to kill.

Though routinely depicted in Euro-American discourse as bloodthirsty savages, Indians also engaged in trade and diplomacy using deeply embedded traditions involving council fires, wampum and gift exchanges, and smoking of the calumet. Indians participated vigorously in trade and commerce, especially the fur trade, obtaining firearms and other European products in exchange for beaver pelts. Indians both allied with Europeans and played them off against each other or against their own indigenous rivals. Various Indian groups conducted painstaking negotiations to remove land from commercialization, often winning concessions from their British and American counterparts. Indeed, "The concessions wrung from British and American governments over the colonial and early national eras are testimony to Amerindian political acumen in the face of daunting pressures."[16]

Following the arrival of Europeans in the Chesapeake region, the Algonquian Indian leader Powhatan initially pursued a diplomatic understanding with the settlers. Powhatan presided over the thirty or so tribes, about 7,500 Indians in total across some eighty miles between the James and Potomac Rivers. In the famous incident of December 1607—a prelude to ethnic violence has been rendered as a love story—Powhatan may have sought to display his prowess to let live or destroy the English colonists when one of his daughters, Pocahontas, saved the English mercenary John Smith from execution. Smith, a veteran of prior warfare against the Islamic Eurasian enemy other, failed to appreciate the gesture, as he viewed the Indians as heathen savages. When conflict later erupted, it was Smith who pioneered the tradition of irregular war in the new world by burning and razing Indian homes and agricultural fields. "Inspired by Smith's success, the Virginia Company institutionalized the measures he had pursued."[17]

Virginia's first governor, Francis Wyatt, concluded in the wake of the conflict that it would be "infinitely better to *have no heathen among us ...* than to be at peace and league with them."[18] While suffering fearful losses of life through war, disease, and starvation, the Jamestown settlers bene-fited from a continuing influx of new colonialists and supplies while the Indians, lacking immunities against the new diseases, perished in droves. As it became clear that the settler invaders intended to drive the Algon-quians off the land, the Indian sachem Opechancanough launched an all-out counterattack. In the last gasp surprise offensive of 1644, Opechanca-nough's warriors killed some five hundred Euro-American settlers. Now equipped with an organized militia in each county and forts all along the James River, the Virginians responded with a campaign of indiscriminate warfare culminating in the summary execution of Opechancanough and the selling of indigenous captives into slavery.[19]

After two generations of bitter conflict, the Tidewater Wars ended in total victory for the Virginians. Virginia society had become militarized through the creation of the militia and the string of fortresses throughout the colony. The campaign of ethnic cleansing—the killing, relocating, and generally driving "hostile" Indians from their midst—established a frame-work for the Euro-American settler colonial project.

Although in other respects New England societies bore little resem-blance to settler colonial patterns in the Chesapeake, indiscriminate warfare against the indigenous other came to characterize both regions. William Bradford, governor of Plymouth, landed with the expectation of encoun-tering "savage people, who are cruel, barbarous, and most treacherous." The New England Amerindians, who had previously encountered Euro-pean explorers, fishermen, and would-be colonists, greeted the mostly Puritan settlers with distrust. Nevertheless, Massasoit, the Wampanoag chieftain, opted to try to work with the fledgling colonists rather than wipe them out, as he surely could have done at the outset. As colonists ar-rived en masse over the next generation, the Massachusetts Indians would be devoid of such options.[20]

After a long period of relative peace, the expanding Bay Colony moved deeper into the interior, bringing on a war of annihilation against the Pe-quot Indians. "Indian villages, and therefore noncombatants, were the main targets of the English in the Pequot War, New England's first large-scale military conflict," John Grenier explains.[21] In May 1637 Massachusetts Bay, joined by Indian allies including the Mohegans and Narragansetts, longstanding enemies of the Pequot, attacked the Pequot village on the Mystic River under the leadership of Captain John Mason, a veteran of English conflict in the Netherlands. Determined to wipe out the settlement of mostly women, children, and old men, Mason fired the village and then relished "the extreme amazement of the enemy and a great rejoicing of ourselves." God had condemned the Indians to the "fiery oven" and their "frying in the fire, and the streams of blood quenching the same" had exacted a "revenge so sweet," the governor of Plymouth exulted. Troops using dogs hunted down survivors and conducted summary executions, sometimes replete with torture as when they tied one Pequot's leg to a post and put twenty men on a rope tied to the other leg as they "pulled him to pieces."[22]

In the late seventeenth century, a final wave of violence in both Virginia and New England cemented Euro-American settler colonialism but not without persistent Indian efforts at homeland defense. In what became a virtual iron law of American history, any impediment to westward expansion could incite civil tumult among the Euro-Americans. Thus in 1676, Virginia Governor William Berkeley tried to limit conflict with Indians by reining in landed expansion. Masses of armed men joined the Henrico planter Nathaniel Bacon in rebellion against the governor and Crown authority. Bacon condemned the Virginia authorities for attempting to discourage attacks against "those barbarous enemies," as he described the Indian other. Bacon launched search and destroy operations into Pamunkey villages and Occaneechee territory, wiping out even Indians who refrained from resistance. As the Indians escaped into the forest, Bacon burned Jamestown before dying suddenly, probably from dysentery. Bacon's demise brought an end to the rebellion, illustrating the determination of growing numbers of armed and violent men to take what they wanted on their self-avowed frontiers.[23]

Almost simultaneously, King Philip's War marked another wave of indiscriminate warfare between New Englanders and the Amerindians. The Wampanoag sachem Metacom, son of Massasoit, had lived and traded peacefully with the Puritans for years and even taken on the European name Philip. Tensions escalated, however, over land encroachments, missionary efforts undermining Indian spiritual and political leadership, and unequal justice. Violence erupted in what would become a familiar and continuous pattern in American history, as an isolated incident escalated into full-blown extirpative war. Spurred on by younger warriors, Metacom, joined by the Narragansett and other tribes, led the resistance.

Having learned some lessons from the Pequot War, the Indians now too fought indiscriminately and left a series of New England towns littered with dead and mutilated bodies and in smoking ruins. The English, however, possessed superior numbers, material resources, and social cohesion that allowed them to prevail. The New England confederation eventually dispatched a one-thousand-man army on a campaign to search out and annihilate the indigenous enemy. The ultimate victory removed Indians as a threat in southern New England, thus furthering the English colonial project. The conflict had been devastating, however, as it inflicted greater casualties in proportion to population than any other war throughout American history.[24]

In order to achieve victory, the English adopted the once condemned and Indian-inspired techniques of irregular warfare. The English under the leadership of Benjamin Church now "skulked" in the woods and launched surprise attacks. Born of King Philip's War, ranging and scalp hunting of the indigenous population soon permeated New England culture. The colonists bulked up enlistments through the incentive of scalp hunting, earning a return of five shillings for the scalp of a common Indian (often regardless of age or sex) to one hundred shillings, or five pounds, for King Philip. "Extirpative war, ranging, and scalp hunting provided both an effective and a financially rewarding means to kill, conquer, and subjugate the Indian peoples of the Eastern seaboard," Grenier explains.[25]

Aided by a Native American traitor, the English located a Narragansett fortress at the Great Swamp east of the Chippuxet River and in a reprise of the Mystic River assault put it to the torch as the Indians sat down for dinner. Some 600 Narragansett—roughly half of them noncombatants—died in the inferno. "They and their food fried together," one Englishman exulted. Several towns had been destroyed and more than five hundred soldiers and some one thousand New England civilians had been killed in King Philip's War. Indian losses were much greater, however, following a campaign of lynching, murder, and enslavement. Metacom, a "great, naked, dirty beast" and thus the personification of the Indian other, was executed, his body drawn and quartered, and his severed head hung from a pole for decades.[26]

King Philip's War left a deep imprint, as it underscored the benefits as well as the traumas of indiscriminate warfare against the savage foe. In the wake of the war the English increasingly viewed "all Indians who resisted English definitions of authority as enemies." The conflict reflected "the unwillingness of the colonists to accommodate Native cultures, economies, and land use" and as such presaged "most if not all of the subsequent major wars between Natives and settlers during the next two centuries of American expansion." Moreover, King Philip's War established a foundation that "would form the basis of American nationalism as it emerged in the late eighteenth and early nineteenth centuries."[27]

Indians and the Imperial Wars

The imperial wars of the next generation, innocuously named after a series of British sovereigns, ensconced extirpative war and further militarized New England society. Periods of peace were unmercifully brief on the American borderlands. These conflicts were King William's War (1689–97), Queen Anne's War (1702–13), King George's War (1744–48), and the French and Indian War (1754–63). The warfare pitted the English, usually aided by the Five Nations of the Iroquois Confederation, against the French and their Indian allies on the Western frontier. The blood-soaked struggles resulted in the deaths of thousands of English, French Canadians, and Indians.

Indian raids and irregular warfare terrorized encroaching English settlements throughout these conflicts. In colonies such as Massachusetts, where one of every four men who took up arms died in the field, the hatred and determination to destroy the indigenous enemy other became deeply enmeshed in culture. With bounties being paid for Indian scalps, the fighting men made no unprofitable distinction between combatants and noncombatants. Indeed, as the incentives ran in the other direction, extirpation became "a legitimate act of war."[28]

The decisive French and Indian War, known as the Seven Years' War in Europe, was global in scope yet originated on the American borderlands. The eventual British victory proved paradoxical, as it led directly to the American anti-colonial revolt. The American Revolution, in turn, led to the devastation of Amerindians, who would be cleansed from New York, the Ohio Valley, and parts of the southern states after already having been driven off of the eastern seaboard.

The British Army's ignorance of irregular warfare combined with contempt for the native savages led to a series of shattering defeats in the early years of the French and Indian War. Before launching his famously ill-fated march on Fort Duquesne in 1755, British General Edward Braddock contemptuously dismissed an offer of alliance from the Delaware Indian leader Shingas. After arriving with his delegation to meet with Braddock in Cumberland, Maryland, Shingas linked Delaware support against the French with securing the lands of upper Ohio for the Indians once the French had been driven from the Forks of the Ohio. Contemptuous of conducting diplomacy with Indians, Braddock added gratuitously, "No savage shall inherit the land." Shingas replied, "If they might not have liberty to live on the land, they would not fight for it," at least not on the side of Great Britain.[29]

Spurned by the British, the Delaware and other tribes instead allied with the French and launched a campaign of terror targeting backcountry settlements. For several years, the borderlands were the "scene of chaos and rout, with colonial forces hardly managing even to hinder the raids." Indian warriors took prisoners and plunder, killing "nearly every male colonist they encountered, often going out of their way to escalate the body count." As they conducted a "psychological terror campaign designed to intimidate and dishearten their opponents," the Indians affirmed the discourse of savagery by mutilating and posing the bodies of many of their victims. Few considered that the Native Americans, increasingly outnumbered by the flood of borderland settlers, employed horror and terror as a deliberate tactic of intimidation, one that often worked by prompting reverse migrations.[30]

In the wake of such sustained violence, borderland settlers increasingly viewed all Indians as bloodthirsty savages. The trope "savages" functioned to deprive Indians of individual and tribal agency or distinctiveness and thus facilitated the indiscriminate killing of them. Theorist of colonialism Albert Memmi described this phenomenon as "the mark of the plural." The same dialectic would play out in other colonial settings and in subsequent American campaigns against Filipino "goo-goos," "Japs," Vietnamese "gooks," and Islamic "terrorists."[31]

In 1757 the slaughter outside Fort William Henry on Lake George, New York, further reinforced the trope of the demon Indian savage. The French under Marquis de Montcalm bombarded and forced the surrender of the English fort, but what followed underscored the Indo-European cultural divide and became a turning point in the war. After accepting Montcalm's terms, the British began their march out of Fort William Henry whereupon Montcalm proved unable to constrain his Indian allies, who descended upon defenseless men and women with knives and tomahawks in order to take their customary captives and trophies. The Abenakis, Ottawa, and Potowatomi, among others, killed 185 and took some 300 to 500 captives. As the Indians saw it, the French had promised them their just reward for joining in the assault before Montcalm reverted to a European-style honorable surrender. Moreover, with the English colonies offering bounties for the scalps of indigenous men, women, and children, the Indians outside Fort William Henry had cause to view their actions as consistent with the prevailing way of war.

What the Anglo-Americans promptly termed "the massacre of Fort William Henry" became a turning point. Like Pearl Harbor or 9/11, it had a galvanizing effect on British North Americans. The slaughter outside the fort, vividly recounted in newspapers across the colonies, led to an upsurge in recruitment of thousands of new militiamen. Proponents of extirpative war ruled the day. After the disasters between the decimation of Braddock and his forces in the Battle of Monongahela on 9 July 1755 and Fort William Henry, the British embarked upon a war without mercy.[32]

With British America fully mobilized, new officers such as James Wolfe and Jeffrey Amherst conducted "wildly violent campaigns" against New France and the Indian "miscreants."[33] Few events better illustrated the embrace of indiscriminate warfare at the moment of British-American triumph than the murderous assault by Rogers' Rangers on the Abenaki village of St. Francis on 4 October 1759. During decades of warfare with the New England settlers the Abenakis had often descended from St. Francis, located north of Montreal, to conduct murderous raids. Major Robert Rogers of Massachusetts, who today "is regarded as the founding father of the U.S. Army's Special Forces units," recruited a force of mostly Scotch-Irish irregulars from New Hampshire, together with some Indian and even a few African-American fighters, to make the audacious trek deep into enemy territory. "Take your revenge," General Amherst charged Rogers, adding the contradictory directive to show "no mercy" and yet to spare women and children.[34]

In an operation much like those that would occur later in places like Sand Creek, Batangas, and My Lai, angry attackers primed for slaughter would make no distinction on the basis of age or gender. Indeed, as so often happened in such attacks warriors were not even present at the village, leaving mostly old men, women, and children to die by the scores if not hundreds as "the well-disciplined assault swiftly degenerated into an uncontrolled massacre." The villagers, who had celebrated a wedding the night before, burned alive in their wooden houses in the sunrise assault or were bludgeoned or shot dead on the spot. Noting that hundreds of scalps hung wafting in the breeze around the village, Rogers' Rangers took their own trophies from the dead and plundered the village of valuable metals and icons. "The American frontier could find and un-tether the savage that lay within even the most civilized of men," Stephen Brumwell observes.[35]

The French and Indian War spurred racial formation within an emergent, distinctly American identity. As the settlers fought off or succumbed to Indian violence, they increasingly identified themselves as another and superior race of "white" people. "Whether publicists wrote of 'the white people' or simply 'the people,' images of a single, suffering peoplehood … came to flourish in the press" of the mid-Atlantic states, Peter Silver found. Moreover, the "white people in this period were nearly always depicted as suffering at Indians' hands rather than triumphing over them." As American identity began to coalesce in the wake of the French and Indian War, "violent self-pity" would become "one of the new nation's most characteristic and long-lasting cultural products."[36]

The French and Indian War simultaneously advanced the process of ethno-genesis in which Indians had begun to take on a collective identity. Religion, especially the teaching of the Delaware mystic Neolin, accented the cultural divide between all "red" Indians and the "white" man. As Neolin's preaching spread across the borderlands, Indians rejected British paternal authority and began to ally more with one another.[37]

The total defeat of France brought an end to the French and Indian War in 1763 yet no end to the violence in North America. Under terms of the Treaty of Paris, the British arrogated to themselves all French territory in North America, including indigenous lands. The Indians had cooperated in the war in the expectation that in return the British would respect their cultures and access to the land. Yet even though Braddock had been killed in the first major battle of the war, his declaration that "no savage shall inherit the land" still prevailed in the minds of Englishmen. The British had erected a chain of forts in the Upper Great Lakes region from 1758 to 1762 and soon cut off trade with the Indians in weapons and gunpowder.

Trade and ceremonial gift giving had long stabilized European-Indian relations in the *pays d'en haut,* as the French had called the "upper country" of the Great Lakes region. Indians remained more numerous and powerful in the region yet since the establishment of the profitable fur trade in the sixteenth century they had become dependent on commerce with the Europeans. Many French traders transcended enemy othering by marrying indigenous women and cultivating a "middle ground" between native and European cultures.[38] Amherst, however, like Braddock before him, came to the mistaken conclusion that the desires of the Indians merited no respect.

British contempt for the savages spurred vicious conflict following the French and Indian War. With Amherst in command, postwar Indian removal emerged first in the South, where British-Americans laid waste to Cherokee villages and killed indiscriminately. High tensions turned to all-out war as the Anglo-Americans summarily executed twenty-two chiefs who had come to negotiate an understanding. Amherst encouraged a military campaign against the Cherokee carried out by South Carolina rangers and their Catawba and Chickasaw warrior allies. In frontier fighting in 1761 Lieutenant Colonel James Grant, sent from New York by Amherst, burned Cherokee villages to the ground and summarily executed non-combatant captives regardless of age and gender. Such actions, combined with disease and famine, devastated the Cherokees.[39]

British-American relations with Indians deteriorated further as a result of the halt to trade and gift giving and the destabilizing flood of new settlers streaming down new roads into the Ohio Valley. Britain showed itself as ungrateful to its Indian allies and as unworthy successors to the French by cutting off trade in high-demand items, notably guns and alcohol. Moreover, Britain proved unable to stem the tide of settler colonialism. "No provincial go-between was immune to the land fever that afflicted British America," James Merrell points out.[40]

Dramatically underestimating the growing Indian unity and capacity for resistance, the British under Amherst soon reeled from an uprising generically though not very accurately known as "Pontiac's Rebellion." Amherst had shrugged off suggestions of Indian violent resistance by citing their "incapacity of attempting anything serious." In any case, he vowed that he would "punish the delinquents with entire destruction, which I am firmly resolved on whenever any of them give me cause."[41] Belying such assurances, on April 27, 1763, the Ottawa chief Pontiac led an assault on the British redoubt at Detroit, sparking violent resistance across the borderlands.

Indian homeland defense set off a new wave of frontier warfare while simultaneously fueling the modernist impulse to exterminate. Declaring, "No punishment we can inflict is adequate to the crimes of those inhumane villains," an apoplectic Amherst urged policy that would "extirpate this execrable race ... I wish to hear of no Prisoners." In a dispatch on 4 May 1763, Amherst asked, "[c]ould it not be contrived to send the Small Pox among those disaffected tribes?" Two months later, Colonel Henry Bouquet responded, "I will try to inoculate the bastards with some blankets that may fall in their hands." Even before Amherst's order, the British deliberately gave infected blankets as gifts to Indians who came to parley before an attack on Fort Pitt. Extirpative biological warfare against the Indian other thus had arrived on the American borderlands.[42]

Stunned by the Indian uprising in the *pays d'en haut,* Britain had no choice but to recede through the establishment of the Proclamation Line of 1763. The line proscribed new trans-Appalachian land grants or purchases and required a permit for trade on the western side of the mountains. The line was a futile effort to curb the flood of settlement and thus to demilitarize the Western frontier. The Proclamation Line placated the Indians but embittered the people who soon called themselves Americans. They did not intend to comply with such a restriction on their mobility or with many other royal proclamations. In time, these Americans would employ indiscriminate warfare to take for themselves what the British had conceded to the Indians. By withdrawing from Fort Pitt and leaving only the paper-thin Proclamation Line as the basis for peace, the British paved the way for the ensuing violence. Emboldened by victory in the French and Indian War and hungry for new lands, settler-invaders with no regard for Indian sovereignty drove into the borderlands.

Thus the end of the French and Indian War—traditionally conceptualized in American history as a period of growing conflict with Great Britain
leading to the Revolutionary War—was also the opening phase of a determined campaign of indiscriminate warfare against Indians. Unremitting
borderland violence had begun to cement a homogenizing discourse that
framed Indians as a unified enemy in the path of civilization and progress.
A violent dialectic emerged; the formation of American national identity
depended in part on this identification of Indians as a unitary and savage
foe. Indian removal and indiscriminate warfare thus became synonymous
with the formation and achievement of U.S. nationalist aspirations.

Indian Removal and the American Revolution

From 1763 to 1783 Indian removal and extirpative warfare evolved in lock-
step with the birthing of the United States. In 1764 the British-Indian agent
and land speculator William Johnson, who had lived among the Iroquois,
respected their culture, and married a Mohawk woman, met with about
two thousand Indians from some twenty-four nations in an effort to bring
peace to the trans-Appalachian borderlands. The parties exchanged gifts
and wampum belts in traditional ceremonies thus cementing an alliance
that would carry through the subsequent Revolutionary War. Peace could
not prevail, however, because the Euro-American settlers showed contempt for both Indian rights to hold land as well as for the British prerog-
ative to draw the Proclamation Line at the mountains. Settler colonialists
argued that a British and Indian alliance in the West was no better than the
preceding French and Indian alliance. If they were barred from westward
expansion, victory in the French and Indian War would hold no meaning
for them.

The steady inflow of immigrants to British America created demographic pressures for landed expansion as well as economic opportunity
for land speculators and settlers. On the eve of the American Revolution,
more than fifty thousand "whites" lived on the trans-Appalachian frontier beyond British ability to control them. The brutal warfare had condi-
tioned most settlers to view the Ohio Valley Indians as savage others who
ought to be removed from the land if not exterminated. As the English
trader George Croghan noted, settlers "thought it a meritorious act to kill
Heathens whenever they were found."[43] Both ordinary settlers and men
of wealth and prominence shared the determination to drive out or kill
Indians in advance of expanding western settlement. Significantly, most
of the colonial elites engaged in land speculation. The Proclamation Line
thus infuriated men such as George Washington, a land surveyor, as well

as Thomas Jefferson, Arthur Lee, Patrick Henry, and other American patriots. The colonial elite and land speculators, as Colin Calloway puts it, "saw tyranny in Britain's interference with their ability to make a [financial] killing in the West."[44]

But the elite men of the cities and plantations were generally not those who performed the bloody work of cleansing the land of the indigenous enemy. "The pressures that inspired Indian hating did not descend from the top down, but arose from the bottom up," Patrick Griffin explains.[45] Thousands of men, women, and children of divergent European ethnicity knew little about land speculation, only that they intended to carve out a stake of their own where they could build farms, homesteads, and outposts for trade. British officials invariably described these squatters as "low" and "the very dregs of the people." British General Thomas Gage held out little hope of peace on the frontier, as the settlers were "too numerous, too lawless and licentious ever to be restrained."[46]

Settler colonialism gained ground in the South, as the besieged Creeks granted the British a huge land cession in 1763 in return for the promise that their remaining lands would be free of Euro-Americans. But no paper agreement could put a stop to the settler colonialists who flooded into Georgia regardless of Creek claims or British paper restrictions. The Cherokee raided borderland settlements but in 1776 the action "provoked a large retaliatory expedition by the southern states, whose militia forces ravaged Cherokee towns and burned crops."[47] Ensconced in Florida since the establishment of St. Augustine in 1565, Spain could hold back the tide of American settlers for another generation or two but no longer, as it turned out.

While conquest of the South would take time, neither the Proclamation Line nor Indian resistance could halt the advance into Pennsylvania, Kentucky, and Ohio. Each became a site of vicious warfare and relentless ethnic cleansing. William Penn had established Penn's Woodlands as a Quaker colony that acknowledged the essential humanity of the indigenous people and sought peace with the tribes. At the same time, however, Penn pursued the incompatible goal of selling off lands to generate revenue. "From the beginning, this practical need abraded uncomfortably with his benign intentions toward the Indians," Eric Hinderaker explains. As Euro-Americans pursued profitable land sales and expansion into new settlements, the Delaware and other Indians "were increasingly forced to adapt rapidly or pick up and move."[48]

Backed by the French in the Seven Years' War, the Indians fought fiercely against the inexorable encroachment and took hundreds of scalps from their settler victims in Penn's woodlands. Such violence dealt a deathblow to already waning Quaker calls for toleration. The contradictions inherent in Penn's dream of peaceful relations with Indians came to an end as Pennsylvanians mustered the militia and volunteers for search and destroy missions. The violent Indian homeland defense ultimately only served to deepen Euro-American determination to cleanse them from the land, a dialectic that would play out in the nineteenth century across the trans-Mississippi West.

Acting within a discourse of Native American terror targeting innocent settlers, the colonists demonized the savage Indians and launched campaigns of extirpation. The colonial press routinely referenced "murder" and "massacre" perpetrated by "barbarians" and "savages" against innocent men, women, and children. Graphic accounts offered "careful descriptions of bashed-in skulls and cut-out tongues. Of sharp objects stuck into eyes and genitals." Accounts often emphasized that the victims were "helpless wives and poor defenseless babes." As Silver explains, "Huge amounts of writing and thinking about Indians after midcentury were ... engineered to overwhelm the reader with emotion at the sight of suffering."[49]

It was not only the loss of friends and loved ones that incited hatred, but the manner in which these people died. Whole families were killed, bodies posed, mutilated, sometimes disemboweled. That fueled the rage of violent redemption. "Every child ... learns to hate an Indian, because he always hears him spoken of as an enemy," explained the settler James Hall. "From the cradle, he listens continually to horrid tales of savage violence, and becomes familiar with narratives of aboriginal cunning and ferocity."[50] Settler colonialists thus condoned Indian killing because of knowledge of whites "being massacred by a barbarous and inhumane enemy" or being "butchered without immediate relief or assistance."[51]

In a cultural dynamic that would play out repeatedly throughout subsequent American history, the demonization and destruction of the savage enemy other helped solidify a common national identity. As Americans framed the Indians as demonic savages bent on their destruction, they put aside their own differences and vowed to destroy the existential threat. "Even as they remained divided on a wide range of social and political questions," Hinderaker explains, "the Euro-American residents of the Ohio valley could unite in support of aggressive national expansion."[52]

American national identity thus evolved, in opposition to British authority as American schoolbooks long emphasized, and also within the context of a murderous race war against the savage Indians. What Silver describes as an "enraptured discourse of fear" and a "horror-filled rhetoric of victimization" became "all but unanswerable as political discourse." As in future American conflicts, "Anyone who professed not to see the dangers it decried, or who seemed not to care enough about the suffering it relentlessly described, was open to the charge of acting against the best interests of 'the white people.'"[53]

The hegemonic discourse of Indian terror against innocents enabled the indiscriminate killing of any and all Indians. In late 1763 and early 1764 a Pennsylvania mob known as the Paxton boys slaughtered twenty Christian Indians. Determined to extirpate "this nest of perfidious enemies," the mob seized fourteen of the Indians from protective custody in Lancaster for summary execution and mutilation. The "piecemeal ethnic cleansing" of the Paxton Boys "crystallized long-simmering hatreds into explicit new doctrines of racial unity and racial antagonism." Declaring that all Indians were "enemies, rebels, and traitors," the Pennsylvania governor made the colony a free-fire zone thereby authorizing settler colonials "to embrace all opportunities of pursuing, taking, killing, or destroying" Indians. The by now time-honored practice of offering bounties to scalp hunters flourished, with a sizable $134 award offered for each male scalp. Pennsylvania encouraged the slaughter of women and children with offers of $50 for those scalps.[54]

In an effort to contain the borderland violence, the British sought to use the longstanding alliance with the Iroquois Confederation to exert influence over less powerful Indian tribes. The Six Nations of the Iroquois sought to maintain their own lands and cultural autonomy through diplomacy with the British at the expense of the Ohio Indian tribes. Accordingly, the British and the Iroquois signed the Treaty of Fort Stanwix (near present day Rome, New York) in 1768. The "Stanwix line" supposedly settled the Euro-Indian boundary line with the understanding that settlement would be limited to the east and south of the Ohio River. However, neither the Iroquois nor the British had the power to rein in the settlers or the Delaware, Shawnee, and Wyandot Indians of that region. "At root, it was a cynical compact born in the mutual weakness of its two major parties: the Iroquois and the British Empire," Richard White explains.[55]

The growing American revolt against British authority ushered in a massive wave of Indian killing. On the eve of the American Revolution, the innocuously titled Lord Dunmore's War erupted when the eponymous Virginia governor had capitalized on the colonial rebellion by setting aside royal decrees against speculation in Indian lands. Virginia surveyors, settlers, and speculators promptly claimed Kentucky lands as their own, precipitating a treaty with the Cherokee but violent resistance by many of the Shawnee. The Shawnee had rejected the Stanwix line under which they would lose their Kentucky hunting grounds.

Dunmore's War began after a spate of indiscriminate killings of Indians in 1774, some perpetrated by drunken settlers. The killings included the murder of the pregnant sister of the Mingo chief Logan, who retaliated by slaughtering a family of settlers and taking the children as captives. Logan took thirteen scalps and declared that he had satisfied the need for retaliation over assaults on his people, as sanctioned by Shawnee cultural tradition. The conflict could have ended there but Dunmore, declaring that the Indians should be "severely chastised," precipitated a wider war by ordering the destruction of entire Shawnee towns and villages and the seizure of their lands. Dunmore thus "demonstrated how murders occasioned by rum and backcountry settlers could serve the desires of more discreet men to become wealthy."[56]

At the very time that Dunmore drove Indians from their villages, the First Continental Congress simultaneously began the process of driving the British from the continent. The American Revolution, framed in historical discourse as a struggle for freedom and self-determination, thus unfolded in concert with indiscriminate violence against the indigenous other. Whereas the Crown had sought to contain and regulate westward expansion, land-grabbing settlers received the backing of local and national revolutionary governments in a "dramatic inversion of the earlier model of imperial development." For squatters who had already begun to settle on the borderlands without authorization, "the language, the ideas, and the urgency of the American Revolution all helped to validate their scramble for western lands," Hinderaker explains.[57]

Revolutionary War discourse further inculcated the binary between the savage Indian other and patriots in pursuit of liberty. Thus the Declaration of Independence excoriated King George for unleashing "on the inhabitants of our frontiers, the merciless Indian savages, whose known rule of warfare is undistinguished destruction of all ages, sexes, and conditions." Subsequent campaigns of Indian removal and extirpation could be elided within a larger frame of the Revolutionary struggle for the triumph of republicanism over monarchy. The British "were a useful enemy," Andrew Cayton explains, "in that they made it easier to reconcile conquest and liberty."[58]

As the British once again turned to alliance with "the savages" to chastise the rebellious colonies the Mohawk leader Joseph Brant (Thayendanegea) spearheaded Indian resistance. Although he could hardly be called a savage, having graduated from the future Dartmouth College and embraced the Anglican Church, Brant recognized that a British victory offered the only hope of containing the relentless American drive against the Indian homelands. The British and their Indian allies sought to destroy and terrorize vulnerable pockets of rebellion in the backcountry in order to undermine morale and divert American military resources from other battlefields.[59]

In July 1778 in the Wyoming Valley of Pennsylvania, Seneca, Onondaga, Mohawk, and Cayuga of the Iroquois Confederation joined British forces under Colonel John Butler in an extirpative assault against settlers. The attack centered on the township of Wilkes-Barre, named for rebellious Whigs in the British parliament and had become an American rebel stronghold. In the wave of murder, torture, scalping, and mutilation that followed, the Indians, Butler's rangers, and Tory allies killed 227 while taking only five prisoners. "The massacre of the Wyoming Valley militia illustrated the savagery of frontier fighting and civil war at their bloody worst," Glenn Williams observes.[60]

The Americans retaliated the next year as George Washington directed General John Sullivan to conduct extirpative campaigns against Loyalists in Pennsylvania and on into the heart of Iroquois country. Sullivan's forces razed some forty Iroquois villages in the Finger Lakes region of New York. As Sullivan reported to Washington, "The immediate objects of this expedition are accomplished; total ruin of the Indian settlement, and the destruction of their crops, which were designed for the support of those inhuman barbarians, while they were desolating the American frontiers." Washington pronounced the success of a campaign that had been designed to "relieve our frontiers from the depredations to which they would otherwise be exposed." The Iroquois, who froze to death or died of starvation in droves, ever after dubbed Washington "the Town Destroyer." Washington's search and destroy campaign bore "striking similarities with other operations conducted by the U.S. Army later in its history," Williams observes.[61]

In the Ohio valley, the effort to cleanse the land of Indians militarized the borderlands, which Americans claimed as their own "frontier." The settler colonialists constructed forts or "stations" as a means of survival as they "carried the military organization of the frontier settlements to a higher plane." As Indian attacks intensified in the summer of 1777, "militia duty became the paramount activity of the Kentucky men." The army bolstered U.S. claims to land, drove settlement patterns, and fueled the nascent market economy of the new nation.[62]

Ohio Valley Indians resisted the mounting American assault on their homelands, hunting grounds, and way of life, yet often diverged on how best to respond. Zealous young warriors sought out the fight while more moderate community elders perceived the threat of Indians being annihilated by the waves of settler colonials. The Shawnee leader Cornstalk blamed some of the violence on the warrior zeal of his own "foolish young men" and embarked on a peace mission in 1777. A settler mob in Point Pleasant responded to his call for nonviolence by imprisoning and then executing and mutilating Cornstalk and his son. "Everyone among the Shawnees knew that Cornstalk had been the tireless advocate of accommodation and peace," John Mack Faragher points out, "and their outrage was immeasurable." Meanwhile, other groups of settlers in and around Fort Pitt killed innocent Delaware and Seneca Indians. As a result of this wave of indiscriminate violence, Indian accommodationists lost ground and violent resistance reigned. The Ohio Indians sought unsuccessfully to recruit Cherokees and Creeks against the Long Knives, explaining it was "better to die like men than to dwindle away by inches."[63]

The American "birth of freedom" from Britain thus coincided with a ferocious race war that pitted American settler colonialists against the savage Indian other. "Backcountry Anglo-American, Scots-Irish, and German-American patriots lost relatives and property to Indians, and most of them became Indian haters," White explains. "Murder gradually and inexorably became the dominant American Indian policy."[64]

The perpetration of one of the most infamous atrocities in American history underscored the point. The massacre, unique in its deliberation and sheer depravity, unfolded in 1782 at Gnadenhutten, a Moravian village on the Tuscarawas River. As the Americans besieged the Delaware Indians, sacking Coshocton, they coldly executed ninety-six noncombatant Christian Indians who had been converted by the Moravian "black coats." After a night filled with terror, song, and prayer, the Indians were executed like farm animals. "Still singing, still crying, the male Moravians were separated from the women and children, and led to two separate houses." One Indian after another was forced to kneel then bludgeoned to death with a heavy cooper's mallet until the executioner's arm tired and he gave way to a second.[65]

In a chilling display of the coexistence of democracy and ethnic cleansing on the American borderlands, the Pennsylvanians had first held a vote on what to do with the Moravian converts. Indiscriminate slaughter won out. The American settler colonialists could perceive Indians only as savage foes regardless of their religion, intentions, or behavior. As one man observed after Gnadenhutten, "On this side of the mountain ... the country talks of nothing but killing Indians and taking possession of their lands."[66]

Indiscriminate ethnic violence raged across the borderlands throughout the Revolutionary War. As Indian prisoners brought no reward, Americans killed them for their scalps, redeemable for cash. When, as often happened, no men of fighting age could be found in a village, the invaders burned the homes and crops, leaving the people to forage or starve. "American troops and militia tracked through the Susquehanna, the Allegheny, the Scioto, Miami, and Tennessee valley, leaving smoking ruins and burned cornfields behind them."[67]

Indian combatants, to be sure, reciprocated the extirpative violence. In 1782, at the Battle of Blue Licks in northern Kentucky, the Shawnee and Delaware soundly defeated the frontier forces after luring them into a fatal frontal assault. The Indians proceeded to slaughter seventy-seven men after giving them a false pledge of quarter. Colonel George Rogers Clark responded with a massive raid into southern Ohio and Indiana, replete with indiscriminate killing of Indian women and children as the war without mercy raged on both sides. "To excel them in barbarity is the only way to make war upon Indians and gain a name among them," Clark averred. In an infamous incident in February 1779, Clark made good on his words through a ritual execution of a young Ottawa named Macutté Mong in a calculated effort to terrorize the British, as he demanded the surrender of their fort. After being struck in the head with the tomahawk outside the gates of the British fort at Vincennes, Macutté Mong withdrew the weapon from his own skull and handed it back to his executioner, mocking his inefficiency. Clark ordered his bludgeoned victim, still alive, thrown into the Wabash River whereupon he drowned. When Clark, "his hands and face still reeking from the human sacrifice," subsequently took the surrender of the fort, he told the British General Henry Hamilton that as to the Indians "for his part he would never spare man, woman or child of them."[68]

The psychic anxieties of borderland violence inculcated the desire to exterminate within the emergent American national identity. Settler colonials embraced "the power that autonomy and violence conferred in a revolutionary crucible," Griffin explains. With government unable or unwilling to defend them on the borderlands, violence and independence of spirit evolved as virtues. Americans would defend themselves on the borderlands and simultaneously preserve their individual rights. "Rights, of course, included the ability to kill Indians."[69]

The American triumph in the Revolutionary War ended the struggle between the Anglos and the Americans and laid the foundation for the continent-wide campaigns of Indian removal and extirpative warfare that followed. The Treaty of Paris in 1783 produced the same result as the one twenty years earlier: Indians, though not defeated militarily, once again were excluded from the white man's diplomacy. The British summarily abandoned even the longstanding Iroquois ally, who would soon be dispossessed.

Conclusions

Euro-American Indian removal and indiscriminate warfare is but one chapter in a massive global history of settler colonialism. In addition to

North America, examples of this type of colonial development include Argentina, Australia, Brazil, New Zealand, and Israel. However, as scholars of settler colonialism have pointed out, "[t]he place of the United States is especially controversial." This controversy reflects the hegemonic sway of mythic American national identity, commonly known as American exceptionalism, and the extent that Americans have elided their history of colonialism. "The true magnitude of the violent encounter with the indigenous inhabitants of North America remains unacknowledged even today," Karl Jacoby points out. "So too are its consequences and contingencies unexplored," despite an outpouring of genocide studies.[70]

History itself has been cleansed, as textbooks and school curricula rarely explicitly address colonialism as an American phenomenon. Even scholars began to employ the term colonialism in an American context only in relatively recent years. While still few in number some scholars have begun to feature ethnic cleansing as an apt description of U.S. colonial policy.[71]

More explicit analysis of colonialism will illuminate the "boomerang effect" suggested by Cesaire, Fanon, and other theorists. Violence on the borderland boomeranged back against Indians as angry whites came to hate the red savages for their violent homeland defense. While many Euro-Americans remained sympathetic to Indian victimization, others saw their destruction, and if necessary their extermination, as inevitable. Indian tactics boomeranged back against them as Euro-Americans learned to skulk in the woods, conduct search and destroy operations, attack villages at dawn, destroy Indian food stores in winter, take Indian scalps, enslave them, deport their children, and above all, relentlessly take Indian land. The United States refused to share space or conduct diplomacy on equal terms with the savage Indian other. As in future American wars, only the unconditional surrender of the enemy could stem the tide of violence.

As noted at the outset, postcolonial analysis encompasses the study of the psychological impact not only on the colonized but on the colonizer as well. While much has been learned about colonialism and its impact on the colonized peoples, less understood "are the cultural and psychological pathologies produced by colonization in the colonizing societies." As Ashis Nandy points out, "Colonizers are at least as much affected by the ideology of colonialism … their degradation, too, can sometimes be terrifying."[72] As historian Geoff Eley points out, "[t]he critical and eclectic appropriation of psychoanalytic theory of various kinds has played a key role, whose potentials historians have begun only slowly to explore."[73] The American borderlands comprised a vast arena of ethnic cleansing and indiscriminate warfare, a Lacanian battleground where Americans acted out the violent desires that would propel their national identity.

The boomerang effect of Indian removal and extirpative warfare on national identity and subsequent U.S. foreign policy has been understudied and undertheorized. Yet as John Ferling argues, "When warfare occurs with considerable frequency, as it did in early America, war shapes the character and identity of a people." Violence against Indians, replete with demonization, racialized discourse, and indiscriminate killing, presaged similar virulent national campaigns against external enemy others throughout American history. As Calloway notes, "[t]he Indian wars, some would say, left a more sinister mark on American culture: a nation built on conquest could not escape the legacy of its violent past."[74]

Americans have mostly elided rather than grappled with the implications of the ethnic violence and indiscriminate warfare. Wars had been waged from the arrival of the first Europeans to the end of the American Revolution yet history has obscured these conflicts. Many of these wars—Philip's, William's, Anne's, Pontiac's, and Dunmore's—took on innocuous personal names or no name at all. This absence of meaningful names reflected "the unspoken recognition that there was little that was noble about them," Cayton observes.[75]

The lack of nobility was one thing, the impulse to exterminate quite another. A consensus emerged among the Americans streaming into the borderlands as well as their backers in the east. The time had passed for trade and diplomacy, compromise and coexistence, with the indigenous peoples. These Americans sought a final solution to the problem that had long plagued the project of settler colonialism on a frontier they called their own.

Notes

1. The literature on this subject is extensive. See Brett Bowden, *The Empire of Civilization: The Evolution of an Imperial Idea* (Chicago: University of Chicago Press, 2009).
2. The frontier in American history and historiography has been heavily problematized since the promulgation of the Turner Thesis in 1893. The best analysis I have found is Kerwin Lee Klein, *Frontiers of Historical Imagination: Narrating the European Conquest of Native America, 1890-1990* (University of California Press, 1997).
3. Frantz Fanon, *The Wretched of the Earth* (New York: Grove Press, 1968), 102; Tzvetan Todorov, *The Conquest of America: The Question of the Other* (New York: Harper & Row, 1984), 5; Kevin Bruyneel, *The Third Space of Sovereignty: The Postcolonial Politics of U.S.-Indigenous Relations* (Minneapolis: University of Minnesota Press, 2007), 8. See also Walter L. Hixson, *The Myth of American Diplomacy: National Identity and U.S. Foreign Policy* (New Haven: Yale University Press, 2008); Fred Anderson and Andrew Cayton, *The Dominion of War: Empire and Liberty in North America, 1500-2000* (New York: Viking, 2005).

4. As I am intending use of the term, "continuity" does not suggest that Indian warfare was literally constant or continuous in that sense. Clearly the occurrence and scope of Amerindian and Euro-American violence varied from place to place and time to time. In some areas many decades could pass between outbreaks of sustained violence. Moreover, Indians and Euro-Americans conducted multiple relationships, notably commerce, that often proceeded in a nonviolent manner. All that said, as I read early American history, violent Indian removal and extirpative war occurred repeatedly and throughout the British colonies until the ultimate end game of Indian removal. I therefore view this phenomenon as continuous over the *longue dureé* of early American history.

5. Malani Johar Schueller and Edward Watts, eds., *Messy Beginnings: Postcoloniality and Early American Studies* (New Brunswick, N.J.: Rutgers University Press, 2003), 2.

6. The definition and utility of "postcolonial studies" has been contested, often virulently, and the literature is large and growing. In the sense I am using the term, postcolonial reflects an approach or methodology and not the temporal meaning suggested by the hyphenated version of the term, post-colonial, or after colonialism. The nonhyphenated version suggests that the impact of colonialism was so great as to be enduring, thus the need to address its impact through the field of postcolonial studies. Works that I have found most useful include Ania Loomba, *Colonialism/Postcolonialism* (New York: Routledge, 1998); Henry Schwarz and Sangeeta Roy, eds., *A Companion to Postcolonial Studies* (Malden, MA: Blackwell Publishers, 2000); Robert J.C. Young, *Postcolonialism: An Historical Introduction* (Malden, MA: Blackwell Publishers, 2000); Ania Loomba, Suvir Kaul, Matti Bunzl, Antoinette Burton, and Jed Esty, eds., *Postcolonial Studies and Beyond* (Durham, NC: Duke University Press, 2005); and Achille Mbembe, *On the Postcolony* (Berkeley: University of California Press, 2001).

7. Settler colonialism refers to the process by which settlers—or more appropriately settler-invaders—sought to, as Caroline Elkins and Susan Pedersen explain, "construct communities bounded by ties of ethnicity and faith in what they persistently defined as virgin or empty land. Indeed, insofar as there was a logic to their approach to the indigenous populations, it was a logic of elimination and not exploitation: they wished less to govern indigenous peoples or to enlist them in their economic ventures than to seize their land and push them beyond an ever-expanding frontier of settlement." Settler-invaders, typically European, arrived with the intent to control space—define it, demarcate it, map it, own it, and secure it through violence if necessary. Examples of this type of colony include Argentina, Australia, Brazil, Canada, New Zealand, Israel, and the United States. The Americans and the other settler-invaders sought nothing less than the physical, geographical, spiritual, cultural, and symbolic *elimination* of the indigenous population. See Caroline Elkins and Susan Pedersen, eds., *Settler Colonialism in the Twentieth Century: Projects, Practices, Legacies* (New York: Routledge, 2005); "Settler Colonialism," *South Atlantic Quarterly* 107, No. 4 (Fall 2008); Patrick Wolfe, *Settler Colonialism and the Transformation of Anthropology: The Politics and Poetics of an Ethnographic Event* (London: Cassell, 1999); The best overview of settler colonialism is Lorenzo Veracini, *Settler Colonialism: A Theoretical Overview* (New York: Palgrave Macmillan, 2010); see also "Settler Colonialism," *South Atlantic Quarterly*, 107, 4 (special edition, Fall 2008); Patrick Wolfe, *Settler Colonialism and the Transformation of Anthropology: The Politics and Poetics of an Ethnographic Event* (London: Cassell, 1999); James Belich, *Replenishing the Earth: The Settler Revolution and the Rise of the Anglo World, 1783–1939* (New York: Oxford University Press, 2009); and John C. Weaver, *The Great Land Rush and the Making of the Modern World, 1650–1900* (Montreal: McGill-Queen's University Press, 2003).

8. Aimé Césaire, *Discourse on Colonialism* (New York: Monthly Review Press, 1972), 35. See also Dominique-Octave Mannoni, *Prospero and Caliban: The Psychology of Colonization*

(Ann Arbor: University of Michigan Press, 1950); Albert Memmi, *The Colonizer and the Colonized* (Boston: Beacon Press, 1965).

9. Loomba, *Colonialism/Postcolonialism*, 145.

10. The literature is vast. For a sampling see Frederick E. Hoxie, "Retrieving the Red Continent: Settler Colonialism and the History of American Indians in the U.S.," *Ethnic and Racial Studies* 31 (2008), 1153–1167; Colin G. Calloway, "2008 Presidential Address: Indian History from the End of the Alphabet; And What Now?" *Ethnohistory* 58 (Spring 2011), 197–211; Jeffrey Ostler, *The Plains Sioux and U.S. Colonialism from Lewis and Clark to Wounded Knee* (New York: Cambridge University Press, 2004); Ned Blackhawk, *Violence over the Land: Indians and Empires in the Early American West* (Cambridge, MA: Harvard University Press, 2008); Pekka Hamalainen, *The Comanche Empire* (New Haven: Yale University Press, 2008); Brian DeLay, *War of a Thousand Deserts: Indian Raids and the U.S.-Mexican War* (New Haven: Yale University Press), 2008; James F. Brooks, *Captives and Cousins: Slavery, Kinship ,and Community in the Southwest Borderlands* (Chapel Hill: University of North Carolina Press, 2002).

11. Charles C. Mann, *1491: New Revelations of the Americas before Columbus* (New York: Vintage Books, 2006), 29.

12. Mark Rifkin, *Manifesting America: The Imperial Construction of U.S. National Space* (New York: Oxford University Press, 2009), 13.

13. Bowden, *The Empire of Civilization*; Nicholas B. Dirks, Geoff Eley, and Sherry B. Ortner, *Culture/Power/History* (Princeton: Princeton University Press, 1994); Geoff Eley and Ronald Grigor Suny, eds., *Becoming National: A Reader* (New York: Oxford University Press, 1996). Also on this topic, works by and about Michel Foucault, too numerous to mention, are indispensable. On racial modernity, see David Theo Goldberg, *The Racial State* (Malden, MA: Blackwell, 2002). See also Joyce E. Chaplin, "Race," in *The British-Atlantic World, 1500-1800*, ed. David Armitage and Michael J. Braddick (New York: Palgrave, 2002): 154–72; Colin G. Calloway, *New Worlds for All: Indians, Europeans, and the Remaking of Early America* (Baltimore: Johns Hopkins University Press, 1997), 10.

14. Peter Silver, *Our Savage Neighbors: How Indian War Transformed Early America* (New York: W. W. Norton, 2008).

15. Stuart Banner, *How Indians Lost Their Land: Law and Power on the Frontier* (Cambridge, MA: Belknap Press, 2007).

16. Paul Grant-Costa and Elizabeth Mancke, "Anglo-Amerindian Commercial Relations," in *Oceanic Empire: Britain's Atlantic and Indian Ocean Worlds*, ed. H.V. Bowen, Elizabeth Mancke, and John G. Reid (Cambridge: Cambridge University Press, forthcoming).

17. Daniel Richter, *Facing East from Indian Country: A Native History of Early America* (Cambridge, MA: Harvard University Press, 2001), 69–81; John E. Ferling, *Struggle for a Continent: The Wars of Early America* (Arlington Heights, IL: Harlan Davidson, 1993), 21.

18. Richter, *Facing East*, 75. [emphasis added]

19. Alan Taylor, *American Colonies: The Settling of North America* (New York: Penguin, 2001), 135.

20. Ferling, *Struggle for a Continent*, 28.

21. John Grenier, *The First Way of War: American War Making on the Frontier, 1607-1814* (Cambridge: Cambridge University Press, 2005), 26.

22. Ferling, *Struggle for a Continent*, 36–38.

23. Taylor, *American Colonies*, 138–57.

24. Richter, *Facing East*, 90–105; Armstrong Starkey, *European and Native American Warfare, 1675-1815* (Norman: University of Oklahoma Press, 1998), 57–82.

25. Grenier, *The First Way of War*, 43.

26. Ferling, *Struggle for a Continent*, 57; Jill Lepore, *In the Name of War: King Philip's War and the Origins of American Identity* (New York: Knopf, 1998).

27. Jenny Hale Pulsipher, *Subjects unto the Same King: Indians, English, and the Contest for Authority in Colonial New England* (Philadelphia: University of Pennsylvania Press, 2005), 112; Daniel R. Mandell, *King Philip's War: Colonial Expansion, Native Resistance, and the End of Indian Sovereignty* (Baltimore: The Johns Hopkins University Press, 2010), 144; Lepore, *In the Name of War,* xiv.
28. Grenier, *The First Way of War,* 43.
29. Daniel P. Barr, "'This Land is Ours Not Yours': The Western Delawares and the Seven Years' War in the Upper Ohio Valley, 1755-1758," in *The Boundaries Between Us: Natives and Newcomers along the Frontiers of the Old Northwest Territory, 1750-1850,* ed. Daniel P. Barr (Kent, OH: Kent State University Press, 2006), 29.
30. Silver, *Our Savage Neighbors,* 35, 57.
31. Memmi, *The Colonizer and Colonized,* 88.
32. Fred Anderson, *The Crucible of War: The Seven Years War and the Fate of Empire in British North America, 1754-1766* (New York: Vintage Books, 2000), 185–201.
33. Grenier, *First Way of War,* 145.
34. Stephen Brumwell, *White Devil: A True Story of War, Savagery, and Vengeance in Colonial America* (Cambridge, MA: Da Capo Press, 2004), 17, 166–67.
35. *Ibid.,* 197, 262.
36. Silver, *Our Savage Neighbors,* xxii, 94, 114.
37. Barr, *Boundaries Between Us,* 59; Nancy Shoemaker, "How Indians Became Red," *The American Historical Review* 102, no. 3 (June 1997): 625.
38. Richard White, *The Middle Ground: Indians, Empires, and Republics in the Great Lakes Region, 1650-1815* (London: Cambridge University Press, 1991).
39. Anderson, *Crucible of War,* 466.
40. James H. Merrell, *Into the American Woods* (New York: Norton, 1999), 295.
41. Barr, *Boundaries Between Us,* 56.
42. Grenier, *First Way of War,* 144–45; Silver, *Our Savage Neighbors,* 132; Anderson, *Crucible of War,* 541–46.
43. R.D. Hurt, *The Ohio Frontier: Crucible of the Old Northwest, 1720-1830* (Bloomington: Indiana University Press, 1996), 56.
44. Colin Calloway, *The Scratch of a Pen: 1763 and the Transformation of North America* (New York: Oxford University Press, 2006), 98.
45. Patrick Griffin, *American Leviathan: Empire, Nation, and Revolutionary Frontier* (New York: Hill & Wang, 2007), 16.
46. White, *Middle Ground,* 317; Calloway, *Scratch of a Pen,* 100.
47. Starkey, *European and Native American Warfare,* 115.
48. Eric Hinderaker, *Elusive Empires: Constructing Colonialism in the Ohio Valley, 1673-1800* (London: Cambridge University Press, 1997), 102, 128.
49. Silver, *Our Savage Neighbors,* 80–83.
50. White, *Middle Ground,* 366.
51. Griffin, *American Leviathan,* 62.
52. Hinderaker, *Elusive Empires,* 226.
53. Silver, *Our Savage Neighbors,* xix–xx.
54. Richter, *Facing East,* 201–8; Silver, *Our Savage Neighbors,* 172.
55. White, *Middle Ground,* 351.
56. Ibid., 362, 364.
57. Hinderaker, *Elusive Empires,* 186–87.
58. David C. Skaggs and Larry Nelson, *The Sixty Years' War for the Great Lakes, 1754-1814* (East Lansing: Michigan State University Press, 2001), 388.
59. Alan Taylor, *The Divided Ground: Indians, Settlers, and the Northern Borderland of the American Revolution* (New York: Vintage, 2006); Eric Hinderaker, *The Two Hendricks: Unraveling a Mohawk Mystery* (Cambridge, MA: Harvard University Press, 2010).

60. Glenn F. Williams, *Year of the Hangman: George Washington's Campaign against the Iroquois* (Yardley, PA: Westholme Publishing, 2006), 131.
61. Ibid., 284–94.
62. Hinderaker, *Elusive Empires*, 193.
63. Ibid., 208, 211; John Mack Faragher, *Daniel Boone: The Life and Legend of an American Pioneer* (New York: Owl Books, 1992), 156.
64. White, *Middle Ground*, 368–77.
65. Skaggs and Nelson, *Sixty Years' War for the Great Lakes*, 187–214; Hurt, *The Ohio Frontier*, 91.
66. Silver, *Our Savage Neighbors*, 276.
67. Colin Calloway, *The American Revolution in Indian Country: Crisis and Diversity in Native American Communities* (New York: Cambridge University Press, 1995), 48.
68. White, *Middle Ground*, 368–77.
69. Griffin, *American Leviathan*, 153.
70. Jacoby, *Shadows at Dawn*, 2.
71. Gary Clayton Anderson, *The Conquest of Texas: Ethnic Cleansing in the Promised Land, 1820-1875* (Norman: University of Oklahoma Press, 2005).
72. Ashis Nandy, *The Intimate Enemy: Loss and Recovery of Self under Colonialism* (Delhi, New York: Oxford University Press, 1983), 30.
73. Geoff Eley, *A Crooked Line: From Cultural History to the History of Society* (Ann Arbor: University of Michigan Press, 2005), 155.
74. Ferling, *Struggle for a Continent*, 6; Calloway, *New Worlds for All*, 114.
75. Skaggs and Nelson, *Sixty Years' War for the Great Lakes*, 382.

Chapter 2

Alterity and the Production of Identity in the Early Modern British American Empire and the Early United States

Jack P. Greene

During a House of Commons debate in November 1775 over what, in light of its army's misadventures in Massachusetts the previous spring, Britain should do to deal with colonial resistance to parliamentary authority, William Innes, MP for Ilchester, spoke at length in favor of strong coercive measures. Emphatically questioning whether the colonists were even "the offspring of Englishmen, and as such entitled to the privileges of Britons," he denounced them rather as a promiscuous "mixture of people" who consisted "not only ... of English, Scots, and Irish, but also of French, Dutch, Germans innumerable, Indians, Africans, and a multitude of felons from this country." Few members of such a population, he insisted, could possibly have a legitimate claim to status as full Britons deserving of the rich inheritance and identity enjoyed by independent Britons in the home islands. Colonial British Americans, he charged, had created and continued to live in societies that bore little resemblance to that of the home island, citing in particular the massive importation of slaves and the "despotic" exploitation of them. Societies thus drawing their "sustenance from the very bosom of slavery," he declared, "surely [have] nothing in them similar to what prevails in Great Britain."[1]

In these remarks Innes built upon a well-established, if diffuse, language of alterity or otherness that dated back to the earliest days of English overseas enterprise. In metropolitan Britain, the celebration of empire as an enormous stimulant to Britain's wealth and a major element in its international stature and the conception of colonization as a noble enterprise

to bring civilization to savage and rude new worlds had never been un-
qualified. If the colonies themselves had been an obvious boon to Britain,
the settlers who inhabited them often seemed, to those who remained at
home or directly interacted with them, to be far less worthy of praise. The
discourses of empire that took shape in Britain during the late seventeenth
and early eighteenth centuries included a dash of heavy-handed skepticism about the character of the settlers who inhabited the plantations and
the societies that they created. From very early on, a significant strand of
metropolitan imperial thought used what modern analysts would call the
language of alterity to depict the colonies as receptacles for those who had
failed at home: the poor, the unemployed, the unwanted, the outcasts, the
very dregs of English society. Throughout the seventeenth and eighteenth
centuries, this language ran as a strong undercurrent in metropolitan conceptions of empire. The colonial process thus involved not just encounters
with exotic indigenous and imported others but also the creation of an
entirely new category of others, lumping together colonial participants
and thereby distinguishing them from the more successful and refined
populations of the metropolis.[2]

While by no means universal, this unfavorable image of colonials and
the social spaces they created was ubiquitous in British publications—in
commercial tracts, critiques of colonial slavery, imperial histories, travel
memoirs, fake choreographies, novels, poetry, plays, magazine and newspaper essays, political pamphlets, and parliamentary speeches—and it
took a variety of forms. Rooted in a conviction that no one would leave
England except under compulsion, this image stressed the lowly social
origins of migrants and their religious and social deviancy. Furthermore,
the distinctly non-English and often unhealthy places where colonials
chose to settle, sharing the wilderness with uncivil savage peoples, and
the questionable societies that they created in the process, seemed to put
these overseas English people in a separate and inferior category. With
little learning or religion (or a deviant form thereof), and with few of
the other cultural amenities of English life, colonial societies were so
crude that cultural degeneration was inevitable, not a few metropolitans
thought. Moreover, the settlers' lowly origins, unsavory characters, and
narrow pursuit of economic gain, metropolitans charged, produced societies deeply dissimilar to what they had left behind. With their populations exhibiting little concern for traditional English social mores, colonial societies seemed to be characterized by vicious labor regimes, sharp
business practices, and political and legal orders catering to the self-
interest of the upstart socioeconomic groups who were dominant within
the colonies, groups bent upon subverting any metropolitan efforts to
regulate them.

These characteristics provided a sturdy foundation for metropolitans to construct a language of alterity for application to the American colonies. Less harsh than the well-developed languages of savagery and barbarity that were only occasionally applied to colonial settlers, and less comprehensively exclusive than the language of alienation used to identify foreigners, this language lacked a contemporary name to encompass all of the many elements that combined to form a language of social derision or condescension that expressed metropolitan misgivings about the genuine Englishness of England's overseas offshoots. Despite the rapid development, especially after about 1720, of these societies into viable economic and political entities with expanding social amenities, competent leaders, and tightening cultural ties with the parent state, such misgivings persisted throughout the colonial era, to the great disquiet of colonial leaders, who, almost as much as they sought to gain fortunes for themselves and their families, were intent upon establishing offshoots of old England in new American worlds. Thus, the continuing process of metropolitan othering did not stimulate the emergence of oppositional identities that would favorably contrast colonial worlds with the metropolis. Even as they created, through a process of cultural adaptation, distinctive provincial identities that were rooted in peculiarities of place, specific socioeconomic and legal structures, and the inhabitants' collective experiences over time, settlers held tightly to their identities as Britons. As a result, metropolitan othering operated throughout the colonial era to reinforce among settler leaders a determination to prove themselves and their societies worthy of the British identity to which they had ever aspired, a situation that did not change until midway through the great debate that led between 1764 and 1783 to the separation of thirteen of Britain's more than thirty American colonies from the British Empire.[3]

Loose and Vagrant People

The stereotype of the colonies as receptacles for those who had failed at home was already deeply entrenched by the middle of the seventeenth century, and by the early 1690s when the economic writer Sir Josiah Child took up the subject, it was commonplace. Child elaborated in some detail upon the view that colonists scarcely came from the cream of old English society. Rather, he wrote, most of the colonies, singling out Virginia and Barbados as examples, had been "first peopled by a sort of loose vagrant People, vicious and destitute of the means to live at home (being either unfit for labour, or such as could find none to employ themselves about, or had so misbehaved themselves by whoring, thieving, or other debauchery, that none would set them on work)." Nor, despite the emigration of some refugees of higher social standing during the English Civil War, in Child's view, were subsequent emigrants to the colonies much different. "The constant supply that the said Plantations have since had," he insisted, "has been by such loose vagrant people ... picked up, especially about the streets and suburbs of London and Westminster, and by Malefactors condemned for crimes, for which by the law they deserved to die; and some of those people called Quakers, banished for meeting on pretence of religious worship."[4]

But it was not just the suspect origins of the colonists that contributed to their poor reputation in England. While promotional writers hailed the colonies as inviting places of opportunity, and chorographers and historians reported on their steady development as improved and Anglicized social and political spaces, other writers, employing a variety of other genres, limned portraits of them as societies so oriented toward the pursuit of economic gain as to be viciously exploitative of all dependent peoples and barren of most traditional amenities of metropolitan English life. The callous mistreatment of servants and slaves was a prevalent theme. For instance, from the 1659 tract of Marcellus Rivers and Oxenbridge Foyle, two men accused of royalism and rebellion and shipped to the colonies as servants, English readers could learn that American planters were the "most inhuman and barbarous persons," who in the quest for riches worked their servants hard, fed them meagerly, and in general reduced them to the "most deplorable, and (as to Englishmen) ... unparalleled condition," treating them no better than beasts.[5]

If Christians had to endure such a harsh labor regime, the African slaves who after 1650 comprised a steadily growing share of the colonial labor force—first in Barbados and the other West Indian colonies and then on the mainland in Virginia, Maryland, and the Carolinas—reportedly fared even worse. For a small but highly vocal group of critics writing between 1670 and 1710, the system of chattel slavery that was developing in the colonies and the social and cultural systems that supported it constituted exhibit A in an emerging portrait of the colonies as places of cultural regress and social deviation from English norms. These included the Anglican minister Morgan Godwin, who had lived in both Virginia and Barbados for extended periods in the 1670s and 1680s, and Thomas Tryon, a merchant and social reformer who had resided in Barbados for much of the late 1660s.[6] These writers were careful not to challenge the legality of slavery, their principal concerns being to awaken the consciences of American slaveholders to the harsh usage that the enslaved endured in the plantations, to persuade slave owners that enslaved people could be instructed in Christianity and converted without material prejudice to their owners' property interests and without subverting colonial societies. They also sought to alert metropolitan readers to the disturbing character of the societies that were taking shape in the English slave colonies, societies that in their covetousness, inattention to religion, brutal labor regimes, disordered families, and sexual licentiousness constituted monstrous distortions of metropolitan English society. Given the colonists' "extraordinary Ambition to be thought well of" in England, Godwin hoped exposing their social deviations in the metropolis and getting them "decryed here" might eventually "shame them into better Principles."[7] In the meantime, however, he denounced colonial societies as "a reproach and dishonour to the *English* Nation, and Government."[8] If the original settlers, as conventional metropolitan images had long suggested, had been people of low social origins and "small Stocks," some of their descendants had "grown wonderfully rich," but they had not improved their character along with their fortunes, and as presented in the works of Godwin and Tryon, the societies they had built did nothing to alter metropolitan conceptions of colonists as the dregs of English society. At the close of the seventeenth century many metropolitans yet held, in Tryon's words, "but an indifferent Opinion of those Settlements" and the settlers who inhabited them.[9]

As slavery became ever more entrenched in the American colonies and the slave trade ever more voluminous and profitable to Britain during the first half of the eighteenth century, overt criticism of slavery and American slave societies became more muted in metropolitan Britain. The conception of the plantations as places of exceptional cruelty and of the Europeans who presided over them as a category of others continued to be fostered by the repetition of the touching story of Inkle and Yariko, first told by Richard Ligon, a visitor to Barbados, in the 1650s in his *A True and Exact History of the Island of Barbadoes*, published in London in 1657.[10] It was repeated and substantially elaborated by the Irish writer Richard Steele in *The Spectator* in 1711. In this story, Thomas Inkle, a young Englishman on his way to Barbados "to improve his Fortune by Trade and Merchandize," escaped an Indian ambush "on the Main of *America*" and subsequently received shelter, sustenance, and affection from Yariko, a young Indian maiden "of Distinction." The two of them fell in love, with Inkle proposing to take Yariko off to England to lead a civilized life with him, and when they finally managed to hail down an English ship Yariko willingly accompanied him to Barbados, where Inkle, a young man bred up on "an early Love of Gain" and worried about the monetary losses he had sustained during his long stay with Yariko, betrayed his lover and, despite the fact that she was pregnant, sold her to a Barbadian merchant as a slave.[11]

As the popularity of this story revealed, metropolitan unease with chattel slavery and the rectitude of colonial settlers overseas never disappeared and could be easily reanimated, as happened briefly in the mid 1730s, when several London magazines published an anonymous speech purportedly written by Moses Bon Sàam, identified as a learned Jamaica Maroon, who called for slave resistance and revived images of American planters as cruel and "insolent *Enslavers*," whose lives of pomp and wantonness were bought by the sweat of the enslaved.[12] This publication stimulated the Reverend Robert Robertson, a longtime resident of Nevis, to produce a spirited complaint about metropolitan condemnations of colonial slaveholders. Acknowledging that the slave system within the colonies and the commercial and naval structures that supported it left no doubt that "very few such Pieces of Wickedness have ever been acted on the Face of the Earth," he insisted that African and British traders bore equal responsibility with American planters for its perpetuation and pointed out that the British government had done nothing to discourage such a profitable system.[13]

In view of the deep complicity of metropolitan Britain in the imperial system of slavery, Robertson protested that the role of American planters in its development had "brought, and daily brings them under the severest Censure in *England*," where, as he complained in another publication six years later, they were invariably stigmatized "as Enemies to the Negroes, Oppressors, ungrateful and merciless Masters, insolent Enslavers, imperious Torturers, Insulters of the Negro Colour, and proud Spoilers of the Work of God, who dare make Beasts of human Forms." This entrenched "[w]ay of thinking or speaking on this Subject" powerfully revealed the profound extent that colonial involvement with slavery had contributed to serve as support for the ancient view that both the white inhabitants of the colonies and the social entities that they had built were distorted and inferior versions of the free society from which they emanated.[14]

Literary works also contributed to this view. Perhaps no such work was more important in cementing the metropolitan image of colonists as others and of colonial societies as only marginally English than the scatological "travel" accounts of the magazine editor and humorist Edward (Ned) Ward. In 1698, he published his widely read *A Trip to Jamaica*, which went through at least seven editions over the next quarter century, and the more modestly successful *A Trip to New-England*, published in 1699. Almost certainly, Ward never visited either of these places, but the appeal of his volumes was not their accuracy but their satiric bite, leaving the reader with a vivid sense that the areas he purported to describe were crude, provincial, socially dysfunctional, and populated by the outcasts of England. Whatever favorable things Ward had to say about either Jamaica or New England, no reader could leave these texts without a profound sense of the extraordinary cultural distance between them and England. In these

largely unflattering assessments of Jamaica and New England, Ward ca-
tered to and confirmed existing stereotypes about the people and societies
of colonial English America. At his hands, Jamaican and New England
colonists appeared every bit as exotic as the Native American Indians or
Africans among whom they lived. By treating two colonies at the end of
a geographic and social continuum that stretched from the wealthy and
slave-rich, tropical and staple-producing island colony of Jamaica to the
well-settled (with Europeans) farming, trading, and religiously oriented
northern continental colonies of New England, these volumes might, had
the second volume been as successful as the first, have led to a series of
"Trips" to all of England's prominent colonies. Ward appreciated that the
colonies were distinctive, one from another, but his larger point was the
more important distinction between England and the colonies as a whole,
each of which, he suggested, represented a peculiar and shocking deviation from metropolitan England. Indeed, in Ward's text, whatever social
continuities existed between metropolis and colonies involved the very
worst features, the underside, of English society.

To the extent that Ward's *Trips* were fictional, they were precursors of
the emergence in the 1720s of the American colonies as an appropriate setting for belletristic literature. The American colonies, specifically Virginia,
and its neighbor Maryland, figured heavily in two Daniel Defoe novels
published in 1722: *The Fortunes and Misfortunes of the Famous Moll Flanders*
and *The History and Remarkable Life of the Truly Honourable Colonel Jacque.*
The first told the story of a child born in Newgate Prison to a mother under
sentence of transportation. Grown up, Moll married several times, became
a highly successful shoplifter, and was eventually caught and sentenced
to transportation to Virginia, where she used her gains from shoplifting
to buy herself and her highwayman husband out of service, established a
successful tobacco plantation, and finally achieved the status of a gentle-
woman.[15] The second was a tale of an unwanted child who turned to a life
of crime and in his late teens was kidnapped and sold as an indentured
servant in Virginia. There he worked hard, caught his master's eye, was
promoted to overseer, and after being discharged from his servitude became a successful planter who, wealthy enough to indulge his desire to
see the larger world, spent a quarter century in Europe as a soldier before
retiring to his plantation in Virginia.[16]

In these two novels, Defoe treated Virginia and Maryland as places of
opportunity and redemption. Six characters, three in each novel, found
themselves transported or kidnapped to Virginia, where they put their
lives of poverty and crime behind them and became respectable property
holders with large independent resources. Indeed, in *Colonel Jacque,* Defoe
explicitly touted Virginia and Maryland as places where English felons

and unfortunates could replicate Jacque's experience, explaining how the customary system of land grants and credit offered to servants upon expiration of their terms provided them with a start on the road to independence and respectability, and having Colonel Jacque express the opinion that "every Newgate wretch, every desperate forlorn creature, the most despicable ruined man in the world, has here a fair opportunity put into his hands to begin the world again, and that upon a foot of certain gain and in a method exactly honest, with a reputation that nothing past will have any effect upon." "Some of the most considerable planters in Virginia, and in Maryland also," the colonel declared, had "raised themselves—namely, from being without a hat or a shoe to estates of £40,000 or £50,000; and in this method, I may add, no diligent man ever miscarried, if he had health to work and was a good husband; for he every year adding more land and planting more tobacco, which is real money, he must gradually increase in substance, till at length he gets enough to buy negroes and other servants, and then never works himself any more." Moll's mother, with whom she is reunited during an early stay in Virginia, tells her daughter much the same thing, recounting how "many a *Newgate* Bird" has become "a great Man" in Virginia. "Several Justices of the Peace, Officers of the Train Bands, and Magistrates of the Towns they live in," she says, have "been burnt in the Hand" as transported fellows.[17]

Yet, if Defoe presented Virginia and Maryland as lands of opportunity for European felons, servants, and free people, his accounts did little to undermine the metropolitan image of the American colonies as places of excessive cruelty and cultural deviance and of American colonists as people of low social origins. Although Moll's mother and Colonel Jacque were fortunate in being bought by men "of humanity," the colonel noted that most "masters in Virginia" were "terrible things," that white servants "worked hard, lodged hard, and fared hard," and that "the cruelty so much talked of, used in Virginia and Barbados, and other colonies, in whipping the negro slaves" was "the accustomed severity of the country." Indeed, the colonel's claim that his reforms in treating slaves with mercy and as rational beings rather than beasts had rendered Chesapeake slavery "less cruel and barbarous" as well as dangerous than it was in Barbados and Jamaica testified to the continuing prevalence of violence and cruelty in the slave systems of the British American world. Similarly, the colonel's description, following his acquisition of a little knowledge, of himself as being "buried alive in a remote part of the world, where I could see nothing at all, and hear but a little of what was seen, and that little not till at least half a year after it was done, and sometimes a year or more," and his reluctance to return, for the same reason, further underlined for readers the cultural distance between Britain and its American colonies.

Furthermore, both Moll's and the colonel's American histories and, more
explicitly, Moll's mother's observation that "the greatest part of the Inhabitants of the Colony came thither in very indifferent Circumstances from
England: that, generally speaking, they were of two sorts, either (1.) Such
as were brought over by Masters of Ships to be sold as Servants ... Or,
(2.) Such as are Transported from *Newgate* and other Prisons, after having been found guilty of Felony and other Crimes punishable by Death,"
could only underline and confirm for metropolitans the appropriateness
of the language of otherness for Britain's American colonists.[18]

Works from other genres published in Britain also spoke to the question
of metropolitans' lack of esteem for colonists and colonies. In 1708, John
Oldmixon produced the first comprehensive history of the British-American Empire, published in two volumes in London and in 1741 revised
and expanded in a new edition. Until 1755, it was the only such history.
In this detailed colony-by-colony account, Oldmixon sought to call attention to "the great Increase in Wealth" enjoyed by Britain as a result of its
successful and expanding empire. As he wrote in his dedication, however, he also conceived of his work as an attempt to show the falsity of the
"Scandal which the Enemies of the Plantations maliciously throw upon
them," including especially charges about the "the vulgar Descent of the
Inhabitants," which he denounced as both "ridiculous" and "unjust." Arguing that some colonists were "descended from ... the most ancient and
honourable Families in *England*," he pointed out that many other colonists
of lesser descent had "by their Prudence and Industry ... rais'd Fortunes"
and "acquire[d] Estates" in America sufficient to "ennoble them" if their
achievements had been made in Britain, observing that such achievements
were the essence of "true Nobility" and infinitely more impressive than
titles derived merely from "a long Roll of *Ancestry*," without respect to
either "Reason or Merit."[19]

Over the next half century, many other British analysts acknowledged
the justice of Oldmixon's protest. The economic writer Malachy Postlethwayt, for example, affirmed that, even though the colonies were "much
frequented by unfortunate persons," such people "oftentimes" eventually
became "wealthy there."[20] "Nothing is more certain, or better known,"
declared an anonymous political writer in 1766 "than that necessity has
been the cause of almost every emigration that has happened, and that the
beginnings of most American properties were remarkably slender."[21] But
these and similar affirmations that the colonies provided opportunities
for both metropolitan outcasts and ambitious settlers did little to transform the negative metropolitan image of the colonial world. Throughout
the eighteenth century, metropolitan publications continued to depict the
colonies as receptacles for the waste population of Britain, who would

never overcome the stains of their social origins nor replicate in America the social milieus that had rejected them at home. Routinely, colonials objected, metropolitan commentators continued to show that they thought "meanly of the Colonies," to "spread the grossest Misrepresentations, and wickedly toil to make the World believe" that American settlers were "a Clan of *Kidnappers, Pickpockets, Knaves,* and *Villains,*" and to stigmatize them with *"the black characters of* Unhospitable, Brutal, Savage, Covetous *and* Barbarous" people.[22] By *"freely bestow[ing]"* such *"Epithets"* upon settlers, metropolitans effectively continued to categorize colonials as others who, despite their mostly British descent, were something less than genuine Britons, "a lower order of men in the scale than Europeans," who, protested one American, deserved little more than "the sovereign contempt of their countrymen" in Britain.[23]

Even Adam Smith subscribed to this image in his *Theory of Moral Sentiments,* published in London in 1759. In a section on the differences in customs between a savage and "a humane and polished people," Smith observed that there was "not a negro from the coast of Africa, who does not," in respect to fortitude, "possess a degree of magnanimity, which the soul of his sordid master is scarce capable of conceiving. Fortune never exerted more cruelly her empire over mankind," he added, "than when she subjected those nations of heroes to the refuse of the jails of Europe, of wretches who possess the virtues neither of the countries which they come from, nor of those which they go to, and whose levity, brutality, and baseness, so justly expose them to the contempt of the vanquished."[24]

Common to all British colonies, the legalization of slavery was the most glaring deviation from metropolitan British social norms, but a variety of other characteristics operated throughout the early centuries of empire to sustain a negative image of the American colonies as not quite British, or even as essentially foreign places, which, even though most of their free inhabitants had originated in Britain, were incapable of reproducing British society. Living in exotic places among the strange peoples whose land they had taken or who had been imported to labor for them, colonial settlers, as depicted from the metropolitan perspective through the language of alterity, seemed to be a separate breed, a mixture of poor laborers, former servants, transported felons, economic and social adventurers, and religious deviants who had been unable to make it in Britain and who had been demographically and culturally contaminated in America through their sexual liaisons with native peoples and imported Africans. That such people should create societies characterized by suspect sexual mores, religious deviance or irreligion, crudity, incivility, provinciality, and long-term cultural degeneration, presided over by social upstarts driven largely by material objectives, was, for metropolitans, only to be expected.

A Humane and Polished People

That elite colonialists should find metropolitan usage of a language of alterity deeply offensive is unsurprising. Having always claimed the traditional rights of Englishmen as an essential part of their inheritance, they had long aspired to metropolitan recognition of their identity as British people living in demonstrably British societies and governed by British institutions. These aspirations had been a powerful consideration in the long-term contests and uneasy negotiations between colonial leaders intent upon preserving entire their constituents' inherited rights and metropolitan representatives charged by the Crown with achieving objectives at times incompatible with those rights.

Of course, champions of the colonies labored to counteract the metropolitan image of the origins of their settler populations and the use of the language of otherness to characterize them. Thus did the Virginia planter Robert Beverley directly address Josiah Child's remarks in his *History and Present State of Virginia*, published in London in 1705. Granting Child's point that "at first" the plantations were "for the most part ... peopled by Persons of low Circumstances, and by such as were willing to seek their Fortunes in a Foreign Country" and acknowledging that no person who "cou'd live easy in England" or had there a "plentifull Estate" would "voluntarily abandon a happy Certainty, to roam after imaginary Advantages in a New World" and confront "the infinite Difficulties and Dangers, that attend[ed] a New Settlement," Beverley insisted that once a regular constitution had been "firmly established" and "after the advantages of the Climate, and the fruitfulness of the Soil were well known, and all the dangers incident to Infant Settlement were over, People of better Condition retir'd thither with their Families, either to increase the Estates they had before, or else to avoid being persecuted for their Principles of Religion, or Government."[25]

Almost six decades later in 1764, the young Virginian Arthur Lee, a student in Edinburgh, sought to answer Adam Smith's charges in *An Essay in Vindication of the Continental Colonies of America*. Perhaps more fully than any other writer published in London up to that time, Lee laid out the elements of the language of otherness that had long been used in the metropolis in reference to the colonies and expressed the depths of colonial resentment at the pervasive metropolitan application of that language to the American colonies and their inhabitants. By implying that American colonists consisted of "the refuse of their respective countries" and that they were "utterly destitute of every virtue, or abandoned to the influence of every infamous and detested vice," Lee complained indignantly, Smith had without "the least shadow of truth," at least in reference to Britain's

American "continental colonies," debased the Americans "into Monsters" who "should be treated with reproaches more rigorous than the severest justice, unmitigated by the least humanity, would utter against the most perfectly vicious."[26]

Such slurs, Lee declared, were "as bitter an invective as ever fell from the tongue of man." In specific reference to his own native Virginia, he contended that "no colony had ever a nobler foundation," its founders being "distinguished, even in Britain, for rank, for fortune, for abilities," and pointed out that the subsequent increase of free inhabitants had mostly come from people "from Britain, and other countries, who chose to seek their fortunes in a new and rising world." He did not deny that Virginia had received its share of transported felons, but insisted that such people, when "transported to a country where there is little opportunity, and still less necessity for stealing," usually reformed and became honest settlers. Moreover, he emphasized, "such persons" had "been rarely the founders of families which became afterwards eminent," and few such families in either Virginia or any of the other American colonies could "be traced from so mean an original." In short, Lee concluded, "the inhabitants of the colonies" were "descended from worthy ancestors, from whom," contrary to Smith, they had not "degenerated." To support this contention, Lee observed that many analysts had acknowledged the colonists "to be, at this period, a humane, hospitable, and polished people" entirely undeserving of "the ignominy of being styled, the refuse of jails, inhuman, brutal, and base." How "the mind of a man of sense, a philosopher, a moralist," could "be so strangely perverted," Lee could explain only by his gullibility in being imposed on by "the reports of wretches" designed "to catch the ear of vulgar credulity."[27]

Arising in colonial societies that, like most early modern European colonies of settlement in the Americas, considered themselves an extensions of the parent state, settler indignation of the sort expressed by Beverley and Lee did not lead to the explicit creation of counter identities constructed to emphasize the positive features of the colonial self. Rather, in the formation of colonial identities the metropolitan center continued to be normative. What colonials so painfully sought from fellow Britons at home was an admission that colonial creations measured up to metropolitan standards. Moreover, the immediate presence in the colonies of culturally different people both indigenous and imported from Africa also operated to sustain the cultural power of the center in the formation of collective identities peripheries.

To be sure, provincial identities differed substantially from one colony to another, but they were all informed by an inherited set of values and institutions that made them both recognizably British and culturally similar, and they all possessed a deep pride in being part of an empire that was comparatively free, commercially successful, and, after Britain's stunning victories in the Seven Years' War, undeniably mighty. In association with the empire they had made rapid strides in economic and cultural improvement and had enjoyed a high degree of self-direction in their internal affairs. That they might maintain their connection with Britain on increasingly favorable and mutually beneficial terms was the animating hope of most colonists in the wake of the Seven Years' War.

A Settled Malice Against the Colonies

The metropolitan administration's efforts to tighten the reins of colonial governance after the Seven Years' War rapidly shattered this expectation. By endeavoring to tax the colonies for revenue and to diminish their authority over their internal affairs in other ways, new metropolitan initiatives effectively rendered the colonists' ancient claims to a British identity and an equality of rights with metropolitan Britons highly problematic. Vigorously resisting such measures, the colonists explicitly challenged metropolitan conceptions of colonies as subordinate appendages of the parent state and roused latent fears that the colonists were intent on achieving an independence that would deprive metropolitans of the vast economic and strategic benefits that colonies supplied. This situation provoked widespread indignation among metropolitans and invited them to lapse into the language of otherness that Britons had long used to identify those who had left the home islands for America and places overseas. The existing language made it easy for resentful metropolitans to condemn the colonists as the descendants of "a set of vagabonds and transports," an "obstinate, senseless, and abandoned set of convicts," to deplore their "baseless ingratitude," to charge them with treason, and to label them as rebels.[28]

The doggedness with which most of the continental colonies resisted each new round of metropolitan efforts to bring them to acknowledge the authority of the British Parliament over their internal affairs only intensified metropolitan resentment toward them. More and more, complained Benjamin Franklin, who resided in London through most of the 1760s and early 1770s, metropolitans used disparaging language to express a "settled Malice against the Colonies." The public papers, he observed, daily printed "Rancorous Libels" against the colonials, dismissing them with the "[g]entle terms of republican race, mixed rabble of Scotch, Irish and foreign vagabonds, descendents of convicts, ungrateful rebels & c.," language that conveyed only the most "violent contempt and abuse." By "lumping all the Americans under the general Character of 'House-breakers and Felons'" and by denouncing them "as 'diggers of pits for this country,' 'lunaticks,' 'sworn enemies,' 'false,' 'ungrateful' … 'cut-throats,'" Franklin protested, metropolitan writers after 1764 had branded them as a people who, though descended from British ancestors, had "degenerated to such a Degree" as to become "the lowest of Mankind, and almost of a different Species from the English of Britain," a people "unworthy the name of Englishmen and fit only to be snubb'd, curb'd, shackled and plundered." By such language, metropolitans continued, as so many had done for the past century and a half, to identify colonists as a category of others, "foreigners" who, however much they might aspire to be British, could never actually achieve those aspirations, and who on the scale of civilization were only slightly above the native Amerindians whose lands they had stolen and the African slaves whose bodies they had expropriated to work for them.[29]

Not all Britons shared this low opinion of colonists, of course, and a vigorous Opposition sought unsuccessfully to counter it within Britain. Well into the mid 1770s, colonial leaders clung to the hope that men more favorably disposed to them might gain power, as they had briefly done during the Stamp Act Crisis in 1765–66, change political course, and create an atmosphere for colonials to achieve the British identity they had long sought. However, as during the crisis over the Coercive Acts in 1774, it became ever more clear that the administration was unlikely to back down from its demands for colonial acceptance of parliamentary authority, more and more Americans began to appreciate that the metropolitan government would never relent from its determination, as the young Alexander Hamilton put it in a 1774 pamphlet, to put Americans "of *all* ranks and conditions, opulent as well as indigent … upon a less favourable footing" even than those dependent people in Britain, who, said Hamilton, quoting Sir William Blackstone, were "*in so mean a situation,* that they are supposed to have no will of their own."[30] If this appreciation finally supplied a context for colonial Americans to begin the slow process of developing a counter identity, British military and naval hostilities, launched in the spring of 1775 in an effort to quell colonial resistance, led directly to the widespread demonization in the colonies of the existing British ruling establishment, the movements for independence in thirteen contiguous continental colonies, and the early articulations of a broader American identity among the revolting republican states.

Yet, this counter identity had two peculiar features. First, although their longstanding mutual attachment to their British heritage and their more recent mutual antagonism to Britain provided the preconditions for a union among the thirteen disparate states, the new American identity that began to take shape after 1765 existed in a symbiotic and unequal relationship with colonial/state identities that were deeply entrenched and, for many decades, infinitely more powerful. Throughout the War for Independence, the Confederation era, and the first three-quarters of a century after the creation of a somewhat stronger national union with the Constitution of 1787, American identity would continue to be subordinated to and mediated through the provincial identities of the several states that composed it, as political leaders would show a preference for provincial over national interests and considerations, in foreign as well as in domestic affairs. Although it would affect political decisions for another century, the American antagonism to Britain developed during the War for Independence lacked the staying power to remain central to the emerging national American identity.[31]

Second, in contrast to later colonial projects that left postcolonial nations with a legacy of exploitation, oppression, and underdevelopment, early modern English/British colonialism in America, at least for free settlers of European descent, was a highly positive experience, something to be embraced, not rejected. Just as the rapid demographic, economic, and political development of the colonies and their growing value to Britain had prevented the widespread metropolitan othering of the colonies from stimulating the development of oppositional identities during the colonial era, so their colonial experience provided Americans with a well-developed framework for self-realization at the provincial level and a blueprint for expansion across a huge continent. Their deep attachment to British ideas of consensual government, rule of law, sanctity of private property, and Protestantism, their self-serving conception of colonization as a noble endeavor to bring civility and civic improvement to previously rude and undeveloped worlds, and the embedded-ness of British institutions and legal culture in their existing polities meant that any emerging counter identity would not require the wholesale repudiation of their British heritage.[32] Indeed, in an emphatic denial of a century and a half of metropolitan othering, Americans after 1776, constructing a new nation, could eschew monarchy and embrace republicanism while still thinking of themselves as the true heirs of British-ness.

Notes

1. William Innes, 8 November 1775, in *Proceedings and Debates of the British Parliaments Respecting North America 1754-1783*, 6 vols., ed. R.C. Simmons and P.D.G. Thomas (White Plains, NY: Kraus International Publications, 1982–86), 6: 203.

2. For a superb study of English/British encounters with non-European worlds, see P.J. Marshall and Glyndwr Williams, *The Great Map of Mankind: Perceptions of New Worlds in the Age of the Enlightenment* (Cambridge, MA: Harvard University Press, 1982). For a collection of illuminating case studies on this subject, see also Martin Daunton and Rick Halpern, eds., *Empire and Others: British Encounters with Indigenous Peoples, 1600-1850* (Philadelphia: University of Pennsylvania Press, 1999).

3. On the importance of metropolitan cultural models for English colonists, see Jack P. Greene, "Search for Identity: An Interpretation of the Meaning of Selected Patterns of Social Response in Eighteenth-Century America," in Greene, *Imperatives, Behaviors, & Identities: Essays in Early American Cultural History* (Charlottesville: University of Virginia Press, 1992), 143–74. On the formation of provincial identities, see Greene, "Reformulando a identidade inglesa na América britânica colonial: adaptação cultural e experiência provincial na construçào de identidades corporativas," *Almanack Braziliense* 4 (November, 2006): 5–36.

4. Sir Josiah Child, *A New Discourse of Trade*, 4th ed. (London, 1695), 197–99.

5. Marcellus Rivers and Oxenbridge Foyle, *England's Slavery, or Barbados Merchandize* (London, 1659), 1–7.

6. Morgan Godwin, *The Negro's and Indian's Advocate* (London, 1680); Morgan Godwin, *A Supplement to the Negro's [and] Indian's Advocate* (London, 1681); Morgan Godwin, *Trade prefer'd before Religion and Christ made to give place to Mammon represented in a sermon relating to the plantations* (London, 1685); Morgan Godwin, "A Brief Account of Religion, in the Plantations, with the Causes of the Neglect and Decay thereof in those Parts," in *Some Proposals towards Promoting of the Gospel in our American Plantations*, ed. Francis Brokesby (London, 1708). The most perceptive analysis of Morgan's writings is Alden T. Vaughan, "Slaveholders' 'Hellish Principles': A Seventeenth-Century Critique," in *Roots of American Racism: Essays on the Colonial Experience*, ed. Vaughan (New York: Oxford University Press, 1995), 55–81. Thomas Tryon's works include: Thomas Tryon, *The Planter's Speech To His Neighbours & Country-Men of Pennsylvania, East & West Jersey* (London, 1684); Thomas Tryon, *Friendly Advice to the Gentlemen Planters of the East and West Indies* (London, 1684); Thomas Tryon, *Tryon's Letters, Domestick and Foreign* (London, 1700). For the fullest analysis of Tryon's writings on the colonies, see Philippe Rosenberg, "Thomas Tryon and the Seventeenth-Century Dimensions of Antislavery," *William and Mary Quarterly*, 61 (2004): 609–42.

7. Godwin, *Negro's and Indian's Advocate*, 13, 22, 39–40; Godwin, *Supplement*, 8.

8. Godwin, *Supplement*, 6; Godwin, *Trade prefer'd before Religion*, 7, 19, 21, 23, 25–26; Godwin, *Negro's and Indian's Advocate*, 160.

9. Tryon, *Friendly Advice*, 122, 160; *Tryon's Letters*, 188, 192.

10. Richard Ligon, *A True and Faithful History of the Island of Barbadoes* (London, 1757), 55.

11. Richard Steele, *The Spectator* 11 (13 March 1711).

12. "The Speech of Moses Bon Sàam, 1735," reprinted in *Caribbeana: An Anthology of English Literature of the West Indies 1657-1777*, ed. Thomas W. Krise (Chicago: Chicago University Press, 1999), 101–7.

13. Robert Robertson, *The Speech of Mr. John Campo-bell, A Free Christian-Negro, to His Countrymen in the Mountains of Jamaica* (London, 1736), 72–73.

14. Ibid., 73; *Gentleman's Magazine* 11 (March 1741): 145.

15. Daniel Defoe, *Moll Flanders*, ed. Albert J. Rivero (New York: W. W. Norton, 2004).

16. Daniel Defoe, *The History and Remarkable Life of the Truly Honourable Colonel Jacque*, in *The Works of Daniel Defoe*, 16 vols. (New York: G. D. Sproul, 1925).

17. Defoe, *Colonel Jacque*, 1: 234–36, 2: 4–5; *Moll Flanders*, 70–71.

18. Defoe, *Captain Jacque*, 1: 198, 204, 231–32, 265; 2: 97–98, 130; *Moll Flanders*, 70.

19. John Oldmixon, *The British Empire in America, Containing the History of the Discovery, Settlement, Progress and Present State of All the British Colonies, on the Continent and Islands of America*, 2 vols. (London, 1708), 1: iv, xxxi, xxxvii.

20. Malachy Postlethwayt, *Universal Dictionary of Trade and Commerce,* 4th ed. (London, 1764), entry: *Plantations.*

21. Anonymous, *Application of Some General Political Rules, To the Present State of Great-Britain, Ireland and America* (London, 1766), 75.

22. Jonathan Blenman, *Remarks on Several Acts of Parliament Relating more especially to the Colonies abroad* (London, 1742), v.

23. Roscommon, *To the Author of those Intelligencers printed at Dublin* (New York, 1733), 2, 8; "A Friend of Liberty, this Colony and all Mankind to Mr. Hall," 20 August 1767, *Providence Gazette* (Providence, RI), 5 September 1767.

24. Adam Smith, *Theory of Moral Sentiments* (London, 1759), 402–3.

25. Robert Beverley, *The History and Present State of Virginia,* ed. Louis B. Wright (Chapel Hill: University of North Carolina Press, 1947), 58, 286–88.

26. Arthur Lee, *An Essay in Vindication of the Continental Colonies of America, From the Censure of Mr. Adam Smith, in his Theory of Moral Sentiments* (London, 1764), iii–iv.

27. Ibid., 10, 18, 22–23, 25, 30–31.

28. Anonymous, *The General Opposition of the Colonies to the Payment of the Stamp Duty, and the Consequences of Enforcing Obedience by Military Measures, Impartially Considered* (London, 1766), 16.

29. Leonard W. Labaree, et al., *The Papers of Benjamin Franklin,* 39 vols. (New Haven: Yale University Press, 1959–), 12: 414; 13: 5, 77, 81, 150; 15:13; 18: 122; 21: 185, 598.

30. Alexander Hamilton, *The Farmer Refuted,* 23 February 1774, in *The Papers of Alexander Hamilton,* ed. Harold C. Syrett and Jacob E. Cooke, 19 vols. (New York: Columbia University Press, 1961–73), 1: 1005–7.

31. For an elaboration of this argument, see Jack P. Greene, "State and National Identities in the Era of the American Revolution," in *Nationalism in the New World,* ed. Don H. Doyle and Marc Pamplona (Athens: University of Georgia Press, 2006), 61–79.

32. On this point, see Jack P. Greene, "Colonial History and National History: Reflections on a Continuing Problem," *William and Mary Quarterly* 64 (April 2007): 235–50, 281–86; Jack P. Greene, "The Cultural Dimensions of Political Transfers: An Aspect of the European Occupation of the Americas," *Early American Studies* 6 (Spring 2008): 1–26.

Chapter 3

Identity, Alterity, and the "Growing Plant" of Monroeism in U.S. Foreign Policy Ideology

Marco Mariano

During his bid for reelection in the fall of 1940, while war was disrupting Europe, Franklin D. Roosevelt chose to focus his Columbus Day speech on hemispheric defense and Pan-American unity. From a train platform he explained to his audience in Dayton, Ohio, that the offensive of the Axis powers in Europe prompted an immediate response by the United States. and the Latin American republics; a joint effort was needed to stop Nazi and Fascist infiltration in the Americas and to mobilize military resources for a total defense of the Western Hemisphere.

As it was often the case in his public addresses, FDR was careful to frame security and foreign matters in a wider, accessible narration on the place of the United States and the American people in the world, and in history. The imagined European other was crucial to his construction of the national self. At a time when the contrast between a war-ravaged Europe infested by dictators and a peaceful democratic America could not be starker, the president recast his view of U.S. national security within the "old world" versus "new world" dichotomy, that had been generated in U.S. culture and diplomatic language across the nineteenth century.

Initially he praised the millions of immigrants from the old world who had "formed, here in the Western hemisphere, a new human reservoir." These new Americans dedicated to the pursuit of new opportunities, peace, and freedom "proudly carried with them their inheritance of culture, but they cheerfully left behind them the burden of prejudice and hate," thus becoming "citizens of the new world." Similarly, FDR constructed the na-

---

Notes for this chapter begin on page 76.

tions of the new world as peace-loving republics bent on the pursuit of progress through friendly cooperation, sharing the same political values since their independence: "No one nation in this hemisphere has any desire to dominate the others. In the Western hemisphere no nation is considered a second-class nation ... The fire of freedom was in the eyes of Washington and Bolivar, and San Martin, and Artigas, and Juarez, and Bernardo O'Higgins, and all the brave, rugged, ragged men who followed them in the wars of independence." But freedom, he warned, was now being threatened by "the foreign plots, the propaganda, the whole technique of underground warfare originating in Europe and now clearly directed against all of the Republics on this side of the ocean."[1]

Finally, once he had articulated his own version of the "two-spheres principle" originally stated in the Monroe Doctrine, FDR went on to reaffirm U.S. opposition to European attempts to establish a "foreign system" in the new world—another Monrovian principle—as he warned the totalitarian powers against any attempt to infiltrate, let alone attack, what he had defined as the "hemisphere of peace": "There are those in the old world who persist in believing that here in this new hemisphere the Americas can be torn by the hatred and fear [which] have drenched the battle grounds of Europe for so many centuries ... 'Divide and Conquer!' That has been the battle-cry of the totalitarian powers in their war against the democracies. It has succeeded on their continent of Europe for the moment. On our continents it will fail."[2]

This 1940 Columbus Day speech, part of FDR's effort to disguise his interventionist agenda in the reassuring mantle of the Monroe Doctrine orthodoxy, reflected widespread U.S. concerns about Italian and German influence in key South American nations like Argentina and Brazil. It also revealed the hemispheric mind-set of a president who loved to display his command of geography. Finally, this speech illustrates the enduring legacy of the Monroe Doctrine as an ideological tool providing domestic cohesion and forging national identity by opposition, and defining the natural place and historical mission of the United States as one against a perceived other in the international arena.

To be sure, such a process of construction of the national self through difference in the realm of international affairs was by no means new in 1823. In fact, the doctrine codified widespread assumptions about the nation's relation to the world, and its legacy continued to display its adaptability vis-à-vis the changing status of the United States in world politics and the changing domestic landscape. Tracing the origins of the Monroe Doctrine in U.S. foreign policy thinking illustrates how this mechanism of oppositional identity construction—that is, asserting a foreign other to define the national self—worked at three turning points in the history of U.S.

foreign relations, namely, the imperial turn of the late nineteenth century, the internationalist turn leading to the U.S. entry to World War II, and the globalist turn during the Cold War.

Revolutionary Seeds

The Monroe Doctrine as both a cornerstone of U.S. foreign relations and a marker of national identity is a demonstration of how nation-states, as Andrew M. Johnston argues, "contain two competing subjectivities, one as states-like-other-states, with a common interest in sovereignty and security" and the other as nations who "are built around particularist identities ... constantly articulating images of themselves, in their history texts, political speeches, popular culture, and so on, in order to create the social unity needed to mobilize power for the state, and to differentiate between inside and outside, us and them." In a context in which states follow a rational-choice approach to power and security, while nations are constantly negotiated and contested as "imagined communities," foreign policy discourse is best understood as a combination of both processes: the outcome of state bureaucracies operating under utilitarian assumptions believed to be universal as well as the particularist "desire to satisfy unstable internal arguments about the character of the nation itself."[3]

This dual dimension of foreign policy is especially evident in the United States, "the imagined community *par excellence*," a nation whose identity is particularly related to practices of cultural representation.[4] Representations of the American self by opposition against an imagined other have been frequent since the revolutionary and early republican years; while the dichotomy between freedom and tyranny was obviously a central tenet of the construction of American identity, "mental maps" also played a crucial role within a political culture in which expansion, security, and freedom were closely interrelated.[5] As the United States was being built as a nation, "space itself, in a way, became the outside counterpoint for the projection of the national self."[6]

In fact, the Monroe Doctrine codified a tradition postulating geographic distance as a defining factor of the separation between the new world and the old, and of American alterity vis-à-vis Europe, as the writings of Thomas Paine, Alexander Hamilton, George Washington, and Thomas Jefferson illustrate in different ways.

Considerations about space, and size, were prominent in Paine's case for a revolutionary turn in the struggle of the North American colonies. In *Common Sense*, he wrote: "It is not in the power of Britain to do this continent justice. The business of it will soon be too weighty, and intricate, to be managed with any tolerable degree of convenience, by a power so distant from us, and so ignorant of us ... To be always running three or four thousand miles with a tale or a petition, waiting four or five months for an answer, which when obtained requires five or six months to explain it, will in a few years be looked upon as folly and childishness." Paine made it clear that the irreconcilable differences between America and Europe were rooted in the natural laws of geography, as well as in the natural right to liberty from the "royal brute." "There is something very absurd," he argued, "in supposing a continent perpetually governed by an island. In no instance hath nature made the satellite larger than its primary planet, and as England and America, with respect to each other, reverses the common order of nature, it is evident that they belong to different systems; England to Europe, America to itself."[7]

A few years later Alexander Hamilton in Federalist No. 11 formulated his own view of America's separateness from, and of the threat posed by, Europe. "The world may politically, as well as geographically, be divided into four parts [Africa, America, Asia, Europe], each having a distinct set of interests," with the latter imposing its "domination" on the other parts. In fact, Europe was a separate "quarter" but it was threatening nonetheless, and distance alone would not guarantee American security and prosperity. According to his federalist outlook, "under a vigorous national government, the natural strength and resources of the country, directed to a common interest, would baffle all the combinations of European jealousy to restrain our growth." As the two sides of the Atlantic were two distinct but interrelated spheres, the external threat of European imperialism made the foundation of a modern American state all the more urgent: "Let the thirteen States, bound together in a strict and indissoluble Union, concur in erecting one great American system, superior to the control of all transatlantic force or influence, and able to dictate the terms of the connection between the old and the new world!"[8]

While Hamilton's quest for a strong federal government was part of a bitter partisan feud on the issue of federalism, Washington's *Farewell Address* (1796) soon came to be revered as a paradigmatic synthesis of U.S. ideals and interests in foreign policy. The construction of American identity by means of opposition to the European other and the rejection of foreign interference as a prerequisite for national security were central tenets of his address, in which notions about space were instrumental in defining the contours of what was established as the natural, as opposed to artificial, place of the United States in the world. In Washington's view, geography contributed to show how U.S. involvement in European affairs was unnatural and therefore harmful:

Europe has a set of primary interests which to us have none; or a very remote relation ... Hence, therefore, it must be unwise in us to implicate ourselves by artificial ties in the ordinary vicissitudes of her politics, or the ordinary combinations and collisions of her friendships or enmities. Our detached and distant situation invites and enables us to pursue a different course ... Why forego the advantages of so peculiar a situation? Why quit our own to stand upon foreign ground? Why, by interweaving our destiny with that of any part of Europe, entangle our peace and prosperity in the toils of European ambition, rivalship, interest, humor or caprice?[9]

Finally, this rigid dichotomy was put to the test by the wave of Latin American independences in the 1810s, introducing a third actor in the stage of Atlantic politics.

Skepticism about Latin Americans' fitness for republican self-government was widespread in the United States, partly due to anti-Catholicism and racial prejudice about miscegenation. In the following decades, American observers read endemic political instability, widespread Catholic influence, the abolition of slavery in several countries, and attempts of monarchic restoration in Brazil and Mexico as proof of the ties that still linked Latin America to the old world.[10] However, it was believed that geographic proximity might prompt some progress at least among the neighboring regions "beneath the United States."

In fact, U.S. visions of Latin America in the early nineteenth century exemplify the complexity of the grammars of alterity. Gerd Baumann and Andre Gingrich argue that the process of selfing/othering does not necessarily reproduce a binary friend-versus-foe dynamic; rather, it depends on the context it is applied to. In this case, according to a Western hemispheric perspective, Latin America was easily depicted as an inferior, distant other within a rigid hierarchy of alterity. On the other hand, according to an Atlantic perspective, the quintessential other was the old continent of Europe, while Latin America started to be cautiously and selectively "encompassed" depending on how its distance from/proximity to the United States was interpreted.[11]

A letter that Jefferson, a strong proponent of continental expansion, sent to Alexander Von Humboldt exemplifies how notions of distance/proximity affected the way U.S. leaders dealt with the Latin American dilemma within the rigid self-versus-other dichotomy, which nicely dovetailed with the relations between the United States and the European imperial powers. Jefferson had very low expectations about the new Latin American republics, except perhaps for those who might profit from their proximity to the United States. In his view, history showed that a "priest-ridden people" marked by "the lowest level of ignorance" were unlikely to maintain "a free civil government." However, he also believed that U.S. "vicinity" to and exchanges with the Latin American republics "may furnish schools for the higher, and example for the lower classes of their citizens. And Mexico, where we learn from you that men of science are not wanting, may revolutionize itself under better auspices than the Southern provinces. These last, I fear, must end in military despotisms" because of the "different casts of their inhabitants, their mutual hatreds and jealousies, their profound ignorance and bigotry."

Even so, he trusted that these new republics were destined to escape the doom of the European balance of power thanks to their separateness from the old world:

> But in whatever governments they end they will be *American* governments, no longer to be involved in the never-ceasing broils of Europe. The European nations constitute a separate division of the globe; their localities make them part of a distinct system; they have a set of interests of their own in which it is our business never to engage ourselves. America has a hemisphere to itself. It must have its separate system of interests, which must not be subordinated to those of Europe. The insulated state in which nature has placed the American continent, should so far avail it that no spark of war kindled in the other quarters of the globe should be wafted across the wide oceans which separate us from them. And it will be so.[12]

While Jefferson's emphasis on the separation between America and the European other contributed to "reflect and form societal ideals and views of the international environment," his confidence in American insularity as a source of security was questioned by the events that reshaped the geopolitics of the Atlantic world in the 1810s.[13] On the one hand, the collapse of imperial Spain and the extension of the republican model to former European colonies confirmed the confidence of the Founding Fathers in the superiority of U.S. institutions, while the opening of new opportunities in terms of trade and influence confirmed their increasing optimism on the glorious destiny of the nation. On the other hand, many in the United States feared that turmoil and instability in the Western hemisphere could pave the way to the maneuvering and intrigue of the major European imperial powers—especially after the latter had solemnly announced their reactionary agenda to the world at the Congress of Vienna. Likewise, old world powers feared that the republican disease might spread across Europe via Spain but, at the same time, hoped that commercial opportunities might open up in Central and South America. The rise of this "Western question" urged the United States to redefine its place and its mission in an evolving Atlantic context; James Monroe's inaugural address of 1823 offered such definition.[14]

Again, geographic determinism was instrumental to the conceptualization of the Atlantic space as a cohesive unit structured by the multiple dynamics of ideological opposition, geopolitical competition, and economic integration. The Monroe Doctrine codified a natural theology in which the natural and the rightful overlapped, and imagined proximity/distance concurred to the definition of identity/difference and threat perception.[15] Distance from Europe, combined with the relevance of European imperial powers for U.S. security and trade, dictated the twin Monrovian principles of U.S. opposition to further colonization in the new world and U.S. noninterference in the affairs of the old world that did not concern U.S. interests.

On the other hand, U.S. proximity with its "Southern brethren" provided a natural and therefore rightful argument for American hemispheric hegemony. According to James Monroe, "With the movements in this hemisphere we are of necessity more immediately connected, and by causes which must be obvious to all enlightened and impartial observers." Or as David Ryan has put it, "Latin America was the object of the document, but the subject was transatlantic relations; the new world versus the old world."[16]

Imperial Offsprings

The long-lasting influence of the Monroe Doctrine is due to the fact that its two-sphere principle continued to affect the American politics of identity in changing ways throughout U.S. history. In 1900, Alfred Tayer Mahan defined it as "an inherent principle of life, which adapts itself with the flexibility of a growing plant, to the successive conditions it encounters."[17] Conditions were definitely favorable during the 1840s when, after two decades of relative neglect, the doctrine was deployed by President Polk to support the manifest destiny of westward expansion (incidentally, Monroe's address featured a sentence including the words "manifestation" and "destiny").[18]

But it was the imperialist turn of the 1890s that prompted not only a massive use of the doctrine in the public discourse, but also a major reinterpretation of its tenets. While the Spanish-American War marked a watershed in the rise of the United States as the undisputed continental power and potential global player, Theodore Roosevelt's corollary transformed the Monroe Doctrine both as a cornerstone of U.S. foreign relations and as an identity-making tool. His "Big Stick" version was part of a new orientalist discourse that recast the place of the United States in the world—from the new, righteous half of a divided West, with Europe as the villain, to the assertive member of an extended, transatlantic West, with "barbarism" as the villain.

The context of this sea change is well known. Since the Civil War, the increase in transatlantic trade, economic integration, and cultural exchanges made possible by technological advance in transportation had linked the United States and Europe in closely knit "Atlantic landscape."[19] At the same time, the age of imperialism contributed to reshape both power relations and mutual images between the new world and the old. Anglo-American rapprochement in the Caribbean and elsewhere was legitimized by a flood of Anglo-Saxon rhetoric, that in turn was part of a "civilizational discourse of conquest and uplifting" with strong, pseudoscientific racial undertones on both sides of the Atlantic.[20] Finally, evolutionism reinforced the ideology of U.S. civilizational imperialism by articulating in secular and transatlantic terms the impulse in U.S. attitudes toward a set predestined path set for other nations and cultures. As Matthew Frye Jacobson puts it, "the ascendant Euro-American fetish of evolutionary development had tremendous consequences for the U.S. encounter with foreign peoples: it provided a narrative for otherwise disparate and disjointed images of the world's nations and tribes … it became a secular counterpart to an earlier religious discourse of the Christian civilizing mission among the 'heathen.'"[21] Finally, the works by Alfred T. Mahan—whose influence on Roosevelt was significant—provided geopolitical underpinnings to the "civilizational" imperialism advocated by reverend Josiah Strong, historian John Fiske, and political scientist John Burgess. In Mahan's view, the United States had to build a strong naval force to expand its regional hegemony and compete with Western powers globally; at the same time, he urged Americans to rediscover their roots in Western civilization and to carry on their uplifting mission: "We stand at the opening of a period when the question is to be settled decisively … whether Eastern civilization or Western civilization is to dominate throughout the Earth," he wrote in 1897.[22] These developments by no means undermined American exceptionalism; in fact they reinforced a wider narrative based on the encounter between a civilized Anglo-Saxon West and a savage barbarian other.

Theodore Roosevelt's world view and foreign policy exemplify how the American grammar of alterity at the turn of century had changed with respect to the 1820s, but at the same time was still being formulated in Monrovian terms. He saw the world as divided in two spheres: a Christian civilization led by the Anglo-Saxon people versus the "waste spaces" of the world dominated by barbarism and despotism. In his *The Strenuous Life* (1899), he lamented that "many of the [Philippine] people are utterly unfit for self-government, and show no signs of becoming fit" and expressed widespread assumptions on the hierarchy of race and civilization: "We have driven Spanish tyranny from the islands. If we now let it be replaced by savage anarchy, our work has been for harm and not for good." Roosevelt expressed how changing notions of threat and of otherness were changing America's self-image—from the new Israel, the revolutionary outpost called to regenerate the world by example, to the new Rome, the world power called to lead the transatlantic West by intervention.[23]

This transformation was codified in his Corollary to the Monroe Doctrine, which combined the cultural premises of civilizational imperialism with the assertive claim of U.S. police powers in the Western hemisphere. As financial instability in the Dominican Republic threatened intervention by European powers to protect their interests, Roosevelt stated in his fifth annual message to Congress that: "chronic wrongdoing, or an impotence which results in a general loosening of the ties of civilized society, may in America, as elsewhere, ultimately require intervention by some civilized nation, and in the Western hemisphere the adherence of the United States to the Monroe Doctrine may force the United States, however reluctantly, in flagrant cases of such wrongdoing or impotence, to the exercise of an international police power." At a time when the international status of the United States was being transformed, the corollary radically altered the meaning of the Monroe Doctrine by claiming for the U.S. exclusive police powers to enforce its principles and by paving the way to a radical change in U.S. attitude toward Latin America. As Walter LaFeber put it, it was an "historic switch in the doctrine's targets, from attacking European states that would interfere with Latin American revolutions to attacking the revolutions themselves."[24] This switch was part of a broader change of attitude toward Latin America and toward other peoples and countries. Compared to the 1820s, Americans were now much less committed to escaping the world, and in fact many believed that the nation was bound to lead it. The "search for order" that characterized the domestic scene in the Progressive era also involved U.S. foreign relations. According to Herbert Croly's "new nationalism," a new world order had to be built by putting aside "some essential incompatibility between Europeanism and Americanism" and rejecting "continental provincialism and chauvinism" and the "sort of religious sanctity" associated to isolationism.[25] Similarly, Roosevelt valued order at the international as well as at the domestic level. He stated in his address to Congress that: "All that this country desires is to see the neighboring countries stable, orderly, and prosperous. And they cannot be happy and prosperous unless they maintain order within their boundaries and behave with a just regard for their obligations toward outsiders." Establishing order, by force if necessary, was part of the mission of the civilized powers in the lands of despotism and lawlessness.

In his view, as in the view of many of his contemporaries, history was a linear succession of stages from barbarism to civilization. In this Spencerian framework, which Roosevelt translated in Monrovian parlance with his corollary, imperial powers were called to favor the expansion of civilization by imposing order; they would "make the rules and punish transgression but, by the same token, would also be obliged to provide protection (as well as education and welfare) and an example to emulate."[26]

To be sure, several dissenting voices questioned the Monrovian revival. In 1896 William Graham Sumner, a prominent conservative critic of the imperialist turn, dismissed what he defined "the proposed dual organization of mankind" as "new spinnings of political metaphysics."[27] However, the imperial rendition of Monroeism was clearly hegemonic at the turn of the century, as it turned out to be flexible and adaptable to the new domestic and international scenario both as a cornerstone of U.S. foreign policy, as we have seen, and as an identity-making tool. Compared to the rigid, binary construction of identity versus alterity that informed the original Monroe Doctrine, here we have a different, more complex orientalist grammar based on the concept of encompassing, that works at two different levels—the lower recognizing difference between "the West and the rest," the higher partially and gradually overcoming difference in the name of universal features, such as the values of Western civilization at the turn of the century, or the stages of modernization and progress after World War II.[28]

This was by no means a totally new development; in fact it was consistent with the missionary impulse of the ideology of U.S. foreign policy. Back in 1816, as Latin American independence was opening the way to greater U.S. influence, Jefferson remarked: "What a colossus shall we be, when the southern continent comes up to our mark!"[29] However, by the end of the nineteenth century the imperialist turn not only multiplied American encounters with other peoples and nations, it also required that what Samuel Flagg Bemis classified as "a great aberration" be incorporated within the benevolent narrative of American exceptionalism. Theodore Roosevelt responded exactly to this urge to differentiate U.S. expansionism from tyrannical old world—especially Spanish—imperialism when he stated in his corollary that U.S. intervention in Dominican affairs "will give the people of Santo Domingo the same chance to move onward and upward which we have already given to the people of Cuba." Finally, as the United States was asserting its imperial role in the Western hemisphere and beyond, images of the other changed accordingly. While advocates of expansionism in Congress, in the press, and in the business community recast the U.S. emancipating mission in paternalistic terms, the Latin American other was often portrayed as the unruly child demanding tutelage and guidance. The prevailing American image was now that of "an infantile and often negroid Latin, [which] provided the justification for Uncle Sam's tutelage and stern discipline."[30]

To sum up, at a time when the place of the United States in the world was going through dramatic changes, U.S. notions of identity/alterity were being reconstructed. Americans were now defining the national self and the foreign other through the ubiquitous concept of civilization, combining the ethics of Christian moralism, the pseudoscience of white supremacy, and the power of economic and technological development. The transatlantic links of religion, race, trade, and empire undermined the rigid new world versus old world dichotomy forged in the revolutionary years, and would eventually dismantle it along the twentieth century. The uncivilized other was to be found South of the border, and the triumphant American giant, far from fearing it, would eventually emancipate it from savagery and despotism. Needless to say, such a dramatic change in mental maps, construction of national identity, and foreign policy priorities required some adjustment. The triumphant outcome of the Spanish-American war led to a twofold aberration: not only was the United States building an overseas colonial empire, it was also stepping out if its traditional, hemispheric "sphere of interest."

As Anders Stephanson put it, "The Philippines presented a particular problem in that they were spatially a part of the old world, the dichotomous other of the 'new.' How was one to square this with the consecrated Monroe Doctrine?"[31] Roosevelt's corollary did the trick by diluting the continental meta-geography of Monroeism in the universal dimension of the civilizational discourse. Isolation had been selfish, the British were showing how empires could be righteous, and the United States seemed to be ready to assume the responsibility of a world power.

Global Ending

In the twentieth century Monroeism continued to provide a powerful ideological framework to the state's quest for power and security as well as to the nation's quest for identity. Perceptions of external threat continued to play a crucial role in the definition of the national interest, while notions of alterity and difference continued to shape the contours of the national imagined community.

By the time the doctrine's centennial was celebrated, the *New York Times* carried a full-page advertisement in which Christian Science founder Mary Baker Eddy revered it as an undisputable sacred text. And on the eve of World War II, when a foreign other was again questioning the place and the mission of the United States in the world, the ideology of Monroeism was again being appropriated and reinterpreted by opponents as well as advocates of the U.S. entry to the war.

In the late 1930s, Theodore Roosevelt's corollary seemed a relic from a distant past. The notion of a group of imperial powers sharing a civilizing mission on behalf of "the West" had been crushed since World War I; the bitter legacy of the first American intervention in a European war had revived old, isolationist suspicions against the old world balance of power, and the failure of the Wilsonian dream of a new world order had paved the way to a nationalist revival with an unmistakable hemispheric tinge; the crisis of 1929 and the Depression led to economic nationalism and the collapse of the transatlantic integration of industrial and financial markets; traditional anti-European attitudes were fueled by the spread of old-fashioned authoritarianism and new totalitarian regimes across the Atlantic in the interwar years; finally, starting in the early 1930s FDR's Good Neighbor policy resuscitated "the original defensive and anti-European conception of the Monroe Doctrine," and added a multilateral twist that marked a significant breakthrough in inter-American relations.[32]

FDR's 1940 Columbus Day speech situated the United States in the international arena as to reflect these shifts. It resorted to the original orientalist model of 1823 that constructed American identity by means of opposition to the European other. However, while FDR updated the two-sphere principle, he was aware that economic and strategic interdependence prevented isolation and made free security and hemispheric self-sufficiency impossible in the modern world. On the eve of World War II, he relied on Monroeism and its dual function as an identity-making tool—by imagining a sense of hemispheric American-ness in opposition to a European other—and as a cornerstone of U.S. foreign policy—by reinterpreting hemispheric defense as the first step toward global commitment.

FDR genuinely shared the "Europhobic-cum-hemispheric" mind-set of influential members of his administration like Under-Secretary of State Sumner Welles and Assistant Secretary of State Adolf Berle, and was attuned to the widespread continentalist revival of the 1920s and 1930s.[33] In a 1939 speech to the Pan American Union he defined the "American family of nations" as sharing a "common civilization under a system of peace" as well as "diversities of race, of language, of custom, of natural resources; and of intellectual forces at least as great as those which prevail in Europe." Against the backdrop of events across the Atlantic, peaceful relations and mutual cooperation were creating a new American identity: "we have begun to realize in Pan American relations what civilization in intercourse between countries really means." And yet, as FDR constructed national identity through difference in characteristic Monrovian fashion, he also stated that such difference could be overcome, and that "civiliza-tion" could and should be reproduced beyond the Western hemisphere: "If that process can be successful here, is it too much to hope that a similar intellectual and spiritual process may succeed elsewhere? Do we really have to assume that nations can find no better methods of realizing their destinies than those which were used by the Huns and the Vandals fif-teen hundred years ago?"[34] Behind closed doors, his language was less empathic but his hemispheric mind-set emerged nonetheless: "For the first time since the Holy alliance in 1818 the United States now faced the possibility of an attack on the Atlantic side in both the Northern and the Southern hemispheres" FDR said in a 1938 cabinet meeting.[35]

As in 1823, the barbarian other situated on the other side of the Atlan-tic was instrumental to forge domestic cohesion and to define the place and the mission of America. As in 1904, however, identity and alterity were constructed in complex, dynamic terms through a discourse of en-compassing, which bridges the gap between barbarism and civilization. In fact, in FDR's Wilsonian understanding of modern interdependence, expansion of civilization against barbarism was not only desirable, but necessary. As Walter LaFeber put it, "[b]y 1941 Roosevelt brought North Americans a long way to accepting a part of Wilson's original vision: to think of the doctrine as intertwined with a global responsibility they would have to assume."[36]

Uses of geography and cartography by policy makers, commentators, and the media were crucial in this transformation of both the ideological use and the popular understanding of the doctrine from the old, reassur-ing idea of separate spheres to the new fear of falling dominoes. "We know that the development of the next generation will so narrow the oceans separating us from the old world, that our customs and our actions are necessarily involved with hers ... within a scant few years air fleets will cross the oceans as easily as today they cross the closed Europeans seas," stated FDR in his 1939 Pan American Union speech, thus echoing Walter Lippmann's influential remarks on the Atlantic ocean as a bridge, rather than a barrier, between the new world and the old.[37]

To be sure, both opponents and advocates of U.S. intervention resorted to arguments about proximity/distance in order to situate the United States and the Western hemisphere vis-à-vis the old world and to advance their conflicting notions of national interest as the natural consequence of America's place in the world. On the one hand, isolationists held on to the traditional understanding of the doctrine based on reciprocal noninterfer-ence as well as on the two-sphere principle, and to a rigidly continentalist mind-set. On the other, many internationalists adhered to the Monrovian dogma of hemispheric defense, but at the same time, reshaped the very notion of hemisphere and of its relation to the world. While experts debunked the myth of continental determinism, FDR literally redrew the contours of the Western hemisphere with a stroke of a pen so as to include Greenland and possibly Iceland, Cape Verde, and the Azores to emphasize that events in Europe were by no means distant and alien to U.S. interests.[38]

Such meta-geographic disputes were part of a wider dispute over the role of the United States in world affairs that reflected competing notions of national identity as the ubiquitous threat posed by a not-so-distant other made it all the more impossible to imagine the national community in purely domestic terms. At a time when the United States found itself threatened not only in its national interests, but also in its fundamental values, the new world/old world dichotomy of the original doctrine perfectly fit the civilizational confrontation underway in World War II. However, Pearl Harbor definitely showed that the new Israel's separation from the rest of the world was an empty illusion and interdependence was the present and the future, as Wilson had anticipated and FDR had famously reminded the American public in his 1937 Quarantine speech: "Let no one imagine that America will escape, that America may expect mercy, that this Western hemisphere will not be attacked and that it will continue tranquilly and peacefully to carry on the ethics and the arts of civilization … It seems to be unfortunately true that the epidemic of world lawlessness is spreading. When an epidemic of physical disease starts to spread, the community approves and joins in a quarantine of the patients in order to protect the health of the community against the spread of the disease."[39] Not surprisingly, the Rooseveltian reinterpretation of Monroeism prevailed in the foreign policy establishment as well as in the public discourse during the war years, as it grounded the rise of the United States as the global leader of the West and the permanent U.S. entanglement with Europe and the world within a traditional narrative of American nationalism.

Finally, after World War II, the orientalist dual world view of Monroeism contributed to shape American Cold War ideology. It continued to rationalize the old tension between regionalism and globalism in U.S. foreign policy by providing a world view in which sealing off the Western hemisphere to foreign influence was consistent with projecting U.S. influence globally. Conversely, it continued to inform U.S. views of and policies toward Latin America. In March 1947, James Reston wrote in the *New York Times* that according to "the tentative conclusions of responsible observers" the Truman Doctrine "like the Monroe Doctrine, warned that the United States would resist efforts to impose a political system of foreign domination on areas vital to our security."[40] It was yet another twist in the history of appropriations and reinterpretations of the doctrine—

one that expunged geographic boundaries and extended the range of U.S. power and interests from the Western hemisphere to a potentially global West. In fact, in the early Cold War years the Soviet threat came to be perceived as both global and absolute; in 1950 the notorious NSC 68 stated that—as the Soviet Union was "animated by a fanatic faith, antithetical to our own"—what was at stake was "the fulfillment or destruction not only of this Republic but of civilization itself." Again, the Monrovian grammar of alterity came to be expedient at a time when national identity was being constructed by opposition to an alien, threatening other. The Cold War order reconfigured the two-sphere principle and the noncolonization principle. As Walter LaFeber points out: "The Monroe Doctrine did not have to be again proclaimed because the 'two camp' division of the world and the de facto economic and military hegemony of the U.S. of the Western hemisphere allowed North American officials to assume the validity of the Doctrine ... the evolving principles of Monroe were not questioned, just extended."[41] The lingering influence of the doctrine was evident also in the way American policy makers shaped inter-American relations throughout the Cold War according to both global considerations and deep-rooted assumptions about Latin American people and culture.

In 1950, when international tension reached an unprecedented peak, American fears of Communist infiltration and subversion south of the border soared to wartime levels. At the same time, the foreign policy establishment was relatively unprepared to tackle hemispheric issues after many years in which Europe and later the Far East had received much greater attention; the days of the Good Neighbor diplomacy were long gone and diplomatic celebrity George Kennan, a Europeanist with very little knowledge of Latin America, was asked to provide a new strategic framework for the region. The outcome was "Latin America as a problem in United States foreign policy," a ten-thousand-word memorandum that recommended a hard-line approach to prevent Communist attempts "to make the Latin American countries pawns in the power aspirations of regimes beyond the limits of this continent." While the "vigor and efficacy of local concepts and traditions of self-government" were the best response to Soviet expansionism, Kennan argued, conditions in Latin America required a different approach. As such concepts and traditions were "too weak to absorb successfully the intensity of the communist attack, then we must concede that harsh governmental measures of repression maybe the only answer." The United States had to support any regime ready to adopt such measures, including those with "origins and methods that would not stand the test of American concept of democratic procedures."[42]

The distance Kennan emphasized in terms of democratic standards paralleled the personal estrangement he felt during the mission through

Latin America he undertook earlier in 1950. In his memoirs he recalled the journey as "anything but pleasant" and concluded that in the region "the handicaps to progress are written in human blood and in the tracings of geography; and in neither case are they readily susceptible of obliteration … and the answers people have suggested to them thus far have been feeble and unpromising."[43] The contrast with the sense of hemispheric "weness" and belonging to a community of nations sharing cultural traditions and political institutions, a feeling that many high-ranking officials in the FDR administration publicly expressed and privately felt, could not be more stark. Latin America was again marginalized as a dubious member of the expanded Cold War West that encompassed the European colonial powers and reiterated "the narrative of freedom and democracy."[44] Racial notions of otherness were now unacceptable, but they reemerged in secret memos like Kennan's, or were voiced implicitly, as in Dwight Eisenhower's remark about Argentinians being "the same kind of people we are."[45]

What Gaddis Smith defined as the "Kennan corollary" to the Truman Doctrine was followed by a string of U.S. interventions in the affairs of Guatemala (1954), Brazil (1964), the Dominican Republic (1965), and Chile (1973), not to mention the heavy-handed approach to Central American crises during Ronald Reagan's "second Cold War." In an address before Congress in 1983, Reagan framed events in Nicaragua and El Salvador in terms of the hemispheric meta-geography of Monroeism: "Central America's problems do directly affect the security and the well-being of our own people. And Central America is much closer to the United States than many of the world trouble spots that concern us. So, we work to restore our own economy; we cannot afford to lose sight of our neighbors to the south. El Salvador is nearer to Texas than Texas is to Massachusetts. Nicaragua is just as close to Miami, San Antonio, San Diego, and Tucson as those cities are to Washington, where we're gathered tonight."[46]

An exception to this trend was the highly ambitious, deeply flawed, and largely unsuccessful Alliance for Progress launched by the Kennedy administration. Yet again, this attempt to reverse recent U.S. policy in the area was articulated in Monrovian terms. The dogma of hemispheric defense was widely used to sell the Alliance for Progress at home and abroad. Harvard historian-turned-presidential adviser Arthur Schlesinger was among the many academics directly involved in Latin American policy in the early 1960s. When he met Bolivian president Paz Estenssoro in a 1961 mission through South America, he made it clear that "where revolution meant healthy social change, the Kennedy administration could be depended on to look on it with sympathy, but not so when revolution meant dictatorship, repression and the entry of alien forces into the hemisphere."[47] At same time, as he made his case for the Alliance for Progress, he pictured Latin America as ready for reform and "modernization" because it was "part of the west, permeated and tantalized by democratic ideals of freedom and progress, where the existence of a common and political inheritance might create the possibilities of partnership and action that did not exist in Asia or Africa."[48]

Latin America was being included again in the civilizational notion of the West, meant as a specific historical and cultural entity and as a distinct political and economic system in the global context. Monrovian orientalist assumptions were implicit, and sometimes explicit, in this world view. At a time when modernization theory à la Walt Rostow was gaining increasing influence in official as well as academic circles, many believed that Latin America was especially positioned to fast-forward in the transition toward modernization. Harvard economist and diplomat Lincoln Gordon wrote in an account of his participation in Kennedy's Latin American task force that: "We believed that most of the region, especially the larger countries of South America and Mexico, were on the threshold of a Rostovian take-off. [There were] institutional and social obstacles, but not cultural ones such as oriental fatalism, sacred cows, or caste system." To Gordon, the Latin American landscape was a familiar one, and was "in sharp contrast with Africa, which still lacked the preconditions for take-off, and South and South East Asia, which would have to overcome ancient cultural obstacles."[49]

Discussing the legacy of the Monroe Doctrine is relevant to the extent that the sacred text of 1823 and its many adaptations and interpretations provided not just a cornerstone of U.S. foreign policy, but also an answer to the question: What is the relationship of the United States to the world?

Such answer was threefold in the original doctrine. First, the division of the world in two spheres created an American identity against a foreign other, and rooted the American experience in the Western hemisphere — that is in the natural, as opposed to artificial, realm of geography. Second, opposition to further colonization reiterated the exceptional historical mission of America and its opposition to European imperialism; in fact it made clear that the United States was willing to lead by intervention, not only by example. Moreover, the doctrine merged geography and history, space and time in a discourse on national security; preserving the geographical separation and carrying on the historical mission was vital to the survival and, later, the expansion of the American republic. It was a "declaration of diplomatic independence" as it framed national security as a natural development of U.S. history and geography which was easily understandable to the American public.

Finally, the doctrine informed an ideology that turned out to be flexible enough to shape the American imagined community in the twentieth century by constructing changing notions of the European other as well as the Latin American other, but also by appropriating selected features of the other to build changing notions of the self and of "the West". As Gretchen Murphy suggested, Monroeism turned out to be compatible with, and in fact has provided the foundations for, different narrations of the American experiment: "the empire for liberty and the postcolonial retreat from old world power, U.S. isolation and expansion, the American missions to reform the world and to escape from history."[50]

Notes

1. "Address of the President from the Rear Platform of his Special Train, Dayton, OH, October 12, 1940," Franklin D. Roosevelt Papers, Master Speech File, box 54, Franklin D. Roosevelt Library, Hyde Park, NY (hereafter cited as FDRL).
2. Ibid.
3. Andrew M. Johnston, *Hegemony and Culture in the Origins of NATO Nuclear First-Use, 1945-1955* (New York: Palgrave Macmillan, 2005), 9–10.
4. David Campbell, *Writing Security: United States Foreign Policy and the Politics of Identity* (Minneapolis: University of Minnesota Press, 1992), 131.
5. Alan K. Henrikson, "Mental Maps," in *Explaining the History of American Foreign Relations,* ed. Michael J. Hogan and Thomas G. Patterson (Cambridge: Cambridge University Press, 1991), 177–92.
6. Anders Stephanson, *Manifest Destiny: American Expansion and the Empire of Right* (New York: Hill & Wang, 1995), 29.
7. Thomas Paine, *Common Sense,* ed. Marc Philp (Oxford: Oxford University Press, 1995), 27.
8. *The Federalist Papers* 11 (http://avalon.law.yale.edu/18th_century/fed11.asp).
9. George Washington, "Farewell Address" (http://avalon.law.yale.edu/18th_century/washing.asp).
10. Michael H. Hunt, *Ideology and U.S. Foreign Policy* (New Haven: Yale University Press, 1987), 100–102.
11. Gerd Baumann, "Grammars of Identity/Alterity: A Structural Approach," in *Grammars of Identity/Alterity: A Structural Approach,* ed. Gerd Baumann and André Gingrich (New York: Berghahn Books, 2004); David Ryan, "US Foreign Policy and the Hierarchy of Alterity: The Decolonization Dilemma," unpublished manuscript courtesy of author.
12. Thomas Jefferson, "Jefferson to Alexander von Humboldt, 6 December 1813" (http://www.let.rug.nl/usa/P/tj3/writings/brf/jefl224.htm).
13. Fabian Hilfrich, "Visions of the Asian Periphery: Vietnam (1964-1968) and the Philippines (1898-1900)," in *America, the Vietnam War, and the World,* ed. Andreas W. Daum, Lloyd C. Gardner, and Wilfried Mausbaack (Cambridge: Cambridge University Press, 2003), 44.
14. Rafe Blaufarb, "The Western Question. The Geopolitics of Latin American Independence," *American Historical Review* 112, no. 3 (2007): 742–63.
15. For a quantitative approach to content analysis on the massive presence of geographic terms and notions in Monroe's State of the Union address see, A.C. Hart, "Geopolitics

and Grand Strategy: Foundations of American National Security" (Ph.D. diss., University of Pennsylvania, 2003), 147.

16. David Ryan, *US Foreign Policy in World History* (London, New York: Routledge, 2000), 51.

17. Quoted in Gretchen Murphy, *Hemispheric Imaginings: The Monroe Doctrine and Narratives of U.S. Empire* (Durham, NC: Duke University Press, 2005), 130.

18. Stephanson, *Manifest Destiny*, 59.

19. Daniel T. Rodgers, *Atlantic Crossings: Social Politics in a Progressive Age* (Cambridge, MA: Belknap Press of Harvard University Press, 1998), 33–52.

20. Stephanson, *Manifest Destiny*, 86.

21. Matthew Frye Jacobson, *Barbarian Virtues. The United States Encounters Foreign Peoples at Home and Abroad, 1876-1917* (New York: Hill & Wang, 2000), 140–41.

22. John L. Harper, *American Visions of Europe: Franklin D. Roosevelt, George F. Kennan, and Dean Acheson* (New York: Cambridge University Press, 1994), 24.

23. Jacobson, *Barbarian Virtues*, 222–23; Stephanson, *Manifest Destiny*, 106, 114–15.

24. Walter LaFeber, "The Evolution of the Monroe Doctrine from Monroe to Reagan," in *Redefining the Past: Essays in Diplomatic History in Honor of William Appleman Williams*, ed. Lloyd C. Gardner (Corvallis: Oregon State University Press, 1986), 132.

25. Stephanson, *Manifest Destiny*, 110.

26. Ibid., 106.

27. William Graham Sumner, "The Proposed Dual Organization of Mankind," in *War and Other Essays*, ed. Albert Galloway Keller (New Haven: Yale University Press, 1911), 271–84.

28. Ryan, "US Foreign Policy and the Hierarchy of Alterity."

29. Stephanson, *Manifest Destiny*, 24.

30. Hunt, *Ideology and U.S. Foreign Policy*, 62.

31. Stephanson, *Manifest Destiny*, 92.

32. Harper, *American Visions of Europe*, 56.

33. Ibid., 54–60.

34. "Address to the Governing Board of the Pan American Union, April 14, 1939," in *The Public Papers and Addresses of Franklin D. Roosevelt*, ed. Samuel Rosenman (New York: Harper and Brothers, 1938–50): 8, 195–99.

35. Harper, *American Visions of Europe*, 68.

36. LaFeber, "The Evolution of the Monroe Doctrine," 134.

37. Marco Mariano, "Remapping America: Continentalism, Globalism, and the Rise of the Atlantic Community, 1939-1949," *Defining the Atlantic Community: Culture, Intellectuals, and Policies in the Mid-20th Century*, ed. Marco Mariano (New York: Routledge, 2010); Alan K. Henrikson, "The Map as an 'Idea': The Role of Cartographic Imagery during the Second World War," *American Cartographer* 2 (1975): 19–53; Karen Wigen and Martin Lewis, *The Myth of Continents: A Critique of Metageography* (Berkeley: University of California Press, 1997).

38. Eugene Staley, "The Myth of the Continents," *Foreign Affairs* 19 (April 1941): 481–94; Robert E. Sherwood, *Roosevelt and Hopkins: An Intimate History* (New York: Harper and Brothers, 1948) 308–13.

39. Franklin D. Roosevelt, "Quarantine Speech, Chicago, October 5, 1937" (http://millercenter.org).

40. James Reston, "Truman's Speech Likened To 1823 and 1941 Warnings", *New York Times*, 13 March 1947.

41. LaFeber, "The Evolution of the Monroe Doctrine," 137.

42. Gaddis Smith, *The Last Years of the Monroe Doctrine, 1945-1993* (New York: Hill & Wang, 1994), 70–71.

43. Ibid., 68. See also Anders Stephanson, *Kennan and the Art of Foreign Policy* (Cambridge, MA: Harvard University Press, 1989), 162–65.

44. Ryan, "US Foreign Policy and the Hierarchy of Alterity."

45. Smith, *Last Years,* 67.

46. Ronald Reagan, "Address before a Joint Session of Congress, April 27, 1983" (http://www.reagan.utexas.edu/archives/speeches/1983/42783d.htm).

47. Arthur M. Schlesinger, Jr., *A Thousand Days: John F. Kennedy in the White House* (Boston: Houghton Mifflin, 1965), 173.

48. Ibid., 177.

49. Michael E. Latham, *Modernization as Ideology: American Social Science and Nation Building in the Kennedy Era* (Chapel Hill: The University of North Carolina Press, 2000), 80.

50. Murphy, *Hemispheric Imaginings,* 153–54.

Chapter 4

Consumerist Geographies and the Politics of Othering

Kristin Hoganson

A s U.S. overseas interests expanded around the turn of the twentieth century, so did understandings of the wider world. Missionaries, government agents, explorers, and academic experts played notable roles in producing geographical knowledge, much of it aimed at expanding U.S. power, whether political, economic, or cultural.[1] But these were not the only or even the most influential sources of information on other peoples and places. Consumerist geographies—produced by cookbook writers, high society gossip columnists, entertainment entrepreneurs, catalog authors, and countless other contributors to popular culture—also shaped conceptions of the other.

In a time period when the National Geographic Society had fewer than fourteen hundred members, millions of Americans (women notable among them) encountered depictions of the foreign in domestic magazines, cooking columns, travel guides, fiction, and trade cards. Department store displays, ethnographic circus exhibits, world's fairs, church bazaars, museum dioramas, zoological gardens, copycat architecture, and handicraft collections offered further glimpses into the foreign. So did immigrant neighborhoods, such as Chinatowns and Little Italys. Native-born Americans encountered the foreign in theatrical costume parties, dances, festivals, and pageants; they tasted it in ethnic restaurants and around the world dinners; they watched it in stereopticon slides and on stage and screen. And just as significantly, they encountered imported things (such as porcelain, silk, and bananas) and things understood to be foreign in origin or style (such as Oriental rugs, French fashion, and curry) in the

Notes for this chapter begin on page 98.

course of daily domestic life. Taken together, these writings, displays, and collections of things constituted a considerable popular geography, no less important in shaping geographic sensibilities than more scientific reports, due to their quotidian nature, reach, and sensory appeal.[2]

At first glance, yesterday's recipes or fashion pages may not seem like geographic texts. Their main purpose, after all, was not to impart geographical information but to facilitate consumption. Yet, like other forms of geography, they provided insights into the earth and its inhabitants — albeit insights that often differed from those provided by more scientific forms of geography. In contrast to geographies that took an aloof perspective, geographies of consumption were often materially based, pleasure oriented, and participatory.[3] Rather than fostering a sense of distance from other peoples, consumer geographies frequently encouraged imaginative identification. The housewife who duplicated dishes produced in other lands had reason to think she had elided the gap between herself and the natives who had originated her recipes; so did the decorator who attempted to create an Eastern milieu or the hostess who threw an exotic theme party. By enjoying the best that the world had to offer, native-born Americans could experience foreignness (or so they were encouraged to believe) firsthand.

In characterizing the information conveyed by domestic manuals, pattern booklets, or amusement park belly dancers as popular geographies, I do not mean to imply that this information was accurate, or even that contemporaries understood it to be fully accurate. But all geographies are inherently inaccurate in one way or another, for they are by definition representational and hence interpretive. The significance of the writings, things, and displays that infused daily life with geographic consciousness lies not in their exactitude but in their ubiquity and in their claims to represent something about the foreign. So what did these consumerist geographies teach? On the one hand, they conveyed lessons of appreciation and receptivity that can be seen as forerunners to the multicultural sensibilities in our own era. But like other geographies of their time, they also taught lessons with far different political implications, lessons of hierarchy and differentiation.

Affiliative Geographies

Consumerist geographies took off in the late nineteenth century due to expanding webs of trade and consumption. Although this time period is known in U.S. history for the massive expansion of exports, imports rose significantly as well, following one step behind the export trade.[4] Department store buyers and import firms were just some of the sources of foreign-made goods. Entrepreneurs sold curios at world's fairs and other expositions, typically offering them at discount rates at the end of the event. The growing numbers of tourists who traveled overseas brought back souvenirs, curios, and luxury items (commonly underreported to U.S. customs agents), and the even greater tide of immigrants who came to the United States brought not only recipes and artisanal skills but also cherished belongings that they occasionally sold in times of need. Other immigrants used their homeland connections to open retail specialty shops or run peddling operations that purveyed (among other things) imported goods. Sailors, soldiers, government officials, missionaries, and commercial travelers also joined the ranks of those who brought novel items to U.S. shores.[5]

The growing availability of foreign-made objects, along with an expansion in the range of places that supplied Americans' wants, led consumerist accounts to pay considerable attention to origins. Agnes Bailey Ormsbee, author of *The House Comfortable*, provided the kind of purchasing advice typical of late nineteenth-century domestic writing. She counseled her discriminating readers to buy Irish and French damask, Scottish linen, English porcelain, Japanese china (she warned against the imitations from New Jersey), Turkish towels, Indian fabrics, Chinese rattan, and Turkistani, Daghestani, Smyrna, and other Oriental rugs.[6] By paying so much attention to origins, decoration experts heightened the appeal of products manufactured outside the United States.

Indeed, shopping columns, decoration essays, and fashion pages devoted so much attention to provenance that it seems likely that a large part of middle-class women's awareness of the wider world was associated with the goods they purchased for their households. Food writers also encouraged readers to identify specific dishes with foreignness by including geographical markers, such as "Delhi curry" and "Polish sauce," by labeling recipes in languages other than English, by insisting on their authenticity, and by describing the origins as well as nature of novel items such as alligator pears (avocados).[7]

Beyond providing a sense of the web of places that supplied the American cornucopia, such coverage of origins also taught lessons about the places from whence things came. On occasion, consumerist writings described the conditions of manufacture, often emphasizing pleasant, home-based methods of artisanal production. Along with providing insights into production, consumerist writings shed light on foreign consumption practices. Accounts that described foreign objects in use in their original surroundings provided consumers with a sense of knowing what the rest of the world was really like, a sense made all the more powerful because of its material grounding. A woman who had a samovar or Japanese fan could more vividly imagine the usages described in print.[8]

But it wasn't just the descriptions that accompanied consumer objects that turned them into sources of geographical knowledge, it was the conviction that things themselves exemplified national characteristics. As one shopping guide put it, Cairo rugs conveyed "an unmistakable sense of the orient."[9] In a similar vein, an article in *The House Beautiful* described a big stuffed Turkish armchair as typifying "the Pagan attitude toward life." An antique walnut chair, by contrast, "reminded us of nothing so much as a dependent dowager or an upper class London land-lady, insistent on her respectability and her social rights. In fact, she was inexpressibly British, and we weren't surprised to learn that, when a young chair, she had come from England to the States."[10] According to anthropomorphized accounts, material objects served as meaningful cultural signs. The things glimpsed in shop windows could thus provide lessons on otherness, even if not part of a geographically themed display or accompanied by lengthy passages of text.[11]

Food writers were particularly insistent that their subject matter could convey ethnographic knowledge in and of itself. As an article in *The Chautauquan* noted, "Perhaps different nations show their identity more in regard to preparing and eating food than in any other particular."[12] To know a people's cuisine was to know their culture, a point underscored by an article calling French sauces "representative of French character and wit, as subtle and piquant."[13] Food writers' search for characteristic national dishes reflected their belief that food provided a key for understanding cultural difference. "What is the French-Canadian dish … that would correspond to the Italian's spaghetti, the Mexican's hot tamales, the roast beef of old England—the national dish as it were?" questioned an article in *Table Talk, The National Food Magazine*. In identifying this dish as either *perdrix aux choux* (pork pie) or *soupe aux pois* (pea soup), the author revealed how French-speaking Canadians differed from their erstwhile compatriots in France. In contrast to their Parisian cousins, the Canadians came across as relatively simple but more robust.[14]

Not surprisingly, geographies aimed at facilitating new forms of consumption emphasized the pleasure that novel goods, tastes, and experiences could convey. Indeed, they often suggested that foreignness contributed to the appeal of imported goods and styles. Thus a catalog company that sold Mexican handicrafts hawked its "zerapes" by insisting that they had "a distinctly foreign air."[15] Similarly, the John Wanamaker's catalog that drew attention to the "large number of Wanamaker buyers who crossed the ocean looking for goods to stock," and the F. P. Bhumgara and Co. furniture advertisements that mentioned the company's offices in Bombay, Madras, Calcutta, and London also reflected the assumption that American buyers appreciated imports.[16] Rather than downplaying its national origins, for fear that xenophobic consumers would shy away, a Japanese mail order firm cast its foreignness as its greatest asset: "'Things Japanese,' that are peculiarly characteristic of Nippon, or as we call them, wasei (native make) can not be obtained in other countries. The original articles must be bought here."[17]

Although advertisements and decoration writings sometimes stressed the cost savings offered by imports, they more frequently associated imports with quality. In an age of machine-made products, many imports seemed appealingly handmade; one-of-a-kind rather than standardized. But if decorators just wanted handmade items, they could have surrounded themselves with cross-stitch, Shaker chairs, and so forth. Advertisements that stressed the desirability of having genuine foreign articles rather than merely attractive or expensive ones assumed that foreignness itself was a large part of the appeal of imports, and they in turn added to the appeal of foreignness by holding it up as a positive attribute.

Consumerist geographies advanced cosmopolitan sensibilities not only by insisting that people from around the world made things well worth having, but also by advancing the notion that good taste crossed borders. Such geographies encouraged U.S. consumers to identify with wealthy consumers elsewhere. A 1910 *Good Housekeeping* article on pottery from Provence showed how wide these imagined communities of consumption could be. Italy, Egypt, Spain, and the South American republics were the greatest importers of this pottery, but the manufacturers exported their wares to "all ports of the seven seas"—to San Francisco, Petersburg, Hong Kong, and New Orleans. Devotees had supposedly "formed a cult—whether they be on Broadway, Piccadilly or the Nevsky Prospekt."[18] Prompted by this article, casserole owners could regard themselves as members of an international community of like-minded consumers. Just as the national marketplace drew late-nineteenth-century Americans closer together, the international marketplace provided a basis for imagining still wider connections.

An article in *The House Beautiful* went so far as to characterize good taste as inherently cosmopolitan. "A thing may be Chinese or German, Norwegian or from the South Seas, and still be recognized by good judges as beautiful or ugly. There is far less diversity of opinion between different nations than one is led to believe, far less than is found in fact in people of the same nation, or even in the members of the same family. An American with a keen sense of beauty is able to appreciate the artistic product of the whole world. There is no geography in art."[19] Despite the protestation that art knew no geography, this article taught a geographical lesson:

those with truly discriminating tastes paid little heed to the boundaries that more narrow-minded people held so dear. If style should be seen as inherently cosmopolitan, then local tastes were a holdover from the past. According to one pamphlet, the interiors of "our forefathers" were relatively simple, from poverty and "from the fact that they were not a much traveling people, and their curiosity about other lands and their inhabitants was not very great." To be modern meant to be comparatively broad-minded: "We, on the contrary, take a very great interest in other peoples and in other countries. ... In our houses we give our love of adventure free play, and like to be reminded at every turn, of the fact that America, big as is her territory, is but a small part of the world."[20]

The association of modernity with cosmopolitanism was just as prevalent in fashion writings as in decoration advice. Although the imagined community of fashion centered on Paris, U.S. writings made it clear that the reach of Parisian fashion extended far beyond Europe. In 1892, for example, the *New York Tribune* ran a gossipy account of a family of well-dressed "South Americans" who lived in Paris a good part of the year. The newspaper's U.S. informant found them "charming" and "noticeable for their perfect taste in gowns."[21] One need not travel all the way to Paris to find well-dressed Latin American women, however. Travel writer Burton Holmes noted that "feminine Buenos Aires naturally takes Paris for her model."[22] In the teens, Havana won a reputation for being a "transplanted Paris," slightly behind the times in women's dress, but still brilliant. Those hoping to spot some local color looked in vain for mantillas at elite Cuban gatherings, for French fashion reigned supreme as the *Tribune* observed: "The Havanese, like her Spanish neighbors in Argentina, Brazil and Chili [sic], lives for and has her very being in beautiful clothes."[23]

Just as the commitment to French fashion proved the modernity of Latin-American women—or at least of those who discarded their mantillas and other items of traditional dress—U.S. fashion writing reported on the appeal of French fashion among women in Asia, the Pacific, and the Middle East. Coverage of Japan's efforts to claim a place "among modern civilizations" emphasized that "a chief phase of the movement is the decision of the Japanese women to adopt the European dress." The empress herself ordered gowns from the leading design house.[24] Similarly, accounts of the modernizing Young Turk movement highlighted Turkish women's Parisian tastes in clothes. The U.S. press also reported favorably on the appearance of Queen Lili'uokalani, who dressed in a tiara and fashionable gowns to prove her royal status to Westerners inclined to see Hawaiians as savages.[25] Through its apparent globality, Paris fashion seemed to connect women from around the world.

The idea that fashion was as capable of drawing women together as it was to demark national differences drew strength from conceptions of feminine universalism. In an 1889 article subtitled "Cosmopolitan Styles," a fashion writer for the *Ladies' Home Journal* said that "the universal desire to dress becomingly is essentially feminine and natural." A year later, another contributor to the *Journal* expressed similar sentiments: "I write and talk to the general woman. She is the woman all over the world who is interested in looking her best."[26] In foregrounding the seemingly borderless world of femininity, the universal understanding of fashion assumed a world in which common values and aesthetics framed rivalries over beauty. Rather than dwelling on the ways that nationality contributed to the divisions among women, this approach to fashion emphasized how taste united them.

Evidence that consumers embraced the idea that true style was not national can be found in attempts to appear cosmopolitan. Most commonly, fashionable U.S. women strove to look French, regardless of the actual origins of their clothes. Recognizing the allure of Paris fashion, department stores pronounced their Paris modes "authentic," fashion writers praised fabric for being "characteristically French," women's magazines provided pictures of French dresses for home sewers to copy, and advertisers trumpeted their wares as "more 'Frenchy' than ever and very 'chic.'"[27] Rising exports of ready-made clothes notwithstanding, in the late nineteenth century, U.S. designers continued to defer to Paris as the ultimate arbiter of style.

Moments of identification can be found not only in fashionable clothing but also in more theatrical displays that blurred the line between the self and other. Wealthy Americans often created a series of national theme rooms—French, English, Egyptian, and so forth—in their palatial Gilded Age mansions. Unable to afford such ensembles, middle-class Americans settled for Orientalist niches, or cosey corners, that featured imported pottery, textiles, brass work, and little Turkish coffee tables.[28] To make the most of such sets—whether high end or middle brow—trendy hostesses staged ostensibly foreign entertainments. Rebie Lowe, an Atlanta woman with an Oriental reception room, exemplifies this phenomenon. She liked to appear in it in "soft, clinging draperies and a Zouave bodice richly embroidered in gold."[29]

Mid-nineteenth-century Americans had sometimes adopted foreign personae in their frolicsome charades and more formal tableaux. By the late nineteenth century, this tentative experimentation with difference had become a virtual movement. Emulating the masked balls of the wealthy, middle-class Americans jumped on the costume party bandwagon. "Won't you come to my party as your other self?" ran an invitation for one such gathering covered by *Vogue*. What did "other self" imply? One woman came "dressed as a typical Irish maid-servant, in heavy shoes, coarse dress and woolen gloves." Taking the plea to come as her other self seriously, she acted the role suggested by her costume. The *Vogue* correspondent caught her, dust brush in hand, talking in brogue to a "swarthy little Italian in a red sweater."[30] Whereas some hosts gave guests the latitude to pick their own personas, others prescribed a theme. Most notably, the orientalism that so appealed to wealthy ball-givers also appealed to the middle-class hosts of costume parties.

Food often played a central role in such exotic entertainments. Like the recipes they accompanied, instructions for serving and eating also taught lessons in foreignness. Hence one cookbook told readers not to cut their spaghetti, so that it could be eaten Italian fashion, wound around the fork.[31] Others urged chopsticks for Chinese food and Japanese tea cups for Japanese tea.[32] Entertaining guides counseled grouping foods together to provide theme meals—for example, combining rice, chopped cabbage with red pepper, drop cakes and tea to produce a "Chinese Affair" or serving Vermicelli Soep, Snijboontjes (Schnitt beans), Aardappelen Met Room Sause (creamed potatoes), and gevulde lamschouder (stuffed shoulder of lamb) to make a Dutch dinner. "National suppers" were "much in vogue" claimed *Good Housekeeping* in 1888.[33] Advice on eating supposedly foreign foods in an appropriately foreign way and in appropriately foreign combinations underscored the premise that one attraction of foreign foods was their very foreignness. They offered an opportunity to experience the exotic.

The appeal of costumes spilled beyond the purview of the parlor into middle-class women's fund-raising fairs. In her book on these events, Beverly Gordon notes that fair givers introduced costuming during the Civil War and soon after it became typical for salespeople to dress up. Although some fairs emphasized historic themes taken from the U.S. past, international themes peaked at the turn of the century. "Italian 'peasants' and wholesome 'Dutch girls' could probably be found at church bazaars in any community in the country," comments Gordon.[34] Ersatz Dutch and Italian maidens had plenty of costumed company: women "personated" places such as Mexico, Turkey, Japan, and China, as well as various European countries in their fund-raising events.[35]

If the organizers of church bazaars and round-the-world dinners are to be believed, food could transport those who tasted it to other places. This was particularly true when it accompanied costumes, performance, and stage settings, but food could also signify foreignness by itself. According to an article in *Good Housekeeping*, the mere sight of macaroni "calls up visions of the blue Bay of Naples, the great smoking peak of Vesuvius in the background."[36] "Will you ply across the ocean?" questioned an article on English dinners that invited readers to use food as a vehicle for fictive travel.[37] Even when consumed in the course of an ordinary family meal, a dish regarded as foreign added a taste of the exotic. Eating spaghetti meant eating Italian, eating frijoles meant eating Mexican. Through food, native-born Americans could literally ingest the foreign. Recalling how her children used to say "I can smell the West Indies" when they ate a coconut, the author of a domestic advice book commented: "No doubt, under its influence, those palm trees, monkeys and negroes, who figure in their illustrated geography, enlarge in their inner consciousness into life and motion."[38] In contrast to geographies that drew sharp lines between the domestic and the foreign, geographies that encouraged the consumption of foreign things and the feigning of foreignness blurred the boundaries between the self and other.

The appreciative lessons taught by consumerist geographies were at odds with ethnographies that depicted non-European peoples more contemptuously. The Japanese won particularly favorable appraisals in consumerist geographies because of their manufactures and artwork. One article praising Japanese design said the "ingenious" Japanese deserved the title "Yankees of the East."[39] Although praising Japanese for their Yankee attributes continued to hold up Western standards as the ideal, other accounts applauded the Japanese for the alternative they offered, for having taught people in the West "a new way to look at life; the beauty of simplification and elimination."[40] "The Japanese way is best," asserted an article extolling Japanese simplicity.[41] The opening of Japan to export trade revealed, as one writer put it, "how absurd were our own systems of decoration with all their barbarous mannerisms and conventionalities, compared to the simple and natural methods employed by these men of the East, whom for ages we had, in our bigoted ignorance, supposed to be little better than savages."[42]

The potential for consumerist geographies to challenge other currents of geographic understanding can also be seen by contrasting the popularity of orientalist consumption with representations of the Middle East. Just as white, middle-class Americans tended to regard East Asians as inferior, they tended to disdain the Middle East as backward. Rather than criticizing European aggression against the Sultan's dominions, Americans increasingly saw Turks as oppressors of subject Christian minorities. They deplored Turkish massacres of Bulgarian Christians in 1876 and Armenians in 1894–95. They protested the slave trade, which continued to flow from inner Africa, through Tripoli, to Constantinople in the early 1870s. And they sent missionaries to the region: in the 1880s, the Ottoman

Empire was the largest foreign mission site for the United States.[43] Yet all the while, middle-class housewives were sewing cushions for sensuous Oriental niches.

In addition to countering the worst views of some non-European groups, consumerist geographies also countered negative views of immigrants. In particular, the immigrant gifts movement that took off in the early twentieth century cast immigrants as cultural resources—because of, not in spite of—their ability to convey foreignness.[44] In stark contrast to the common claims that immigrant servants were slovenly, irresponsible, and inefficient, and that immigrant girls should learn American methods of cookery under the tutelage of home economics instructors, food writers often held up immigrant women as talented cooks. "To us Americans come every year hordes of foreigners who have foods and different ways of cooking and preparing them that are new to us. If we are ready to learn from all of them we can enrich our diet incalculably," wrote the authors of a 1914 cooking manual.[45]

This appreciation for foreign culinary expertise is perhaps most striking in writings on Chinese foodways. Although European Americans often derogated Chinese-Americans as rat eaters, Chinese chop suey establishments had become a central touristic attraction in U.S. Chinatowns by the 1890s.[46] After visiting joss houses and opium dens, European-American tourists sat down for steaming plates of pork, onions, rice, bamboo sprouts, beef, and chicken, "served with much gravy."[47] The influence of these restaurants radiated out beyond the Chinatowns where they were situated. A *Ladies' Home Journal* article titled "Rice as the Chinese Prepare It" claimed to reveal the "detailed process, learned firsthand from a Chinese restaurant proprietor." The piece again held up Chinese-Americans as cultural resources by counseling readers to "[b]uy at a Chinese shop, or restaurant, a jar of the sauce that they always serve with the rice to their countrymen. It is a strange, dark reddish brown liquid, very salty and pungent."[48]

By heralding immigrants as cultural resources, writings on immigrant gifts echoed the consumerist tone of touristic writings that emphasized the picturesque and spectacular, rather than the troubling or the distasteful. As the members of a travel club reported, their imaginary tours had taken them "through Germany; not to show us, indeed, the Imperial Empire of the Kaiser so much as the Germany dear to the heart of the lover of art, romance and story and the picturesque."[49] A touristic outlook meant seeing the world through the lens of art appreciation. It meant searching for the sublime and the marvelous. After all, why bother to visit a place with no redeeming virtues? A basic premise of the tourist mentality was that any place worth visiting must have something to offer. Hence touristic accounts countered condemnation with more appreciative assessments.

Mexican hotel rooms might lack baths and other modern amenities, but the costumes were picturesque and the people hospitable.[50] So-called "old stock" Americans might think little of the Italian immigrants who were pouring into the United States in the late nineteenth century, but tourists raved about their homeland. As a member of the Atwater, Ohio, Monday Afternoon Club enthused: "We are perfectly in love with our first glimpse of Italy."[51]

Just as touristic writings insisted that travel was broadening, travel club members insisted that their trips, if only of the armchair variety, had made them open-minded. After five months of studying Italy, one club reported: "Our prejudices have disappeared."[52] Other club members echoed these sentiments, insisting that their travels had taught them to sympathize with the nations under study. Indeed, some club members went so far as to say that they had learned to identify with the people in the lands they visited. As an Iowa woman wrote: "Since our circle has taken up the Bay View course, the enthusiasm has grown so strong that it threatens to convert us all into Germans."[53] By teaching travelers to appreciate and even identify with different people, imaginary travel joined with other forms of consumerist geographies to plant seeds of cultural relativism.

The celebration of otherness found in touristic and other consumerist accounts had its share of critics. These included Amelia Muir Baldwin, a Boston-born interior decorator and needle tapestry designer who as an older woman taught Americanization courses to immigrants. Baldwin called for racially and culturally appropriate interiors in a 1916 essay. "In our own houses we are certainly happier if we have a background which expresses something of ourselves, racially and individually … a Turkish harem, however well done from a decorative point of view, is ill adapted to the uses and ideals of domestic life in this country." She went on to object to the French style as "foreign to our genius."[54] Those who called for more national styles (such as the colonial revival, mission, and arts and crafts) instead of eclectic interiors, for a rationalized American cuisine (rather than unscientific meals), and for democratic American fashions (in lieu of aristocratic French designs), regarded appreciative consumerist geographies as a threat to efforts to draw sharper lines between the nation and the rest of the world. Such critics believed that the consumerist appreciation of novelty and difference, celebration of transnational standards of taste, and willingness to fake racial and civilizational as well as national hierarchies. By insisting that taste should be national, by which they meant that it should be shared by everyone assumed to belong to the nation and that it should indicate specifically national sensibilities, critics of consumerist cosmopolitanism strove for a sharper delineation of self and other that would maintain the racial and class distinctions that figured so largely in geographic accounts less focused on pleasure than were geographies of consumption.

Geographies of Differentiation

Although consumerist geographies can be seen as wellsprings of cultural relativity and multicultural mind-sets, they were not always out of sync with geographies bent on establishing national and racial hierarchies. Both those who prided themselves on their cosmopolitanism and those who fretted about cosmopolitan consumption overlooked the many limits to this cosmopolitanism, the many ways that consumerist geographies disparaged the other while advancing conceptions of white supremacy and U.S. national superiority.

Although consumerist literature could wax enthusiastic about the cultural attainments of foreign artisans, consumerist accounts did not always depict foreign production or producers favorably. Significantly, household goods made by Africans living south of the Sahara and other groups assumed to be at the very bottom of the racial hierarchy received little favorable mention in decorating columns. Cosmopolitan decorators may have prized antelope skins, but they scorned black Africans for failing to produce attractive domestic accouterments. White householders may have displayed a Zulu shield or basket as part of an eclectic ensemble, but they did not produce southern African rooms alongside their Moorish, Japanese, and Norwegian rooms. The white housewives who hailed difference and through their cooking, entertaining, and masquerades also drew the line at blackness. They did not craft central African reception rooms so they could better pretend to be Congolese. To embrace foreign styles, to fake foreignness in American homes, meant to acknowledge that the foreign had something to offer, and the overarching power of domestic white supremacist ideologies precluded appreciation of black African attainment.

Southern Africa was not the only part of the world that merited little positive consumerist coverage. Cookbooks published numerous recipes attributed to British India, but not to the Philippines, thus suggesting the difficulties in quickly ingesting those islands. Despite the nation's increasing ties to the Caribbean and Philippines, white American women masqueraded far more as Europeans than as people from the nation's new island acquisitions and other economic dependencies. They might relish Caribbean sugar and bananas, but not yet Cuban music or Philippine piña cloth.

As the comparative lack of attention to the cultural production of southern Africa, the Philippines, and the Caribbean reveals, consumerist geographies cited the ability to make things that were palatable to U.S. consumers as markers of civilization. But even people who made things worth having did not necessarily win high esteem. It was not unusual for consumerist accounts to mix praise for specific cultural attainments with mention of various deficiencies. The Arab may have been "the greatest of decorators," as one account claimed, but he was also (according to the same article) "the fiercest of fanatics … the most treacherous of foes."[55] Another article that mixed admiration and disdain contrasted the Oriental, "steeped in moral degradation, but with intuitive perception of grace of line and harmony of color," with the Scot—"noble, true, generous—but whose highest art achievement has been the combining of ugly checkered squares."[56] As this comparison of Oriental grace and Scottish plaids suggests, the ability to produce beautiful things did not necessarily imply civilizational distinction. Indeed, practical-minded Americans sometimes dismissed artistic handiwork as only a minor attainment. At the turn of the century, many white Americans supported industrial education for people of color at home and in U.S. dependencies, thinking that manual work would teach discipline and work habits without challenging racial hierarchies.[57] Much of the appreciation of handicrafts made by poor, colonized, and dark-skinned workers can be seen as consistent with this logic.

Although foreign entertainments celebrated different foods and practices—the spaghetti wrapped around forks, the ostensibly Chinese cuisine with chopsticks—more critical veins of consumerist geography did not invite U.S. consumers to fake foreignness. Some of the most horrified accounts of other practices can be found in food writings. Reports that West Africans ate without tablecloths, knives, forks, or plates suggested that such uncouth eaters were barbarous in comparison to those who did.[58] Likewise, articles claiming that Hindu women had to watch their men folk eat and then make do with the leftovers presented India as devoid of chivalrous respect for women.[59] (Contemporary etiquette in the United States demanded that the men should never sit down until the women had taken their places.)[60] Like the domestic scientists who were working so hard to rationalize and control American cooking, cookbook ethnographers claimed that other people had curious habits that contrasted with the implicitly normative ones they espoused. According to their accounts, other people ate strange things, like Japanese miso—"a peculiar affair."[61] They ate certain foods at odd times: the Norwegians finished off leftover fish at breakfast; the Swedes ate their soup at the end of dinner, instead of at the start.[62] They ate inappropriate amounts: the English sipped so much heavy port and brandied sherry that it proved "most pernicious and dangerous."[63] Even when such writings purported to be neutral in tone, their implied comparisons could convey the impression that divergent foodways should be regarded as aberrations from the white, middle-class, U.S. norm rather than equally meritorious customs.

If some accounts just depicted foreign foods and eating habits as non-normative, or beyond that, as a trial to the traveler, other writings on foods conveyed the impression that foreign foods were far beyond the pale. Like the European explorers who had earlier shocked readers with reports of cannibalism, late-nineteenth- and early-twentieth-century food writers made others seem barbarous by reporting on their tastes. "Many animals and insects are used as food in different parts of the earth, of which the mere mention is enough to create disgust and abhorrence," noted a treatise on "curious dishes and feasts" from across the world. "The flesh of the sloth, lizard, alligator, snake, monkey, and kangaroo are eaten in South America; the grasshopper is roasted and eaten by the North American Indian, and the eggs of various insects are prepared and eaten by other savages."[64] Eskimos and other people of the Arctic were often targets of such criticism. A housekeeping manual described their diet as "oleaginous to a degree that sounds revolting and almost incredible to a person that rarely sees ice more than six inches thick."[65] The Chinese also won particular opprobrium for eating rats, bats, snails, shark fins, dogs, cats, and living shrimp, still jumping in the bowl. "I could not put one of these live things into my mouth," commented the author.[66] Although the eating habits of non-Europeans received the most unfavorable publicity, disdain for foreign foodstuffs applied to Europeans as well. The French, Spaniards, Italians, and Belgians troubled some sensibilities because of their fondness for snails.[67] German sausages filled with horse flesh and French *patés de foie gras* concocted from enlarged goose livers (a dish described as "fatal to many epicures") also elicited disgust.[68]

Critical appraisals of foreign food ways went beyond coverage of taboo ingredients to include stomach-turning methods of preparation, or lack thereof. Groups ranging from the Abyssinians in the South to Eskimos in the North and Japanese in the East were excoriated for eating raw animal flesh.[69] Even the English reportedly favored "large bleeding, steaming lumps of almost raw meat."[70] If some favored foods that had barely ceased breathing, others ate foods aged to the point of spoilage. Hindus supposedly ate "rancid butter, the Chinese feasted on rotten eggs, and Norwegians enjoyed a cheese more moldy than milky. One particularly sickening article in the *New York Tribune* reported on a Paris restaurant that served woodcock and pheasants killed six weeks earlier to a patron fond of high game. The decomposing flesh had to be eaten with a spoon.[71] The critiques of foreign food preparation went so far as to involve cruelty. To make whiter veal, claimed one account, French butchers hung calves up by the hind legs and let them bleed slowly to death. The author's comment—"This barbarious [sic] method is practiced universally in France, but the laws of this country prevent its open practice here" — conveyed a sense of national superiority typical of many writings on foreign foodways.[72]

This sense of national superiority carried over to writings emphasizing a lack of sanitation in foreign food preparation. Housewives concerned with cleanliness could only be repulsed by assertions that Italians exposed their macaroni to dust and "odors of every kind" when they hung it up to dry.[73] "A traveler says that one look at the making of macaroni was enough to prevent him from ever eating any more of it," reported *Good Housekeeping*. "The workmen were seen to carry the tubes on their naked, dirty, sweaty shoulders and backs." (Such assertions led fastidiously sanitary cooks to wash their macaroni before boiling it).[74] Another traveler reported on the disgusting methods of the tea manufactory in Foochow. After weighing the tea, the workers passed it to "the man at the fires, who spread it on a dirty stained cloth laid over the boiling water." Once heated, it was "thrown at a man some feet distant, who emptied the smoking contents into a wooden mold. A fellow workman placed this under a ponderous lever, moved by a gang of almost naked men."[75] The Ceylon and India Tea Company played on such suspicions of filthy foreign conditions by depicting tea from China being prepared by hand, a pig at the heels of the scantily clad Chinese workmen. The accompanying text hawked tea from Ceylon and India, saying that since it was prepared by machinery, it was free of "all contamination from nude perspiring 'yellow men.'"[76]

If the specter of bodily contamination was not enough to thoroughly nauseate the middle-class housewife, another ground of criticism had to do with poisonous fixatives. Cooking expert Maria Parloa warned that French and English companies relied on harmful copper sulfates to preserve the color of their tinned peas.[77] Similarly, grocer's manuals denounced adulterated imports — such as cayenne tainted by brick dust, ferruginous earths, vermilion, and red lead.[78] Significantly, U.S. cooking writings neglected to mention the European restrictions on American foodstuffs on the grounds that they were adulterated and diseased. The pitiful state of U.S. manufacturing standards can be seen in the nineteenth-century ketchup industry. Tomato canneries made the sauce from the rotten, worm-ridden, and green leavings collected from the floor, throwing in some toxic preservatives to keep the mixture from spoiling. An 1896 study of preserves and ketchups in California found that forty-eight out of fifty-five contained injurious ingredients. American consumers were not oblivious to domestic manufacturing conditions. Over half the states had passed pure food and drug laws by 1895; *The Jungle's* horrific depiction of the meat-packing industry prompted Congress to pass a Pure Food Act in 1906.[79] And yet food writings persisted in associating impurity and filth with foreignness.

The writings emphasizing the unsavory nature of foreign foodstuffs and the problematic ways of preparing them made it seem that white, native-born, middle-class U.S. housewives were worlds away from other people and fortunately so. In contrast to other people given to disgusting tastes, barbarous habits, unsanitary conditions, and dangerous practices, U.S. cookbook readers could regard themselves as more tasteful, cultivated, clean, and educated. They also could see themselves as comparatively wealthy. In explaining why foreigners ate foods that middle-class Americans would not touch, cooking ethnographers blamed taste, the caloric demands of extreme climates like those found in the Arctic, and scarcity. Italian peasants are so abstinent, claimed an article in *Good Housekeeping*, that one almost forgets that they eat. "The bit of black bread may be washed down by a flask of thin sour wine, but macaroni is a luxury; and that there is even an actual dinner in any American or English sense is quite problematical."[80] The American housewife who read such accounts could feel blessed to reside in a land of comparative abundance.

In addition to claiming abundance as an element of national distinctiveness, U.S. consumerist geographies insisted that Americans' ability to draw on distant streams of production further marked their privileged standing in the global scheme of things. A woman shopper who offered advice in *The House Beautiful* illustrates the sense of national privilege taught by consumerist geographies: "The chief thought in the mind of the woman who goes out to buy curtains and draperies ... must be one of thankfulness that she lives in this particular age of the world, for never before were there so many interesting things from which to choose." She went on to mention Japanese, Persian, Scottish, and Madagascar fabrics. Shifting her attention to dishes and cutlery, she continued in awe: "From the four corners of the earth come marching long processions of tableware." The mistress of the house could "make of her dining-table, spread with appropriate wares, a part of a Dutch room, or a Spanish room, or a German room, or a Japanese or a Chinese room. Or, if she wants to make her dining room merely quaint and homey, with a bit of the bizarre [sic] flavor that seems always to add just the necessary tang to bungalow furnishing, she can pick and choose from the offerings of half the nations of the earth."[81] As envious window shoppers well knew, not everybody could bring the world home. But cosmopolitan decorators could and did.

This access to global production stood in stark contrast to the consumption opportunities of many of the world's peoples, as represented by U.S. consumerist geographies. To take one example, despite the ostensibly global reputation of the Paris fashion industry, not all women dressed according to the latest Paris look. A *National Geographic Magazine* article on Bulgaria, for example, juxtaposed pictures of women college students in "European dress" with "uneducated" peasant women in local styles.[82] The point was not the beauty of Bulgarian design, but the vast gulf in culture and outlook between those who had access to world-class style and those who did not. Folk costumes might be picturesque, admitted these accounts, but in contrast to fashionable dress, they were parochial, backward, and lower-class.

Though European peasant women struck many ethnographic writers as throwbacks to a more localized age, women in Africa, Asia, Latin America, and the Pacific generally struck them as most backward of all. To be sure, some won recognition for adopting Paris fashions, but these women came across as elite path breakers. As an article on Mexican women noted, "The people who can afford it wear the Frenchiest of French creations in the way of hats," but the majority of women just wore light scarves. Indeed, the "great middle class," clad only in sandals, still went without stockings.[83] These Latin American women were a far cry from their compatriots who shopped in Paris. The same held true for Hawaiians. Despite Queen Lili'uokalani's impressive wardrobe, the dress worn by most of her countrywomen "would not be tolerated in the state of Kansas," according to travel writer Burton Holmes.[84] Folk clothing, however attractive at its finest, could also connote poverty, hard labor, ignorance, backwardness, and stagnation. If the fashionable world was the world of the appropriators, the rest of the world was appropriated—the source of the design motifs adopted by the world's elite. To buy into the fashion system centered in Paris thus meant to distinguish one from penurious, colored, and colonized people.

Decorating experts advanced the idea that U.S. consumers were especially privileged by describing their purchases as exercises of power. They recounted stories of precious Oriental rugs that had come onto the market because of the dire poverty of their original owners, who had no choice but to relinquish their treasures to wealthy Western buyers. Missionaries in Persia found opportunity even in famine: "it is wonderful how every commodity is sold for a mere song," one reported.[85] That international exchanges were not always regarded as equal can be inferred as well from the words used to describe them. Contemporaries claimed that the markets of the East had been "ransacked" for products; that Europeans relinquished their many treasures to the "hordes of Americans who come armed with the invincible dollar." They referred to foreign goods as "plunder" and "trophies of travel."[86] "It is not unusual for a buyer to invade the dwelling of a Persian gentleman and bid for his dishes or the rugs on his floors or walls," claimed an article in *House and Garden*. "The wretched part of it is that he very often gets them. Persia is being stripped with all the rapidity possible."[87]

The assumption that American shoppers could buy whatever they wanted exaggerated the strength of all but the fattest pocketbooks. Nevertheless, decoration writings and laden shop counters taught American consumers that their nation's relative wealth put them in a position of power in the international marketplace. As they cast the United States as the destination of long processions of tableware, they cast the world's peoples as service providers, important to U.S. consumers only for their ability to gratify consumerist desires. An advertisement for Indian tea that depicted an Indian man serving a white Western woman encapsulated the lessons of these consumerist geographies. To consume novel foods was to become the woman in the advertisement—the beneficiary of global networks of wealth, power, and labor. This woman would appreciate the subheading chosen by the *National Geographic Magazine* for its article on American food: "The World Our Servant."[88]

The tendency to evaluate other peoples based on their potential as service providers is particularly noticeable in touristic writings. Whereas commercially oriented ethnographies focused on the productive capacities of various peoples and politically minded ethnographies focused on their potential for self-governance, travel ethnographies paid relatively greater attention to how other peoples would affect the tourist experience. Would they delight the eye? Would they prepare good meals? Would they provide clean rooms? Would they deal honestly with a stranger? Could an English speaker understand them? Like all ethnographies, tourist ethnography assumed an implicit audience, and in this case, the judge was the leisure traveler. Tourist ethnography valued the knowledgeable guide, the accomplished cook, the indefatigable chair carrier, the efficient porter, the dirt-chasing hotelier, and the helpful official. It valued them all the more if they came cheaply. While tourists might admire artistic, technological, spiritual, military, and other accomplishments, they reserved some of their most heartfelt appreciation for the pleasingly servile native. "Search the world through, and where will you find servants such as these?" questioned John Stoddard in a lecture on Japan. "From the first moment when they fall upon their knees and bow their foreheads to the floor, till the last instant, when they troop around the door to call to you their musical word for farewell—'Sayonara,' they seem to be the daintiest, happiest, and most obliging specimens of humanity that walk the earth."[89] Conversely, travelers damned those who had not gratified their desires. A travel book on Mexico characterized "peons," especially those in small towns and country places, as "usually very stupid." What gave rise to this impression? "When visiting Puebla, I asked several if they could direct me to the post-office, but was unable to make any of them understand."[90]

The trope of the foreigner as service provider intersected with imperialist lines of thought that regarded the natural resources and productive capacity of much of the world as ripe for exploitation by the great powers.[91] Consumerist geographies were imperial in more than just their associations, however: they often celebrated the imperial world system that made the world's treasures available to U.S. consumers. They credited curry to British imperialism, Central Asian rugs to Russian railroad expansion, and tropical fruits to U.S. governmental agents in the Caribbean.[92] The women who sold cocoa in round-the-world church bazaars dressed as Dutch maidens, not Javanese.[93] Thus even as consumerist geographies opened the door to appreciating global cultural production, their tendency to frame the matter as the result of European imperialism limited the cosmopolitanism of their visions.

The limits to their purported cosmopolitan can be seen by taking a second look at efforts to feign foreignness. The white, middle-class American women who crafted cosey corners in their parlors did not get their ideas straight from Turks or Egyptians. They got them via Europe, which had a long history of orientalist design, with aristocratic cachet. Perhaps the best known orientalist spectacle was Brighton Pavilion, built by King George IV in the 1790s. Following the royal lead, aristocrats added Arabian halls, Indian drawing rooms, and Moorish billiard rooms to their mansions in the late nineteenth century. Maude Andrews, who wrote a series of travel articles for the *Atlanta Constitution* in 1896, was struck by a Turkish room in London: "sumptuous, restful, exquisite—nothing in it, I assure you, like the cosey oriental corners we see copied out of newspapers and fashion books." She may have disdained cosey corners for being lowbrow, but these too had European connections—the 1892 Exhibition of Rooms at London's Crystal Palace had one on display.[94]

Constructing a cosey corner meant more than mimicking the wealthy within the United States: like the rich who hired decorators to compose lavish oriental retreats, the middle-class American women who draped their corners in fabric and piled cushions on the divan demonstrated a sense of European sophistication through their exhibitions of oriental exoticism. The American housewives who constructed orientalist cosey corners did not produce an unmediated Eastern decor but a colonial decor, one that emerged from the crucible of empire and was as much European as "oriental." Just as the spreading reach of Western ships had contributed to the rage for chinoiserie in the eighteenth century, a sense of affinity with Western imperialism contributed to the orientalism of the nineteenth. Like the public exhibitions that endorsed Western imperial power, orientalist cosey corners revealed an enthusiasm for empire, if only secondhand.

From Pleasure to Privilege and Power

If missionary geographies were about conversion, political geographies about governance, and academic geographies about systematic classification, then consumerist geographies were—despite their overlaps with other forms of geographical knowledge—fundamentally about pleasure. This included the pleasure of novelty and difference, both of which entailed an appreciation of the foreign and often some amount of identification with producers and consumers beyond the borders of the United States. But consumerist geographies also contributed to the pleasure of distinction by teaching that not all people produced things worth having, that not all people had access to global production, and, ultimately, that Americans should feel fortunate in their ability to command the labor of so many other peoples. Consumerist geographies aimed at U.S. audiences insisted that Americans were exceptionally cosmopolitan when it came to consumption, never mind that any cosmopolitanism that is not reciprocal is not really cosmopolitanism at all.

Notes

1. On geographic knowledge advancing power, see Gilbert G. González, *Culture of Empire: American Writers, Mexico, and Mexican Immigrants, 1880-1930* (Austin: University of Texas Press, 2004); Ricardo D. Salvatore, "The Enterprise of Knowledge: Representational Machines of Informal Empire," in *Close Encounters of Empire: Writing the Cultural History of U.S.-Latin American Relations,* eds. Gilbert M. Joseph, Catherine C. LeGrand, and Ricardo D. Salvatore (Durham, NC: Duke University Press, 1998), 69–104; Catherine A. Lutz and Jane L. Collins, *Reading National Geographic* (Chicago: University of Chicago Press, 1993); Susan Schulten, *The Geographical Imagination in America, 1880-1950* (Chicago: University of Chicago Press, 2001); Matthew Frye Jacobson, *Barbarian Virtues: The United States Encounters Foreign Peoples at Home and Abroad, 1876-1917* (New York: Hill & Wang, 2000); Paul Kramer, "Making Concessions: Race and Empire Revisited at the Philippine Exposition, St. Louis, 1901-1905," *Radical History Review* 73 (Winter 1999): 74–114.
2. On the National Geographic Society, see Lutz and Collins, *Reading National Geographic,* 21. See also, William Leach, *Land of Desire: Merchants, Power, and the Rise of a New American Culture* (New York: Pantheon Books, 1993); Donald W. Curl, *Mizner's Florida: American Resort Architecture* (Cambridge: MIT Press, 1984); John Sweetman, *The Oriental Obsession: Islamic Inspiration in British and American Art and Architecture, 1500-1920* (Cambridge: Cambridge University Press, 1988); Janet M. Davis, *The Circus Age: Culture and Society under the American Big Top* (Chapel Hill: University of North Carolina Press, 2002); Robert W. Rydell, *All the World's a Fair: Visions of Empire at American International Expositions, 1876-1916* (Chicago: University of Chicago Press, 1984); David Brody, *Visualizing American Empire: Orientalism and Imperialism in the Philippines* (Chicago: University of Chicago Press, 2010); Beverly Gordon, *Bazaars and Fair Ladies: The History of*

the American Fundraising Fair (Knoxville: University of Tennessee Press, 1998); Steven Conn, "An Epistemology for Empire: The Philadelphia Commercial Museum, 1893-1896," *Diplomatic History* 22 (Fall 1998): 533–63; William W. Fitzhugh, "Ambassadors in Sealskins: Exhibiting Eskimos at the Smithsonian," in *Exhibiting Dilemmas: Issues of Representation at the Smithsonian*, ed. Amy Henderson and Adrienne L. Kaeppler (Washington, DC: Smithsonian Institution Press, 1997), 206–45; Elizabeth Hanson, *Animal Attractions: Nature on Display in American Zoos* (Princeton: Princeton University Press, 2002); Nigel Rothfels, *Savages and Beasts: The Birth of the Modern Zoo* (Baltimore: Johns Hopkins University Press, 2002); Donna Haraway, "Teddy Bear Patriarchy: Taxidermy in the Garden of Eden, New York City, 1908-1936," in *Cultures of United States Imperialism*, ed. Amy Kaplan and Donald E. Pease (Durham, NC: Duke University Press, 1993), 237–91; Steven Hoelscher, *Heritage of Stage: The Invention of Ethnic Place in America's Little Switzerland* (Madison: University of Wisconsin Press, 1998); Catherine Cocks, *Doing the Town: The Rise of Urban Tourism in the United States, 1850-1915* (Berkeley: University of California Press, 2001); Anthony W. Lee, *Picturing Chinatown: Art and Orientalism in San Francisco* (Berkeley: University of California Press, 2001); Ivan Light, "From Vice District to Tourist Attraction: The Moral Career of American Chinatowns, 1880-1940," *Pacific Historical Review* 43 (August 1974): 367–94; Reid Mitchell, *All on a Mardi Gras Day: Episodes in the History of New Orleans Carnival* (Cambridge, MA: Harvard University Press, 1995); Donna R. Gabaccia, *We Are What We Eat: Ethnic Food and the Making of Americans* (Cambridge, MA: Harvard University Press, 1998); William C. Darrah, *The World of Stereographs* (Gettysburg: W. C. Darrah, 1977); Stephan Oettermann, *The Panorama: History of a Mass Medium* (New York: Zone Books, 1997); John F. Kasson, *Amusing the Million: Coney Island at the Turn of the Century* (New York: Hill & Wang, 1978).

3. On promontory perspectives, see Mary Louise Pratt, *Imperial Eyes: Travel Writing and Transculturation* (New York: Routledge, 1992).

4. U.S. imports rose from $354 million in 1860 to $1.9 billion in 1914. In the same period, exports rose from $316 million to $2.4 billion. Stuart Weems Bruchey, *Enterprise: The Dynamic Economy of a Free People* (Cambridge, MA: Harvard University Press, 1990), 296–300; Mira Wilkins, *The History of Foreign Investment in the United States to 1914* (Cambridge, MA: Harvard University Press, 1989), 142. On imports, see, Department of the Treasury, *Commerce and Navigation of the United States* (Washington, DC: Government Printing Office, 1865), 243, 345, 350–51; Department of Commerce, *Commerce and Navigation of the United States* (Washington, DC: Government Printing Office, 1920), 40–41, 100, 101–2.

5. On buyers, see *Wanamaker's Catalog* (Philadelphia: John Wanamaker's, 1908), inside cover; "F.P. Bhumgara and Co.," *Decorator and Furnisher* 29 (October 1896): 31. On world's fairs, see "The Closing Days of the Exposition," *Atlanta Constitution*, 5 January 1896. On import firms, see Mari Yoshihara, *Embracing the East: White Women and American Orientalism* (New York: Oxford University Press, 2003), 31–38; Frederic A. Sharf, "Bunkio Matsuki,: Salem's Most Prominent Japanese Citizen," *Essex Institute Historical Collection* 129 (April 1993): 135–61; Cynthia A. Brandimarte, "Japanese Novelty Stores," *Winterthur Portfolio* 26 (Spring 1991): 1–26; *Entrance to Vantine's, the House of the Orient* (New York: A.A. Vantine, n.d.). On tourist acquisitions, see Margaret Greenleaf, "Chinese Spirit in Furnishing," *House Beautiful* 36 (June 1914): 32. On underreporting, see Andrew Wender Cohen, "Smuggling, Globalization, and America's Outward State, 1870-1909," *Journal of American History* 97 (September 2010): 371–98. On immigrants who peddled their belongings, see Mary Alden Hopkins, *House Beautiful* 46 (December 1919): 388–89. On immigrant retailers and peddlers, see "The Shopping Guide, *House Beautiful* 31 (January 1912): vii. On other travelers who brought goods back, see Hester M. Poole, "House Decoration Rich and Rare," *Good Housekeeping* 1 (19 September 1885): 2.

6. Agnes Bailey Ormsbee, *The House Comfortable* (New York: Harper and Brothers, 1892).

7. On curry, see *The New Cyclopaedia of Domestic Economy and Practical Housekeeper*, ed. E.F. Ellet (Norwich, CT: Henry Bill Publishing Co., 1873), 221. On sauce, see Gesine Lemcke, *European and American Cuisine* (New York: D. Appleton and Co., 1906), 94. On names, see "Home Interests," *New York Tribune*, 20 January 1884. On the authenticity of recipes, see Louise Rice, *Dainty Dishes from Foreign Lands* (Chicago: A.C. McClurg & Co., 1911), 46, 56–57. On alligator pears, see Maria Parloa, *Miss Parloa's Kitchen Companion* (Boston: Estes and Lauriat, 1887), 88–91, 435.

8. S.G. Benjamin, "How Persian Rugs are Made," *Decorator and Furnisher* 29 (November 1891): 56. See also, "In Metropolitan Shops," *House Beautiful* 24 (January 1908): 38; "Eastern Rugs and Carpets," *Decorator and Furnisher* 2 (May 1883): 56; "Salon in a Private Residence in Cairo in the Moorish Style," *Decorator and Furnisher* 27 (November 1895): 52.

9. Hester M. Poole, "Household Decoration," *Home-Maker* 2 (July 1889): 288.

10. "Miss Muffin and Mr. Turk," *House Beautiful* 41 (March 1917): 210.

11. Leach, *Land of Desire*, 79–83, 102–3, 145.

12. "German-American Housekeeping," *Chautauquan* 3 (May 1883): 442–45.

13. "All Good Epicureans Go to Paris before They Die," *Vogue* 44 (August 1, 1914): 40.

14. Estelline Bennett, "What the French Eat in the North," *Table Talk* 42 (February 1917): 15–16.

15. Francis E. Lester Co., *Catalogue* (Mesilla Park, New Mexico, 1904), 17.

16. *Wanamaker's Catalog* (Philadelphia: John Wanamaker's, 1908), inside cover; "F.P. Bhumgara and Co.," *Decorator and Furnisher* 29 (October 1896): 31.

17. Matsumoto-Do, *The Book of Genuine Things Japanese* (Tokyo: The Matsumoto-Do [ca. 1911]), i.

18. Isabel Floyd-Jones, "The Potters of Golfe-Juan and Vallauris," *Good Housekeeping* 50 (March 1910): 347–51.

19. Oliver Coleman, "Taste," *House Beautiful* 12 (September 1902): 242–44.

20. *The Housekeeper's Quest: Where to Find Pretty Things* (New York: Sypher and Co., 1885), 6.

21. "Here Is a 'bit,'" *New York Tribune*, 18 September 1892.

22. Burton Holmes, *Burton Holmes Travelogues* vol. 13, 1917 (Chicago: The Travelogue Bureau, 1920), 149.

23. "Havana a Second, Almost a Gayer, Riviera," *New York Tribune*, 23 January 1916.

24. Gail Hamilton, "A New Year Suggestion," *Los Angeles Times*, 23 January 1916; Diana de Marly, *The History of Haute Couture, 1850-1950* (New York: Holmes and Meier, 1980), 132.

25. "The Naked Truth about the Turk and His Harem," *Chicago Tribune*, 6 October 1912; Charlotte Jirousek, "The Transition to Mass Fashion System Dress in the Later Ottoman Empire," in *Consumption Studies and the History of the Ottoman Empire, 1550-1922*, ed. Donald Quataert (Albany: State University of New York Press, 2000), 201–42, 234–26; Noenoe K. Silva, *Aloha Betrayed: Native Hawaiian Resistance to American Colonialism* (Durham, NC: Duke University Press, 2004), 177–80.

26. Mrs. Jas. H. Lambert, "Dress Material," *Ladies' Home Journal* 6 (June 1889): 12; Mrs. Mallon, "For Woman's Wear," *Ladies' Home Journal* 8 (December 1890): 23.

27. On authentic, see "Gidding," *New York Tribune*, 23 March 1916; Ada Bache Cone, "Evening Gowns," *Atlanta Constitution*, 3 January 1892. On home sewers, see Margaret Bisland, "Fashions and Fabrics," *Good Housekeeping* (October 1899), 171, cited in Rob Schorman, *Selling Style: Clothing and Social Change at the Turn of the Century* (Philadelphia: University of Pennsylvania Press, 2003), 53. On Frenchy, see "Parisian Fall Styles in Women's Dresses at the Frohsin Store!" *Atlanta Constitution*, 8 September 1912.

28. "A Dining Room in the English Style," *Decorator and Furnisher* 31 (August 1898): 178; "An Italian Renaissance Dining-Room," *Decorator and Furnisher* 29 (December 1896): 69;

"A Dutch Corner," *Decorator and Furnisher* 30 (September 1897): 165; Jonathan A. Rawson Jr., "A Consistent Dutch Dining-Room," *Country Life in America* 22 (1 October 1912): 48; F.J. Wiley, "Original Design for a Dining Room in the German Renaissance," *Decorator and Furnisher* 19 (February 1892): 213. On French, English, Japanese, and Mooresque boudoirs, see *Decorator and Furnisher* 19 (February 1892): 163. On cosey corners, see Carrie May Ashton, "Home Workshop. Cosey Corners," *Decorator and Furnisher* 19 (October 1891): 69; Charlotte Robinson, "A Moorish Recess," *Decorator and Furnisher* 20 (August 1892): 189–90; Marion A. McBride, "Cosey Corners," *Decorator and Furnisher* 25 (October 1894): 18; Laura B. Starr, "Cosy Nooks and Corners," *Decorator and Furnisher* 15 (November 1889): 43.

29. "The Closing Days of the Exposition," *Atlanta Constitution*, 5 January 1896.
30. Mitchell, *All on a Mardi Gras Day*, 53, 107; Ward McAllister, *Society as I Have Found It* (New York: Cassell Publishing, 1890), 326, 336–37, 370; Sarah Leyburn Coe, "A Personality Party," *Vogue* 35 (12 February 1910): 12.
31. Mrs. D.A. [Mary Johnson Bailey] Lincoln, *Mrs. Lincoln's Boston Cook Book* (Boston: Roberts Brothers, 1888), 309.
32. Mary Dawson and Emma Paddock Telford, *The Book of Parties and Pastimes* (New York: William Rickey and Co., 1912), 168–69; "Chat," *Demorest's Family Magazine* 29 (November 1892): 51.
33. "Church Socials from Over the Seas," *Ladies' Home Journal* 31 (February 1914): 73; Ada Marie Peck, "Salads," *Good Housekeeping* 7 (23 June 1888): 76–77, 88.
34. Gordon, *Bazaars and Fair Ladies*, 131.
35. "Second Day of the Fair," *Times Picayune*, 3 February 1896.
36. Marie Gozzaldi, "Macaroni, and How to Cook It," *Good Housekeeping* 9 (1 March 1890): 205–6.
37. Olive Logan, "About English Dinners," *American Cookery* 1 (December 1876): 195–96.
38. Mrs. C.S. Jones and Henry T. Williams, *Household Elegancies, Suggestions in Household Art and Tasteful Home Decorations* (New York: Henry T. Williams, 1875), 258.
39. "Japanese Art Works," *Decorator and Furnisher* 5 (January 1885): 144.
40. Alice Van leer Carrick, "The Furniture of the Allies: Japanese Furniture," *House Beautiful* 45 (June 1919): 366–68.
41. Helen Watterson, "On Over-Decoration," *Atlanta Constitution*, 6 March 1892.
42. Frédéric Vors, "House Japanese Decoration," *Art Amateur* 1 (July 1879): 53–55.
43. James A. Field, Jr., *America and the Mediterranean World, 1776-1882* (Princeton: Princeton University Press, 1969), 307, 339, 347, 445.
44. Robert Bruce Fisher, "The People's Institute of New York City, 1897-1934: Culture, Progressive Democracy, and the People," Ph.D. diss., New York University (1974), 89–90; Diana Selig, *Americans All: The Cultural Gifts Movement* (Cambridge, Mass.: Harvard University Press, 2008).
45. Elizabeth Condit and Jessie A. Long, *How to Cook and Why* (New York: Harper and Brothers, 1914), 2.
46. On rat eating, see John Kuo Wei Tchen, *New York before Chinatown: Orientalism and the Shaping of American Culture, 1776-1882* (Baltimore: Johns Hopkins University Press, 1999), 265; Light, "From Vice District," 384; Mary Ting Yi Lui, "'The Real Yellow Peril': Mapping Racial and Gender Boundaries in New York City's Chinatown, 1870-1910," *Hitting Critical Mass* 5 (Spring 1998): 107–26.
47. On gravy, see William Brown Meloney, "Slumming in New York's Chinatown," *Munsey's Magazine* 41 (September 1909): 818–30.
48. Herbert Copeland, "Rice as the Chinese Prepare It," *Ladies' Home Journal* 25 (June 1908): 50.
49. "Travel Class 1902-1903," Yearbooks, Hyde Park Travel Club Records, Chicago Historical Society, Chicago, Illinois.

50. Geo. De Haven, "A Day in the Mexican Capital," *Outing* 16 (September 1890): 419–29.
51. "Just among Ourselves," *Bay View Magazine* 9 (December 1901): 117.
52. "Around the Study Lamp," *Bay View Magazine* 9 (April 1902): 341.
53. "Just among Ourselves," *Bay View Magazine* 5 (March 1898): 202. On becoming "all but Spaniards," see "Around the Study Lamp," *Bay View Magazine* 6 (April 1899): 248.
54. Amelia Muir Baldwin, "Interior Decoration, A Form of Expression," folder 15, box 1, Amelia Muir Baldwin Papers, Arthur and Elizabeth Schlesinger Library on the History of Women in America, Cambridge, Massachusetts.
55. "An Oriental Interior," *Decorator and Furnisher* 18 (August 1891): 172–73.
56. Mary Parmele, "Some Thoughts upon Life and Art," *Decorator and Furnisher* 4 (May 1884): 63.
57. Glenn Anthony May, "The Business of Education in the Colonial Philippines, 1909-30," in *Colonial Crucible: Empire in the Making of the Modern American State*, eds. Alfred W. Mc-Coy and Francisco A. Scarano (Madison: University of Wisconsin Press, 2009), 151–62.
58. "West African Diet," *Good Housekeeping* 3 (29 May 1886): 49.
59. *Breakfast, Dinner, and Tea: Viewed Classically, Poetically, and Practically, Containing Numerous Curious Dishes and Feasts of All Times and All Countries* (New York: D. Appleton and Co., 1875), 255.
60. Marion Harland and Virginia Van de Water, *Everyday Etiquette: A Practical Manual of Social Usages* (Indianapolis: The Bobbs-Merrill Co., 1905), 165.
61. K. Sano, "How a Japanese Lady Keeps House," *House Beautiful* 14 (November 1903): 351–54.
62. Alice M. Ivimy, "A Norwegian Morning Meal," *Good Housekeeping* 51 (August 1910): 221; "The Cuisine in Sweden," *Household* 12 (July 1879): 152.
63. George L. Austin, *Dr. Austin's Indispensable Hand-book and General Educator* (Portland, ME: George Stinson and Co., 1885), 320.
64. On cannibalism, see Felipe Fernández-Armesto, *Near a Thousand Tables: A History of Food* (New York: Free Press, 2002), 22; *Breakfast, Dinner, and Tea*, 255.
65. Josehp B. Lyman and Laura E. Lyman, *The Philosophy of House-Keeping: A Scientific and Practical Manual* (Hartford, CT: Goodwin and Betts, 1867), 39.
66. From bats to fins, see *Breakfast, Dinner, and Tea*, 258–59; "A Dinner of Rat, Cat, and Tipsy Shrimps," *New York Tribune*, 15 February 1880.
67. "Snails as an Article of Food," *Household* 12 (January 1879): 8.
68. On horse flesh, see Juliet Corson, *Family Living on $500 a Year* (New York: Harper and Brothers, 1888), 89. On patés, see *Breakfast, Dinner, and Tea*, 117.
69. *Breakfast, Dinner, and Tea*, 263; Emma Shaw Colcleugh, "The Eskimo Woman as I Found Her," *Ladies' World*, (December 1896), 10; "Some Japanese Etiquette," *Good Housekeeping* 2 (20 March 1886): ii.
70. Rice, *Dainty Dishes*, 8.
71. On butter, see "Human Food," *Cottage Hearth* 2 (March 1875): 71. "The Chinese Cuisine," *New York Tribune*, 1 February 1880; Alice M. Ivimy, "A Norwegian Morning Meal," *Good Housekeeping* 51 (August 1910): 221; "Parisian Restaurants," *New York Tribune*, 25 July 1880.
72. "Home Interests," *New York Tribune*, 5 October 1884.
73. Lucy Langdon Williams Wilson, ed., *Handbook of Domestic Science and Household Arts for Use in Elementary Schools* (New York: Macmillan, 1900), 73.
74. "Macaroni," *Good Housekeeping* 9 (17 August 1889): 170. On washing, see Corson, *Family Living*, 39.
75. Lucy S. Bainbridge, *Round the World Letters* (Boston: D. Lothrop and Co., 1882), 178.
76. "Ceylon and India Tea," *Ladies' World*, February 1897, 7.
77. Parloa, *Miss Parloa's Kitchen Companion*, 86.
78. New England Grocer Office, *The Grocer's Companion and Merchant's Hand-Book* (Boston: Benjamin Johnson, Publisher, 1883), 7.

79. Andrew F. Smith, *Pure Ketchup: A History of America's National Condiment with Recipes* (Columbia: University of South Carolina Press, 1996), 35, 59, 64, 67; Upton Sinclair, *The Jungle* (New York: Doubleday, Page, and Co., 1906).

80. Helen Campbell, "The American Housekeeper in Italian Kitchens," *House Beautiful* 10 (June 1901): 9–11.

81. Florence Finch Kelly, "Bungalow Furnishings and Fitments," *House Beautiful* 36 (June 1914): 24–28.

82. Hester Donaldson Jenkins, "Bulgaria and Its Women," *National Geographic Magazine* 27 (April 1916): 377–400, 382.

83. Jean Urquhardt, "A Girl's Life in Old Mexico," *Ladies' World*, October 1897, 13.

84. Burton Holmes, *Burton Holmes Travelogues*, vol. 11 (Chicago: The Travelogue Bureau, 1920), 11.

85. Katherine Louise Smith, "Oriental Carpets and Rugs," *House Beautiful* 6 (September 1899): 171–78; "The Romance of the Rug," *Decorator and Furnisher* 14 (April 1889): 11; "The Famine in Persia," *Times-Picayune*, 4 March 1880.

86. On ransacked, see W.L.D. O'Grady, "Influence of Oriental Art on Modern American Decoration," *Decorator and Furnisher* 4 (November 1884): 211. On armed, see Almon C. Varney, *Our Homes and Their Adornments* (Detroit: J.C. Chilton, 1882), 280. On plunder, see Laura B. Starr, "An Indian Room," *Decorator and Furnisher* 14 (May 1889): 38. On trophies, see Mary Gay Humphreys, "House Decoration and Furnishing," in *The House and Home, a Practical Book, in Two Volumes*, vol. 2, ed. Lyman Abbott et al. (New York: Charles Scribner's Sons, 1896), 103–78.

87. John Kimberly Mumford, "Glimpses of Modern Persia," *House and Garden* 2 (September 1902): 429–36.

88. G.F. Heublein and Brothers Advertisement, "Try a Cup of Real Indian Tea," *Vogue* 44 (14 November 1914): 113; William Joseph Showalter, "How the World is Fed," *National Geographic Magazine* 29 (January 1916): 110.

89. John L. Stoddard, *John L. Stoddard's Lectures*, vol. 3 (Chicago: Geo. L. Shuman and Co., 1917), 183.

90. W.E. Carson, *Mexico: The Wonderland of the South*, 1909, rev. ed. (New York: Macmillan for the Bay View Reading Club, 1914), 105.

91. Michael Adas, *Dominance by Design: Technological Imperatives and America's Civilizing Mission* (Cambridge, MA: Harvard University Press, 2006).

92. Flora Michaelis, "Anglo-Indian Pickles and Chutneys," *Delineator* 74 (October 1909): 322; "A Curry," *New York Tribune*, 19 June 1892; Nupur Chaudhuri, "Shawls, Jewelry, Curry, and Rice in Victorian Britain," in *Western Women and Imperialism: Complicity and Resistance*, ed. Nupur Chaudhuri and Margeret Strobel (Bloomington: Indiana University Press, 1992), 231–46; Lizzie Collingham, *Curry: A Tale of Cooks and Conquerors* (New York: Oxford University Press, 2006), 115–18; Elizabeth E. Bacon, *Central Asians Under Russian Rule: A Study in Cultural Change* (Ithaca, NY: Cornell University Press, 1966), 67; Mary Hamilton Talbott, "'New' Fruits and Vegetables," *Good Housekeeping* 51 (August 1910): 213; Jeffrey Charles, "Searching for Gold in Guacamole: California Growers Market the Avocado, 1910-1914," *Food Nations: Selling Taste in Consumer Societies*, ed. Warren Belasco and Phillip Scranton (New York: Routledge, 2002), 131–54.

93. Caroline French Benton, "The Chocolate Table," *Fairs and Fetes* (Boston: Dana Estes and Co., 1912).

94. John M. MacKenzie, *Orientalism: History, Theory and the Arts* (Manchester: Manchester University Press, 1995), 81; John L. Stoddard, *Red-Letter Days Abroad* (Boston: James R. Osgood and Co., 1884), 145; Laura B. Starr, "Sir Frederick Leighton's Arab Hall," *Decorator and Furnisher* 27 (March 1896): 171–72; John Sweetman, *The Oriental Obsession: Islamic Inspiration in British and American Art and Architecture, 1500-1920* (Cambridge: Cambridge University Press, 1988), 192–97; Maude Andrews, "Maude Andrews in London," *Atlanta Constitution*, 12 July 1896.

Chapter 5

Others Ourselves
The American Identity Crisis after the War of 1898

Michael Patrick Cullinane

The War of 1898 and subsequent Philippine-American War were important events in the conception of American identity and foreign policy. As a consequence of these wars, the geography and demographics of
the United States changed. Acquisition reshaped American jurisdiction,
extending the reach of U.S. sovereignty to the Far East and further into
the Caribbean. Ten million Filipinos and two million Puerto Ricans, after
1898, came under the sway of American authority. The expansion simultaneously occurred at a time of national transformation at home, making the
acquisition of territory part of a broader reimagination of American identity. Americans asked themselves probing questions about their nation
and state, including: How are the borders of the nation defined? Where is
the "United States"? Who is an American? How should the United States
govern citizens? What is foreign and what is domestic?

The identity of a community is often created or re-created in reaction
to perceived threats and the conceptualization of a national identity can
equally be conceived as such. Nations may regard themselves at least
partly through an idealization of what they are not. Such national identity
formation is comparable to Hegel's master-slave dialectic that describes
the construction of individual identity and the likely crises that can emerge
from its construction. In Hegel's writing, the identities of the "slave" and
the "master" are entirely reliant on each other. Without the slave there
is no master, and vice versa.[1] With the disappearance of one, the identity
of the other inevitably changes. This sort of identity formation is particularly important in the study of international relations and foreign policy, because, as David Campbell points out, foreign policy is inherently a

Notes for this chapter begin on page 121.

boundary-building exercise. "The sovereign domain, for all its identification as a well-ordered and rational entity," Campbell argues, "is as much a site of ambiguity and indeterminacy as the anarchic realm it is distinguished from."[2] The conception of a nation requires this sort of interaction. Thus, like Hegel's master and slave, national identity is constantly evolving in relation to a perceived other.

The "great debate" in American foreign policy at the turn of the twentieth century sparked a crisis over national identity. The great debate pitted advocates of imperialism against so-called anti-imperialists after the War of 1898. Imperialists advocated the acquisition and government of new overseas territories. Anti-imperialists opposed both acquisition and government of these territories. The contentions and advocacy by both groups challenged the understanding of the national self and as a consequence also challenged the view of the foreign other. Imperialists and anti-imperialists more typically expressed their arguments as protecting American values and dispelling those ideas and actions that were un-American. This constituted two competing tropes of self and other and allowed both groups to promote their vision of American foreign policy. Interestingly, American foreign policy was not only conceived as a reaction to the incorporation of new people or territory, but it was more positively conceived through domestic debates over national identity. Accordingly, the other in the great debate existed in a domestic sense, represented by Americans acting in a perceivably un-American fashion. The opponents and proponents of U.S. imperialism built their campaigns around the idea that each advocated foreign policies adverse to American values.

Not incidentally, behind the promotion of imperialism and anti-imperialism were two very different conceptions of the United States' global mission. Imperialists promoted intervention on the grounds that it extended American values. Consequently, wars and the acquisition of territory, in their mind, would bring American liberties to those places of the world dubbed by Theodore Roosevelt as "waste spaces."[3] In terms of identity, imperialists imagined the United States as the world's liberator delivering democracy, civil liberties, and the rule of law to places where tyranny and arbitrary rule were present. To anti-imperialists, promoting liberty was no less important. The imposition of American institutions and ideas, however, was not a policy they subscribed to. The United States, anti-imperialists imagined, was an exemplar of democracy, civil liberty, and law. In order for American ideas to spread and take root abroad, they needed to be adopted willingly by foreigners, and anti-imperialists believed American imposition was akin to supplanting one brand of tyranny for another. Furthermore, in terms of geopolitical strategy, these anti-imperialists saw risks, confident the United States would fatefully clash with other empires and build alliances, contrary to the nation's diplomatic traditions of isolation and maintaining no standing armies. In these ways, anti-imperialists were convinced that territorial acquisition after 1898 was un-American.

Imperialists and anti-imperialists attempted to convince the American public that their policies were truly American by depicting their adversaries as un-American. Both sides used Filipinos, one as an image of a foreign other and the other as akin to Americans. The first section of the chapter investigates the juxtaposition of these perceptions through the image of Emilio Aguinaldo. In the mind of Americans, Aguinaldo was a dictator and a revolutionary hero. The second section of the chapter delves into the cooperation between American and Filipino anti-imperialists to further understand the transnational nature of foreign policy advocacy in this era. Reciting these narratives expressed by imperialists and anti-imperialists makes clear that foreign policy inherently intersects with the conception of a national identity.

The Filipino Other

One way imperialists attempted to depict the Filipino revolutionaries as others was by denying the ideological links they shared with Americans. The American liberal tradition that celebrated the rule of law through constitutional and republican institutions was an ideology the Filipino revolution also aspired to. Historian Bonifacio S. Salamanca argues that Filipinos had a particular intellectual attraction to the American Revolution that stemmed from an affinity for the ideas of the Enlightenment and the rights of man. "On the whole," Salamanca writes, "Filipino aspirations were concerned primarily with individual freedoms, the relation of individuals in society to their political institutions, the proper functions of government, the limits of governmental authority in a free society [with] the emphasis on political rights."[4] Well-educated Filipinos—better known as *ilustrados*—were well versed in European and American liberal philosophy. In fact all the key intellectual figures of the Philippine revolution— men like José Rizal, Marcelo del Pilar, Graciano Lopez-Jaena, and Mariano Ponce—wrote exhaustively about individual and national rights. One obvious example of this affinity for American history and liberal ideology came on 12 June 1898 when the Philippine Revolutionary Army, under the leadership of General Emilio Aguinaldo, read out the Declaration of Philippine Independence. Aguinaldo announced what the revolutionaries considered to be the end of Spanish rule in the archipelago and the birth of the Philippine Republic.[5] Aguinaldo was an adherent to Enlightenment ideas and worked hard to cultivate a liberal image of himself and the new Philippine Republic as a means of satisfying like-minded *ilustrados* and Americans. When Aguinaldo declared the First Philippine Republic, he said it was done "in the same manner as God helped weak America in the last century when she fought against a powerful Albion, to regain her liberty and independence … He will also help us today in the identical undertaking, because the ways of Divine justice are immutably the same in rectitude and wisdom."[6] Yet the United States refused to recognize the Declaration in such terms or the legitimacy of the new Republic. Filipino revolutionaries nevertheless pursued their plans for self-government. Aguinaldo, acting as a provisional dictator for ten days after the Declaration was made, announced several decrees that demonstrate his appreciation of American-styled republican democracy. In his brief tenure as dictator Aguinaldo established provincial electorates, provincial governments, a federal congress and executive, police, and a provisional judiciary, and organized mechanisms for the redistribution of Spanish property.[7]

On June 23, after proclaiming the creation of the provisional revolutionary government, Aguinaldo stepped down as dictator. Following his renunciation of the dictatorship, the Philippine revolutionary government was organized around a presidency (to which Aguinaldo was appointed) and four secretaries with national portfolios. A national congress of elected provincial representatives oversaw the executive. The structure was remarkably similar to the three branches of the American government, and included a system of checks and balances.[8] Despite these steps taken to establish a federal republic in the archipelago, the United States negotiated a peace treaty with Spain without consulting the new Philippine Republic. The treaty transferred national sovereignty of the Philippines to the United States in return for $20 million.

Still undeterred in their quest to create a republic styled on the United States, Aguinaldo and the Philippine government dispatched its first diplomat, Felipe Agoncillo, to the United States in an attempt to convince the McKinley administration of the sensibilities of Philippine independence. Agoncillo's approach to making such a case was to regularly enunciate the common struggle against oppressive empires—the Philippines from Spain in 1898 and American independence from Britain in 1783. On the vessel that took him to the United States Agoncillo told American General Francis Greene, "the Filipino people were merely following the American example … hence there was no reason for the United States to deny the Filipinos the right to be free."[9] Dubious whether the United States shared the same values as the Filipino revolutionaries, Agoncillo noted that "great nations, being convinced of their power … do everything for their own interest."[10] Regardless of his doubts, Agoncillo throughout the transpacific voyage exploited the seeming ideological and historical bonds to several American politicians and military officers.

Back in the Philippines, Aguinaldo was working to enact a Philippine constitution. By January 1899 it had been completed. The constitution furthered Agoncillo's diplomatic case. The Malolos Constitution more comprehensively outlined the structure and responsibilities of the Philippine government and its ratification not coincidently occurred at the same time the U.S. Senate debated Philippine independence. It was, if only in part, designed to illustrate the Philippine Republic's admiration and emulation of the American republic and its constitutional government.

Contrary to the pronouncements of Aguinaldo and the establishment of a Republic in the archipelago, American imperialists portrayed the revolutionaries as the enemies of self-determination and democracy. Emilio Aguinaldo, as the leader of the revolution, was targeted specifically. He became a touchstone for imperialist propaganda. The fact that Aguinaldo briefly ruled as a self-proclaimed dictator was particularly seized on. Imperialists exaggerated the image of Aguinaldo as dictator, but could also point to Aguinaldo's rise through the revolutionary ranks as evidence of his authoritarian proclivities. The McKinley administration described Aguinaldo's leadership of the revolutionary Katipunan organization as one seized through assassination. Again, this was an exaggerated interpretation of Aguinaldo's rise to power, but one based in the truth of actual events. When Filipino nationalists set up their first provisional government in 1897, Andrés Bonifacio, the founder of the movement, was expected to win the presidency. In the election, however, Aguinaldo earned more votes. Bonifacio attempted to dissolve Aguinaldo's leadership in spite of his loss. In retaliation Aguinaldo had him arrested and charged with conspiracy to overthrow the revolution. Bonifacio was sentenced to death, a punishment the revolutionaries generally believed to be fitting.[11] American imperialists used the execution to assert that Aguinaldo was a despot whose leadership was the result of a coup rather than an election. This interpretation—along with Aguinaldo's ten-day dictatorship— helped legitimize the imperialist argument that Filipinos needed tutoring in American-styled self-government.[12]

Among American anti-imperialists, a contrary image was being constructed. For them Aguinaldo was a republican hero and they portrayed him as a model practitioner of the liberal ideology inspired by the American Revolution. During the Senate debates over the Treaty of Paris, which would ratify the acquisition of Philippine sovereignty, anti-imperialists made much of Aguinaldo's rhetoric and that of Filipino *ilustrados*. Senators who pledged to vote against the Treaty argued the liberties sought by American colonialists during their revolution were comparable, if not identical, to the liberties being fought for by Filipino revolutionaries.[13] Anti-imperialist senators even went so far as to compare Aguinaldo to George Washington. Just as Washington presided over the Continental Congress and the Continental Army, so too did Aguinaldo preside over the drafting of the Philippine Constitution and over the Philippine Army. Anti-imperialist and popular philosopher John Howard Moore was among those who counterattacked the propagandists claiming Aguinaldo a dictator. Moore dubbed him "the George Washington of the antipodes," declaring a "peerless a heart beats in the bosom of that dauntless young Malay as ever pulsated in the breast of the great Virginian."[14] For anti-imperialists the Philippine Republic was not the antithesis of the American ideological tradition; it was the embodiment of it.

How Americans viewed Aguinaldo is representative of the broader domestic debate between imperialists and anti-imperialists and how American national identity was forged. The debate was not restricted to character assassinations of foreign others or the rush by anti-imperialists to defend Filipinos as American-esque. Imperialists and anti-imperialists saw each other as un-American others. For example, the anti-imperialists could not resist making unflattering comparisons to President McKinley. One of the most popular diatribes against the president came from Mark Twain, who wrote perhaps the most scathing anti-imperialist essay on McKinley. His prose—"To the Person Sitting in Darkness"—was published in the widely circulated *North American Review,* and Twain celebrated American-styled civilization and democracy but condemned those who "adulterate it." In his satirical story he metaphorically defined the United States as a corporation exporting liberty to the world. Twain, however, charged McKinley with exporting a fraud. The liberty that America promised Filipinos was "merely an outside cover, gay and pretty and attractive, displaying the special patterns of our Civilization," Twain wrote, "while *inside* the bale is the Actual Thing ... There must be two America's, one that sets the captive free, and one that takes a once-captive's new freedom away from him, and picks a quarrel with him with nothing to found it on; then kills him to get his land."[15] This oft cited and analyzed prose is consciously facetious, but "To the Person Sitting in Darkness" neatly summarizes the conflict facing American identity and the foreign policy of "benevolent assimilation." According to Twain the "true" America represents rights, liberty, equality, and consent. The other America, or the imperial America, has manipulated these values primarily to serve material interests. McKinley in the prose is the agent of imperial America and Twain refers to him only as the "Master of the Game." The "game" is the global competition for power and wealth. Twain mockingly asserts the "Master" will take his place in the "Trinity of our national gods ... each bearing the Emblem of his service: Washington, the Sword of the Liberator; Lincoln, the Slave's Broken Chains; the Master, the Chains Repaired." For anti-imperialists like Twain, McKinley is conceivably the most contradictory figure of America's liberal tradition, not Aguinaldo. For such anti-imperialists, McKinley represented the opposite values of those identified with Washington or Lincoln. Rather than allowing Aguinaldo to impart the virtues of American liberty, anti-imperialists believed McKinley's foreign policy was restricting the expansion of American liberty in the Philippines.

At first glance, the image of McKinley repairing the slave's chains may seem an embellished attempt to visualize an un-American image of the president, but McKinley's neglect of African-Americans at home and of chattel slavery abroad made Twain's portrayal more thought provoking. Domestically McKinley failed to denounce lynch law in the South and in northern cities there were race riots only months before his reelection in 1900. Abroad, his record was even worse. In August 1899 General John Bates signed a treaty with the Sultan of Sulu, a monarch of a small island group in the southwestern Philippine archipelago. The treaty initiated American sovereignty over the Sultan's territory in exchange for a royal stipend and other allowances, including giving "any slave in the Archipelago of Jolo ... the right to purchase freedom by paying to the master the usual market value."[16] The treaty legally recognized the practice of slavery and slave trading and represented the McKinley administration's most legal and official complacency toward slavery within American sovereign jurisdiction. Twain's image of McKinley as the "Master" with the slave's "chains repaired" was one that gained resonance among anti-imperialists after his abetting of the nation's most heinous form of exclusion.

It was uncharacteristic of literary authors of the time to pillory a president as dramatically as Twain had, and rather than attacking the president personally, most anti-imperialists focused instead on condemning his policies. Specifically, the policy of "benevolent assimilation" was parodied as incongruent with American identity. The policy called for the United States to occupy, pacify, and govern the Philippine archipelago, "substituting the mild sway of justice and right for arbitrary rule."[17] Imperialists presented the Philippines as a lawless set of islands inhabited by barbarian races. John Proctor, a close Republican friend of imperialists like Secretary of State Hay and soon-to-be President Theodore Roosevelt, called benevolent assimilation a policy of "peace and progress" that stood for "freedom from oppression."[18] Proctor and his imperialist friends believed benevolent assimilation was the genuine extension of American self-determination and argued that such freedoms could only be realized after years of "self-development" because the Filipinos were "peoples who have for centuries been subjected to misrule and oppression and have yet to learn the principles of self-government."[19]

Undoubtedly an element of racial inferiority existed in this imperialist logic. Rudyard Kipling's "White Man's Burden" was published just as the debates in the Senate over acquisition were at their peak. Filipinos were, as Kipling's poem recalls, seen by imperialists as "Half-devil and half-child."[20] Benevolent assimilation was thus a necessary but gentle American tutelage that would assimilate a racial other into an American protégé. But just as Kipling's poem served as the poetic essence of imperialism, representing expansionist desires and disseminating racial distinctions between Filipinos and Americans, anti-imperialists used the same medium to denounce the president's policy. Over twenty high-profile poetic responses were made in the months after Kipling's poem was published. These poems often used Kipling's title or a variation of it like "The Brown Man's Burden" or the "Poor Man's Burden" to suggest the burden of imperialism was not only that of the "white" man.[21]

Ultimately anti-imperialists viewed the policy of benevolent assimilation not as one that would assimilate a racial or ideological other, but one in which the United States was transforming its own identity in an attempt to subjugate people who were already of like mind. William Graham Sumner, the famous American intellectual and ardent anti-imperialist declared the United States the loser in the War of 1898. Though the United States won the military stakes, Sumner declared the United States lost the war by "throwing away some of the most important elements of the American symbol and ... adopting some of the most important elements of the Spanish symbol." In his speech to the Phi Beta Kappa Society at Yale, Sumner announced that America has been "conquered by [Spain] on the field of ideas and policies."[22] The United States, he argued, has prided itself on ideas like self-determination that were different from those of the "old world," but the acquisition of the Philippines "was a gross violation of self-government."[23] His close friend and fellow Boston anti-imperialist, Charles Francis Adams, made a similar contention. "The very word 'imperial' is, indeed, borrowed from the Old World" Adams posited; "[t]hus, curiously enough, whichever way we turn and however we regard it, at the close of more than a century of independent existence we find ourselves, historically speaking, involved in a mesh of contradictions with our past."[24] Acknowledging that the United States had a long history of expansion including the Northwest Territory, Louisiana Purchase, war with Mexico, and even overseas locations like Samoa or Hawaii, activists like Adams and Sumner still deemed "benevolent assimilation" an anomaly. "Benevolent assimilation" was to them oppressive militarism that supplanted the traditional spread of liberal and anti-colonial government by popular consent. The Philippines would be ruled as a colony, not as an equal state or incorporated as an equal territory of the United States. It was the advent of an American colonial policy that Sumner and Adams believed would transform the United States into the "old world" empire it had for so long chastised as something antithetical to national identity.

After the ratification of the Treaty of Paris and the subsequent outbreak of hostilities between Filipino revolutionaries and American soldiers stationed in Manila, these intellectual arguments over the identity of the United States spilled over into perceptions of patriotism. In times of war—more so than in times of peace—support for America's troops is often a test of "true" patriotism. The term itself—"patriot"—can be defined as one who is loyal or faithful to a nation or community, making it a useful idea in distinguishing between conceptions of "self" and "other." Patriotism inherently defines a community and implies one's willingness to serve or act in the name of the common good of that defined community. In the months preceding the declaration of war against the Spanish, there was a consensus among Americans that national patriotism was a service to humanity, not a desire to glorify or aggrandize the nation. The War of 1898 was premised on the humanitarian suffering of the Cuban people at the hands of the Spanish. Starvation, concentration camps, and years of warfare had contributed to the death of hundreds of thousands of Cubans. In his War Message to Congress, President McKinley defined America's "patriotic considerations" as "a duty imposed by our obligations to ourselves, to civilization, and humanity to intervene with force ... to secure a full and final termination of hostilities between the Government of Spain."[25] On this point there was little disagreement that intervention was an act of humanitarianism. The long and ineffective diplomatic wrangling with Spain, the security threat highlighted by the destruction of the *U.S.S. Maine* and the barrage of reporting on the Cuban independence movement only strengthened the call on American policy makers to intervene. Even most anti-imperialists supported the invasion of Cuba. Mark Twain called the War of 1898 "the worthiest one that was ever fought ... It is a worthy thing to fight for one's freedom; it is another sight finer to fight for another man's. And I think this is the first time it has been done."[26] Anti-imperialists also supported the rallying cry of American patriotism. The venerable anti-imperialist Carl Schurz admitted, "In spite of all efforts to avert it, war does come," and "the duties of patriotism are the same for all ... Patriotism ... demands that we should all unite with the same faithful devotion in doing the best we can to make the shortest possible work of the struggle."[27]

Schurz, however, also warned of a "false patriotism" that is common during wartime. He declared that "false" patriots include "unscrupulous spectators" who seek to sweep away the machinery of government in a bid to serve material interests, "aided by the disreputable politicians ... who expect the loudest kind of war patriotism will lift them into popular favor."[28] True patriotism, Schurz asserted, had two enemies during wartime, "the foreign enemy abroad" and a domestic enemy who used the idea of patriotism to further its own material ends. At the time of the War of 1898, Schurz included in this class the sugar trusts and plantation owners who had a stake in developing Cuba's sugar industry. He included all the members of the Fifty-fifth Congress who were up for reelection. They had as much to gain politically as the sugar industry had to gain economically.

To ensure the United States remained true to this notion of patriotism, Schurz argued, the Teller Amendment—which declared American intentions to leave Cuba an independent state after the war—was attached to the congressional declaration of war. As the war with Spain ended and the conflict with the Filipinos began, anti-imperialists enshrined Schurz's idea of "false patriotism" in the platform of their movement. The Platform of the Anti-Imperialist Leagues called the occupation of the Philippines "open disloyalty to the distinctive principles of our government."[29] One anti-imperialist speaking at a large meeting of activists said, "We are told by those that do not agree with us [that] those that favor the conquest of the Filipinos ... have the 'true American spirit,' while those that think otherwise are false to patriotism."[30] The crowd booed. Anti-imperialist activists worked hard to distinguish themselves as the true patriots and utilized Carl Schurz's famous 1872 quip about patriotism as their defense: "My country, right or wrong; if right, to be kept right; and if wrong, to be set right." The anti-imperialist movement circulated thousands of business cards at rallies and through the mail with Schurz's face and these words.

Imperialists had a similar campaign to promote their foreign policy as patriotic. Even before the acquisition of the Philippines, imperialists adopted a rhetoric that was capable of deflecting the challenge of anti-imperialists. While anti-imperialist Senators argued that America's republican style of government precluded the acquisition of colonies, Senator Orville Platt, a Republican imperialist from Connecticut, called such logic open treachery. Sovereignty dictates "the right to acquire territory," Platt argued, and sovereignty, he determined, was derived from the "right to govern" making the U.S. Congress the ultimate judge of any terms of acquisition. Platt assumed that "sovereign" rights are "unlimited" and thereby all nations have the power and right to acquire territory.[31] His rhetoric was couched in clever language. If anti-imperialists denied the United States had the right to acquire territory they would be denying America's equal rights among nations. Essentially, Platt was suggesting that anti-imperialists were admitting national inferiority. Platt's argument infuriated anti-imperialists, primarily because it relied on the abundant war fever and jingoism of the time to define national patriotism. Congressional politicians were most susceptible to Platt's attack because not appearing patriotic in an election year threatened their return to Congress. Those Congressmen who rejected Platt's argument about sovereignty most vociferously took a drumming in 1898 and 1900. In Indiana and South Dakota, anti-imperialist Senators David Turpie and Richard Franklin Pettigrew lost to candidates that were more emphatically "patriotic" and outwardly imperialistic.

The conceptual representations of Filipinos had real consequences for national identity and foreign policy. Imperialists were ultimately more successful in claiming the sobriquet of "patriot" and subsequently successful in depicting anti-imperialists as un-American. Through this, their notions about the national self gained traction.

Transnational Collaboration

The name calling, ideological wrangling, and political grandstanding was only one way in which American foreign policy and national identity were challenged after the War of 1898. These intellectual conflicts also inspired anti-imperialists to take up the Filipino cause more directly by collaborating with Filipinos in the Philippine-American War. For many anti-imperialists the war was unjust and one being waged against an ally cut from the same cloth as the United States. As a consequence of this thinking anti-imperialist activists operated alongside Filipino revolutionaries to oppose American imperialism.

American anti-imperialists even fought American soldiers on the front lines. Within the ranks of Aguinaldo's Revolutionary forces were scattered some American soldiers who defected from the U.S. Army. The most famous case of defection was David Fagen, an African-American corporal in the U.S. Army who fought in Cuba before being deployed to the Philippines. Fagen's decision to leave the U.S. Army was primarily a result of the way African-Americans were treated in armed service and in domestic life. A native of the South, Fagan was born into the post-Reconstruction era and a victim of the period's Jim Crow laws. In the U.S. Army Fagan and African-Americans were segregated. Discrimination and prejudice, according to one soldier, "followed the Negro to the Philippines, ten thousand miles from where it originated."[32] In addition to such discrimination, African-Americans also objected to the similar prejudices and discrimination directed at Filipinos. White American soldiers referred to Filipinos in the same way they referred to African-Americans at home, as "niggers" or "gugus." The disdain for African-Americans and Filipinos brought these two demographics closer together in Fagan's mind, and for many African-Americans the imperialist depiction of Filipinos as a foreign other was not convincing because they were being described in terms familiar to them. Emilio Aguinaldo recognized this soon after the war began and spoke about the potential advantages of having African-American soldiers defect. In 1899 he offered any defectors from the U.S. Army—particularly African-Americans—commissions as officers in the Filipino Revolutionary Army. Those who took him up on his offer were few, but Fagen's decision to desert became a significant event because he rose to the rank of Captain in Aguinaldo's army. Filipino troops under the leadership of Captain Fagen engaged the U.S. Army on several occasions in 1900. Most notably his troops clashed with Frederick Funston, then Colonel of the Twentieth Kansas Infantry Regiment that would come to capture Aguinaldo in 1901.[33] Funston was unable to capture Fagen and the growing myth of the African-American defector made for explosive stories in the notoriously sensationalist American press. Rumors about Fagan's capability as an officer circulated among soldiers and struck fear into the U.S. Army's top brass that one renegade could spark widespread African-American desertion.[34] It was not until the end of 1901—months after Aguinaldo had been captured and many revolutionary leaders had surrendered—that stories of Fagen faded from the newspapers. In December 1901 it emerged that Fagen was killed by a Filipino hunter who recognized him as the famous deserter and sought to collect the bounty for his capture or death. The hunter shot and killed Fagan, decapitated him, and delivered his head to the American forces as proof of the deserter's demise.[35]

Fagen's story is not altogether unique. All wars have deserters and defectors. In total the U.S. Army estimated there were twenty deserters from 1899 to 1900 in the Philippine-American War. The figures, however, are an underestimate. They were produced to obscure the fact that soldiers not only fled the war, but took up arms with the enemy.[36] In fact there were more defectors than deserters, and for most it was not a matter of race. According to Army records many defectors and deserters were white and expressed a sense of solidarity with the Filipinos. Colorado Regular James Reid noted a marked difference between the war in Cuba and the war in the Philippines. For Reid, fighting Spain in Cuba was a battle for humanity. "We are not nearly as anxious to fight these people as some people may think we are," he said, "and we do not enter any of the fights with the same spirit we did when fighting the Spaniards."[37]

Anti-imperialists at home tried to exploit such sentiments and encouraged soldiers to desert. Edward Atkinson, a Boston textile manufacturer and economist, publicized statements made by disillusioned soldiers in an attempt to stall Army recruitment. Atkinson published a series of pamphlets from May 1899 to October 1900 entitled *The Anti-Imperialist* and designed to articulate the way in which war with the Filipinos was out of kilter with American values. Much of Atkinson's argument centered on the economic drawbacks to war and the political contradictions, but it also contained a call to all soldiers abroad to stop fighting and for those considering enlistment to resist. According to Atkinson, fighting in the Philippines would lead to infections including "well-known kinds" of disease like fever and malaria, and worse. Atkinson wrote that the war would transform healthy young men into aged disease-ridden invalids. Venereal disease, Atkinson believed, would ravage U.S. soldiers as it had British soldiers fighting in tropical places. Sexually transmitted and tropical diseases would "work corruption of the blood to the third and fourth generation," he wrote, "ending in [the] degeneracy" of American posterity.[38] The Philippine environment would literally deform future Americans, mutating their physical identity.

Atkinson attempted to communicate these stories to American soldiers fighting in the Philippines and potential recruits. He found limited success. He distributed over one hundred thousand pamphlets throughout the United States, becoming the most widely circulated anti-imperialist pamphleteer. Atkinson also attempted to mail hundreds of the pamphlets to soldiers in the Philippines, but only a handful reached them. He was refused overseas mailing lists by the government and the majority of the pamphlets he posted to the archipelago were seized by the government censor.[39] It is unlikely that the propaganda led to many defections in the Army, but it does indicate that anti-imperialists were taking strides to disrupt the imperialist policy at home and abroad.

Even for those American soldiers that did not desert or take up arms with Filipinos, the image of the Filipinos as an enemy remained difficult to accept. The cruelty of the war and atrocities practiced by some U.S. soldiers alienated other soldiers. Some U.S. soldiers indiscriminately burned Filipino villages. Torture of natives suspected of being insurgents was widespread and conducted in a variety of gruesome ways. Filipino women were raped and molested, contributing to a sense among soldiers who did not commit these acts that the United States was not actually bringing American-styled self-government to the archipelago, but practicing a barbarism completely contrary to the impression of America they held.[40]

Some American soldiers posited that the climate, the methods of fighting, or even the rice wine that they drank had transformed once mild-mannered Americans into savages.[41] Whether the environment was to blame, or the soldiers themselves were, the aggression and inhumanity led many soldiers to believe their comrades in arms were acting in ways entirely un-American. Herbert Welsh, a Philadelphia anti-imperialist and newspaper editor, collected stories of several American soldiers to use in the Congressional investigation into the atrocities in the Philippines. These stories exhibit the conflict soldiers felt. For example, Private Fred Newell recounted an episode where a rural Filipino farmer gave his hungry squad a chicken dinner and fresh water after a long trek through the jungle. Newell found the act to be one of generosity and indicative of a U.S.-Filipino friendship. An officer in his squad, however, did not have the same regard for the farmer. After eating the chicken he wanted to shoot the farmer. The officer told the soldiers that all Filipinos in the hills were insurgents. Newell protested and shielded the Filipino, telling the officer "You'll have to shoot me first." A few of Newell's fellow soldiers also protested the officer's conclusion noting the "fair treatment" he had shown them. Other soldiers, however, agreed with the officer that all Filipinos in the hills were insurgents. The platoon was split. In a compromise, the farmer was allowed to live, but relocated to an American concentration camp and his home burned down.[42] In another case, Private Albert L. Cross told Welsh, he asked to be excused from an episode of torture known as the water cure in which gallons of salty water were funneled into the stomach of a Filipino priest and expunged with a harsh blow to his abdomen. The torture killed the priest. Cross, along with several other witnesses, admitted to sympathizing with the priest. They reported to anti-imperialists that the behavior of their fellow soldiers was un-American.[43] One of Cross's friends in the squad, Walter H. Snow, admitted about the priest: "I felt sorry for him and used to give him food—tho' there were strict orders against it."[44] Even among soldiers who were unwilling to defect or dessert, there was significant disagreement about how the war was being executed.

The accounts of torture and mistreatment depicted a different image of the United States in the Philippines from that of the imperialists. General MacArthur attempted to show that U.S. forces were benevolent and kind. Under oath in the Senate, MacArthur told investigators that American soldiers were treating Filipinos "the same as our own people. A wounded enemy is a guest. A prisoner is a guest … That was the spirit in which they were treated … everywhere."[45] Throughout 1902 and 1903 the anti-imperialists successfully dispelled MacArthur's notion that Filipinos were treated like Americans. By collecting testimony of thousands of soldiers who witnessed torture the anti-imperialists supplied Senate investigators with contradictory evidence with which anti-imperialist Senators cross-examined U.S. military and civilian governors. The investigation had interesting repercussions. The American public was angered with the seeming hypocrisy of McKinley's policy of benevolent assimilation. As a result, imperialists were forced to denounce the acts of torture and court-martial the worst offenders. Collecting the stories of torture and broadcasting the contradictory nature of the imperialist policy was one of the anti-imperialists greatest successes in challenging the president's policy.[46]

In addition to their activism, anti-imperialists worked closely with Filipinos to build transpacific operations capable of exhibiting common bonds between the two peoples. In 1901 and 1902, anti-imperialists began to operate wartime missions to the Philippines as a means of forging greater links of solidarity with Filipino intellectuals who sought independence. These trips abroad were highly controversial because they challenged the depiction of Filipinos as the enemy other during the war. Americans suspected that anti-imperialist missions gave hope to revolutionaries that there were significant numbers of Americans who sympathized with their cause. The truth was that even among anti-imperialists there were only a few who were willing to so openly align themselves with Filipinos. A good example of this is the trips taken to the Philippines by Fiske Warren, a Boston paper manufacturer and executive committee member of the New England Anti-Imperialist League. In May 1901 Warren traveled to the Philippines with Sixto Lopez, a member of the Philippine revolutionary government in exile. Warren's mission was to find Filipinos that were dedicated to independence and interested in working with men of similar mind in the United States, or as Warren said, to speak for the "other side, in behalf of mutual co-operation in what after all is a common cause."[47] President of the Anti-Imperialist Leagues, George Boutwell, made clear his disapproval of the trip, insinuating that Warren was more concerned with the fortunes of Filipinos than Americans and that it would be detrimental to the anti-imperialists' image in the minds of the American public.[48] Warren and Boutwell clashed regularly on the question of transpacific solidarity. Partly to save the anti-imperialist movement any embarrassment and partly to protest those like Boutwell who opposed solidarity, Warren resigned his place on the League's executive committee. Not long after he quit, Warren embarked on his first trip to the Philippines. His visit to the archipelago was largely unsuccessful in convincing many Filipinos to take up the cause of independence with American anti-imperialists. His trip did, however, introduce sympathetic Americans to many revolutionary Filipinos who already were convinced of the merits of working with

Americans. These Filipinos would later collaborate with members of the anti-imperialist movement.

In 1901 and 1902, though, Warren's visit was dubbed by imperialists as an attempt to rile Filipino resistance to the American occupation and thus a direct and treasonous attack on American soldiers. In Manila, American officials made accusations against Warren's character; soldiers searched his luggage and described finding "treasonable and inflammatory proclamations," discounted by Warren as "souvenirs," but did little to help his push for solidarity.[49] As Boutwell suspected, Warren's trip to the Philippines with a Filipino compatriot during a time of war only helped give a sense that anti-imperialists had little regard for the sake of American troops fighting there.

Warren's trip, though it sought to incite a more widespread alliance between American anti-imperialists and Filipinos, does illustrate an interesting shift in the perception of Filipinos as others. On the first trip he made in 1901, the press was critical of Warren, but on his subsequent journeys to the islands (1905 and 1907–08) there was almost no controversy. With the war's end in 1902 (at least its official end—guerrilla fighting continued for several years) as well as the establishment of the Philippine Assembly in 1907, working with Filipinos became much more acceptable. Arguably, such collaboration was public policy by 1907. The Assembly immediately became a legitimate hub of opposition to imperialism. Created by the Roosevelt administration, imperialists could not disparage the Assembly without criticizing their own policies of democratic tutelage in the islands. The legitimacy of the Assembly and the support it had from the Roosevelt administration made it "a forum for the expression of official views" and allowed anti-imperialists to engage with Filipinos without being tarred as unpatriotic traitors.[50] The Filipinos were still conceived as others by imperialists, but had become a partner in their own transformation from un-American to American-styled.

By 1905, the only real issue that imperialists and anti-imperialists differed on in relation to the Philippines was the timeline for the completion of the transformation. The Roosevelt administration and like-minded imperialists agreed with the anti-imperialists that independence would be the ultimate outcome, but they differed substantially on when it would be declared. Anti-imperialists, like Fiske Warren, who worked closely with Filipinos, argued for "immediate" independence and contended that Filipinos had learned all they could learn from the United States by 1905. The Roosevelt administration and its supporters advocated "eventual" independence and a further period of tutelage. By 1907, the two major political parties in the Filipino Assembly mirrored these perspectives. The

Nacionalistas Party was a proponent of "immediate" independence and the Progresista Party (the old Federalista Party) proposed "eventual" independence.[51] The U.S. colonial period in the archipelago, after the establishment of the Philippine Assembly, no longer resembled one of a master and a slave or that of self and other. And while opposition to anti-imperialist solidarity waned in 1901 and 1902, political collaboration increased after the war's end. With the end of the war, the caustic rhetoric about patriotism that created the notion of the Filipinos as an enemy other, evaporated. This sentiment was replaced with recognition of a degree of sameness through republican institutions.

Conclusion

Identity formation being as much about the self as it is about the other illustrates in the case of the anti-imperialists just how much Americans were capable of viewing their fellow countrymen as foreign beings. Anti-imperialists argued this about imperialists, who they believed threatened the intellectual identity of the American mission as well as U.S. prosperity and posterity in their advocacy of overseas acquisition and war. Imperialists for their part felt threatened by the anti-imperial perception of the United States. The evidence of this domestic identity crisis among Americans can be seen in the intellectual and operational acts that these two opposing activist groups perpetuated. Especially the anti-imperialists, who worked with Filipinos and articulated their argument alongside Filipinos, create an image of imperialists as un-American. Anti-imperialists equally illustrate the capacity of Filipinos to be as American as Americans.

Most interestingly, perhaps, is that the identity crisis facing Americans ceased when imperialists stopped demanding that Filipinos constituted a foreign other. The creation by the United States of the Philippine Assembly for the Filipinos, in particular, brought these two national states (and thereby identities) closer than ever before. Filipinos now operated within an American-styled republican and democratic system. Imperialists were no longer able to depict them as polar opposites with institutions like these. And with imperialists more closely aligned with Filipinos in a way that anti-imperialists had long advocated, the anti-imperialists were left without an antithetical other in domestic politics. The dialectic of self and other had largely been synthesized and disagreements between imperialists and anti-imperialists over the future of the Philippines were marginal. Both agreed on independence for the archipelago. By the time the Philippine Assembly was inaugurated the anti-imperialist movement was largely disbanded. Though many anti-imperialists continued to fight for immediate and complete independence for the Philippines, the bulk of anti-imperialists were content to see the archipelago gradually gain its independence. Consequently the "great debate" over U.S. foreign policy and national identity degraded into a minor disagreement that had little impact on the minds of most Americans.

Notes

1. The idea of the master-slave relationship has been greatly expanded on and recrafted by Jean-Paul Sartre, Michel Foucault, and Edward Said, among other philosophical thinkers. See, G.W.F. Hegel, *Phenomenology of Spirit,* trans. A.V. Miller (Oxford: Clarendon Press, 1977); Jean-Paul Sartre, *Being and Nothingness,* trans. H.E. Barnes (London; New York: Routledge, 2003); Edward Said, *Orientalism* (New York: Vintage Books, 1978).
2. David Campbell, *Writing Security: United States Foreign Policy and the Politics of Identity* (Minneapolis: University of Minnesota Press, 1998), 63.
3. Theodore Roosevelt, *The Winning of the West* (New York: G. P. Putnam's Sons, 1896): 1, 1.
4. Bonifacio S. Salamanca, *The Filipino Reaction to American Rule, 1901-1913* (Quezon City: New Day Publishers, 1968), 18–21.
5. "The Philippine Declaration of Independence, June 12, 1898," in *The Laws of the First Philippine Republic: 1898-1899,* ed. Sulpicio Guevara (Manila: National Historical Commission, 1972), 185–202.
6. "Message of General Aguinaldo on the Proclamation of the Republic, at Malolos, Bulacan, January 23, 1899," in *The Philippine Insurrection against the United States: A Compilation of Documents with Notes and Introduction,* ed. John R.M. Taylor (Manila: Eugenio Lopez Foundation, 1971): 3, 95.
7. "Decree of June 18, 1898," in *Organization for the Administration of Civil Government, Instituted by Emilio Aguinaldo and his Followers in the Philippine Archipelago,* ed. John R.M. Taylor (Washington, DC: Government Printing Office, 1903), 8–9.
8. "Decree of June 23, 1898," in *Organization for the Administration of Civil Government,* 10–11.
9. Esteban De Ocampo, *First Filipino Diplomat: Felipe Agoncillo, 1859-1941* (Manila: National Historical Institute, 1977), 84–85.
10. Taylor, *The Philippine Insurrection Against the United States,* 247–48.
11. Teodoro Agoncillo, *The Revolt of the Masses: The Story of Bonifacio and the Katipunan* (Quezon City: University of the Philippines, 1956), 213–16; Teodoro Kalaw, *The Philippine Revolution* (Manila: New Day Publishers, 1969), 65–71.
12. The *New York Sun* was among the most persistent imperialist newspaper to attack Aguinaldo in this way. "Aguinaldo a Dictator," *New York Sun,* 23 July 1898; "Aguinaldo as Dictator," *New York Sun,* 30 July 1898; "Aguinaldo as a Schemer," *New York Sun,* 12 September 1898.
13. *Congressional Record,* 55th Cong., 3rd sess., 12 December 1898 and 6 January 1899, 93–96, 432–38.
14. John Howard Moore, "America's Apostasy," *Chicago Chronicle,* 6 March 1899. For further anti-imperialist associations of Washington with Aguinaldo see, "Aguinaldo and Anti-Imperialism," *New York Times,* 25 April 1901; James M. Freeman, *True Story of the Capture of Emilio Aguinaldo, Self-Styled George Washington of the Philippines* (Knoxville, TN:

Trent Publishing, 1927), 57. *Harper's Weekly* and imperialists mocked the association. "A Portrait of George Washington Found near Faneuil Hall," *Harper's Weekly*, 24 February 1900.

15. Mark Twain, "To the Person Sitting in Darkness," *North American Review* 172, no. 531 (February 1901), 165, 170.

16. "The Bates Treaty of 1899, Conditional Agreement between Brig.-General John C. Bates, Representing the United States, and the Sultan of Jolo (Sulu), August 20, 1899," in *The Statutes at Large of the United States of America from March 1897 to March 1899 and Recent Treaties, Conventions Executive Proclamations, and the Concurrent Resolutions of the Congress* (Washington, DC: Government Printing Office, 1899): 30.

17. William McKinley, "Benevolent Assimilation Message, December 21, 1898," *A Compilation of the Messages and Papers of the Presidents* (http://www.gutenberg.org/files/13893/13893-h/13893-h.htm).

18. John R. Proctor, "Isolation or Imperialism," *The Forum* 26 (September 1898), 14–26.

19. Ibid.

20. Rudyard Kipling, "The White Man's Burden," *McClure's Magazine*, February 1899.

21. See, Ernest H. Crosby, "The Real 'White Man's Burden,'" *New York Times*, 15 February 1899; Howard S. Taylor, "The Poor Man's Burden," *The Public*, 18 February 1899; W.A. Croffut, "The White Man's Burden," *Washington Post*, 19 February 1899; Harold Mac-Grath, "The White Man's Burden," *Syracuse Herald*, 19 February 1899; John White Chadwick, "The Black Man's Burden," *Later Poems* (Boston: Houghton, Mifflin and Co., 1905), published originally on 21 February 1899; W.J. Henderson, "Our White Man's Burden," *The Criterion* (February 1899); Paul P. Randall "The Poor Man's Burden," *Chicago Broad Axe*, 2 March 1899; Alice Smith-Travers, "The White Man's Burden," *The Freeman*, 4 March 1899; J. Dallas Bowser, "Take Up the Black Man's Burden," *Colored American*, 18 March 1899; Henry Slade Goff, "Take Up the Strong Man's Burden," *Farm Stock and Home* (March 1899); H. Blount, "Take Up the White Man's Burden," *Illinois Record*, 1 April 1899.

22. William Graham Sumner, "The Conquest of the United States by Spain," *Yale Law Journal* 8 (1898–99), 168.

23. Ibid.

24. Charles Francis Adams, *Imperialism and The Tracks of Our Forefathers: A Paper Read by Charles Francis Adams Before the Massachusetts Historical Society, December 20, 1898* (Boston: Dana Estes and Company, 1899), 25.

25. William McKinley, "War Message, April 11, 1898," *A Compilation of the Messages and Papers of the Presidents* (http://www.gutenberg.org/files/13893/13893-h/13893-h.htm).

26. Mark Twain, *The Letters of Mark Twain*, ed. Albert Bigelow Paine (New York: Harper Brothers, 1917), 663.

27. Carl Schurz, "About Patriotism," *Harper's Weekly*, 16 April 1898.

28. Ibid.

29. Anti-Imperialist League, "Chicago Liberty Meeting, April 30, 1899" (http://www.antiimperialist.com/documents/leaguepublications/13-leagues-under-activism/82-centralleaguedocs)..

30. Ibid.

31. *Congressional Record*, 55th Cong., 3rd sess., 19 December 1898, 292.

32. Michael C. Robinson and Frank N. Schubert, "David Fagen: An Afro-American Rebel in the Philippines, 1899-1901," *The Pacific Historical Review* 44, no. 1 (February 1975): 71.

33. Funston's memoirs recall the encounters with Fagen. Frederick Funston, *Memories of Two Wars: Cuban and Philippine Experiences* (Lincoln: University of Nebraska Press, 2009), 376–80.

34. Robinson and Schubert, "David Fagen," 77–80.

35. Ibid., 80–82.

36. Robert Fantina, *Desertion and the American Soldier, 1776-2006* (New York: Algora Publishing, 2006), 87–88.
37. Veltisezar Bautista, *The Filipino Americans: Their History, Culture, and Traditions, 1763-Present* (Naperville, IL: Bookhaus Publishing, 2002), 66.
38. Edward Atkinson, "The Anti-Imperialist," 1, no. 2 (3 June 1899), 18 (http://www.antiimperialist.com/images/Individual-Documents/the%20anti-imperialist%201%20no.%201%20and%202.pdf).
39. Frank Freidel, "Dissent in the Spanish-American War and the Philippine Insurrection," *Proceedings of the Massachusetts Historical Society* 81 (1969), 178–80.
40. See, Michael Patrick Cullinane, *Liberty and American Anti-Imperialism, 1898-1909* (London: Palgrave, 2012).
41. Hoganson, *Fighting for American Manhood*, 184–99.
42. "Statement of Fred F. Newell," *Herbert Welsh Papers*, Box 84, Philippines: 1899, Historical Society of Pennsylvania.
43. "Statement of Albert L. Cross," *Herbert Welsh Papers*, Box 84, Philippines: 1899, Historical Society of Pennsylvania.
44. "Statement of Walter H. Snow," *Herbert Welsh Papers*, Box 84, Philippines: 1899, Historical Society of Pennsylvania.
45. Sen. Doc. 331, "Affairs in the Philippine Islands," 57th Cong., 1st sess. (Washington, DC: Government Printing Office, 1903), 871.
46. See, Michael Patrick Cullinane, *Liberty and American Anti-Imperialism, 1898-1909* (New York: Palgrave, 2012).
47. "Fiske Warren's Philippines Visit," *Springfield Republican*, 14 June 1901.
48. New England Anti-Imperialist League, *Record Book of the Executive Committee Meetings of the Anti- Imperialist League, 1899-1901* (Boston: New England Anti-Imperialist League, 1902).
49. "Sixto Lopez to William Augustus Croffut, January 7, 1902," *William Augustus Croffut Papers*, Box 1, General Correspondence: January 1–January 15, 1902, Library of Congress; "Had to Take Oath," *Boston Journal*, 19 October 1901.
50. Salamanca, *The Filipino Reaction to American Rule*, 57–58.
51. Jim Zwick, *Confronting Imperialism: Essays on Mark Twain and the Anti-Imperialist League* (West Conshohocken, PA: Infinity Publishing, 2007), 10–12.

Chapter 6

The Others in Wilsonianism

Lloyd Ambrosius

President Woodrow Wilson affirmed modern liberalism as the founda-tion for America's foreign policy when he led the United States into World War I. Liberal ideals, that he proclaimed as potentially applicable throughout the world, should define America's wartime purposes and guide its postwar peacemaking. In his war message he called for mak-ing the world "safe for democracy." In subsequent speeches he outlined his vision of a new world order that, he hoped, would replace the old, discredited European order that had collapsed in 1914. The president's liberal vision, later known as Wilsonianism, was apparently universal. His rhetoric suggested that it could apply to all nations. Yet in practice he did not believe in the universality of his modern liberal principles and did not plan to implement them for the benefit of all peoples. Although appar-ently universal, Wilson's vision left some peoples on the outside, at least for the foreseeable future. He saw real or potential enemies, whether at home or abroad, as disqualified, in some way, from full participation in his new world order. Unless or until they conformed to his vision, if they ever could, these others would be kept out. Thus, a fundamental paradox of apparent universality and actual exclusivity characterized Wilsonianism.

Wilson's liberal ideology shaped his progressive presidency in the United States and abroad. He had defined a program of New Freedom during the 1912 presidential election and implemented it as his domestic agenda during the first years of his administration. Similar goals charac-terized his foreign policy as he called for peace, human rights, and equal-ity among nations in a new world order. He defined four key tenets of Wilsonianism in his famous Fourteen Points address and in subsequent wartime speeches in 1918. First, he called for the self-determination of nations. This principle combined the traditional concept of state sovereignty that had prevailed in European international relations since 1648 with the American (and also Western European) idea of democracy. Accordingly, all peoples were entitled to self-rule or popular sovereignty. Second, Wilson advocated an "open door" for international trade and investment across borders. Breaking down national or colonial barriers to commerce and finance would open the world to American-style capitalism. Third, the president proposed a new system of international collective security. His emerging idea of the League of Nations would become the central feature in his peacemaking after the war. Fourth, Wilson's vision of a new world order affirmed and depended upon the idea of progressive history. He wanted to reform international relations to replace the old order with a new one, while guarding against radical or revolutionary changes—or at least against such extreme changes as defined by the norms of the United States. He sought orderly progress toward his liberal goals at home and abroad.[1]

Wilson outlined his global agenda of reform in his Fourteen Points address to a joint session of Congress on 8 January 1918. Emphasizing its ostensibly universal applicability, he proclaimed: "What we demand in this war, therefore, is nothing peculiar to ourselves. It is that the world be made fit and safe to live in; and particularly that it be made safe for every peace-loving nation which, like our own, wishes to live its own life, determine its own institutions, be assured of justice and fair dealing by the other peoples of the world as against force and selfish aggression. All the peoples of the world are in effect partners in this interest, and for our own part we see very clearly that unless justice be done to others it will not be done to us." Peaceful nations were entitled to freedom at home and security against aggressive neighbors. "An evident principle runs through the whole program I have outlined," he affirmed. "It is the principle of justice to all peoples and nationalities, and their right to live on equal terms of liberty and safety with one another, whether they be strong or weak."[2] The war, he asserted, should end with the creation of this kind of new world order.

Wilson's principles of global reform maintained America's traditional antipathy toward the old world, thereby combining exclusivity with universality. Since the United States had gained its independence from the British Empire in the eighteenth century, Americans had drawn a contrast between the new and old worlds as a defining feature in their nationalism, marking an ideological—as well as geographical—division between the new nation and old Europe. This contrast had justified America's isolationism during the nineteenth century and continued to influence its global role during the Great War. Wilson's policy of neutrality from 1914 to 1917 expressed his traditional belief that the United States should not entangle itself in Europe's wars and diplomacy. When Imperial Germany's submarine warfare finally convinced him in 1917 to intervene in the world war, the president still saw the United States as different from the others of the old world. America represented the values of freedom and democracy for all nations, not the special or selfish interests of the European belligerents on either side, whether the Allies or the Central Powers. Although the United States would align with the United Kingdom and France against Germany, it would do so only as an "associated power" and not as an ally. It would seek to transform international relations, thus presumably avoiding the entanglement in the old world that earlier American presidents since George Washington had warned against.[3]

In his address to Congress on 2 April 1917, while calling for a declaration of war against Germany, Wilson defined America's purpose. To protect and promote his liberal ideals, he thought the United States should now intervene in the war. It should fight for a new world order against the enemies of this global mission. Germany's unrestricted submarine attacks against neutral as well as belligerent ships challenged Wilson's "open door" vision of the international economy. "The present German submarine warfare against commerce is a war against mankind. It is a war against all nations," he claimed. To protect freedom for all nations, he called for the United States to join a new democratic partnership—not one of Europe's old alliances—to restore and preserve world peace. "A steadfast concert for peace can never be maintained except by a partnership of democratic nations," he explained. "No autocratic government could be trusted to keep faith within it or observe its covenants." Russia's revolution that replaced the Romanov czarist regime with a new provisional government encouraged Wilson to believe that history was moving in the right direction. "Russia was known by those who knew it best to have been always in fact democratic at heart," he asserted. "The autocracy that crowned the summit of her political structure, long as it had stood and terrible as was the reality of its power, was not in fact Russian in origins, character, or purpose; and now ... the great, generous Russian people have been added in all their naive majesty and might to the forces that are fighting for freedom in the world, for justice, and for peace." The Russians could now join the Americans, alongside the British and the French, to defend democracy and create a peaceful world. "We are glad ... to fight thus for the ultimate peace of the world and for the liberation of its peoples, the German peoples included: for the rights of nations great and small and the privilege of men everywhere to choose their way of life and of obedience. The world must be made safe for democracy. Its peace must be planted upon the tested foundation of political liberty."[4] A new ideological and military partnership of democratic nations would create this new world order.

Wilson heralded America's purpose in the Great War as a providential mission. What Americans had achieved at home and elsewhere in the new world in the name of the Monroe Doctrine would now define their global role. As he explained on 30 May 1917, "we are saying to all mankind, 'We did not set this Government up in order that we might have a selfish and separate liberty, for we are now ready to come to your assistance and fight out upon the field of the world the cause of human liberty.' ... Such a time has come, and in the providence of God America will once more have an opportunity to show to the world that she was born to serve mankind."[5] It was the nation's calling to redeem others.

America's God-given mission, in Wilson's view, promised to transcend the historic failures of the old world's statecraft. On 11 February 1918, he explained "the United States has no desire to interfere in European affairs or to act as arbiter in European territorial disputes." It should remain aloof from Europe's traditional system of international relations, he believed, as it was this that had produced the war. "This war had its roots in the disregard of the rights of small nations and of nationalities which lacked the union and the force to make good their claim to determine their own allegiances and their own forms of political life," he asserted. "Covenants must now be entered into which will render such things impossible for the future; and those covenants must be backed by the united force of all the nations that love justice and are willing to maintain it at any cost." The new world order, Wilson emphasized, would guarantee "essential justice" and peace, replace "the great game, now forever discredited, of the balance of power," ensure "every territorial settlement ... for the benefit of the population concerned," and provide each "well-defined national aspiration ... the utmost satisfaction." In short, it would fulfill the "true spirit of America ... for justice and for self-government."[6]

Throughout the war Wilson reiterated this contrast between the new and old worlds. Europe still represented the other in his traditionally American nationalist thinking. On 27 September 1918, he summarized the kind of peace he favored. He advocated "impartial justice" with "no special or separate interest." Within the new League of Nations that he envisaged, there should be "no leagues or alliances or special covenants and understandings" and "no special, selfish economic combinations." Instead of secret accords, "all international agreements and treaties" should be known to the entire world. This new diplomacy would fulfill rather than abandon the American diplomatic tradition. "We still read Washington's immortal warning against 'entangling alliances' with full comprehension and an answering purpose," Wilson emphasized. "But only special and limited alliances entangle; and we recognize and accept the duty of a new day in which we are permitted to hope for a general alliance which will avoid entanglements and clear the air of the world for common understandings and the maintenance of common rights."[7]

The new world order, with its League of Nations, would transcend the old European statecraft of military alliances and balances of power that had culminated in the Great War. Wilsonianism thus promised a new internationalism without requiring the United States to sacrifice its historic aloofness or isolation from the old world. The president stressed this point at a plenary session of the Paris Peace Conference. "In coming into this war," he reminded the delegates on 25 January 1919, "the United States never for a moment thought that she was intervening in the politics of Europe or the politics of Asia or the politics of any part of the world. Her thought was that all the world had now become conscious that there was a single cause which turned upon the issues of this war. That was the cause of justice and of liberty for men of every kind and place."[8] He invited the Allies to join the United States in this global transformation.

After the United States entered the world war, Wilson denounced Imperial Germany as the principal enemy. It became the foremost other. Although the president generally distrusted the old world, Germany's autocratic and militaristic government ranked as his chief nemesis. It directly threatened his new world order. Wilson blamed Kaiser Wilhelm's government but not the German people. "The military masters of Germany denied us the right to be neutral," he asserted in his Flag Day address on 14 June 1917. "They filled our unsuspecting communities with vicious spies and conspirators and sought to corrupt the opinion of our people in their own behalf." The German government dominated not only its own people but also the other Central Powers. "The war was begun by the military masters of Germany, who proved to be also the masters of Austria-Hungary." German leaders sought to extend their power well beyond their homeland. "Their plan was to throw a broad belt of German military power and political control across the very center of Europe and beyond the Mediterranean into the heart of Asia; and Austria-Hungary was to be as much their tool and pawn as Serbia or Bulgaria or Turkey or the ponderous states of the East." Imperial Germany's global ambitions not only involved military force but also subversive activity in the United States and throughout Europe. "The sinister intrigue is being no less actively conducted in this country than in Russia and in every country in Europe to which the agents and dupes of the Imperial German Government can get access." Wilson framed the challenge as a Manichaean choice. To counter Germany's autocratic and militaristic regime, he called upon all democratic nations to fight against this global challenge. He affirmed that "this is a People's War, a war for freedom and justice and self-government amongst all the nations of the world, a war to make the world safe for the peoples who live upon it and have made it their own, the German people themselves included." The president expressed his firm resolve to win this war. "For us there is but one choice. We have made it," he avowed. "Woe be to the man or group of men that seeks to stand in our way in this day of high resolution when every principle we hold dearest is to be vindicated and made secure for the salvation of the nations."[9] After winning the war against Imperial Germany and the other Central Powers, the democratic partners under American leadership should establish a new world order to preserve the peace.

Russia's Bolshevik Revolution in November 1917 challenged Wilson's plan for a global democratic partnership. In a message to Russia on 26 May, while still expecting the provisional government to establish a liberal democracy, he had affirmed: "We are fighting for the liberty, the self-government, and the undictated development of all peoples, and every feature of the settlement that concludes this war must be conceived and executed for that purpose."[10] But the Bolsheviks replaced the provisional government with their new Socialist or Communist regime under Vladimir Lenin's leadership. Contrary to the president's expectation of orderly progress toward liberal democracy in Russia, its radical new government now became another enemy other. He discounted the authenticity of this dangerous development, viewing the Bolsheviks as German agents or dupes and thus regarding them as illegitimate representatives of the country. Refusing to recognize the Bolshevik government, he continued to hope that moderate liberals would defeat the radicals and keep Russia as a democratic partner.[11]

Shortly after the Bolsheviks seized power in Petrograd, Wilson identified them with Imperial Germany and denounced them as opponents of his new world order. Speaking to the American Federation of Labor convention on 12 November 1917, he expressed his amazement that the Bolsheviks or "any group of persons should be so ill-informed as to suppose, as some groups in Russia apparently suppose, that any reforms planned in the interest of the people can live in the presence of a Germany powerful enough to undermine or overthrow them by intrigue or force." He thought that "any body of free men that compounds with the present German Government is compounding for its own destruction. But that is not the whole of the story. Any man in America or anywhere else that supposes that the free industry and enterprise of the world can continue if the Pan-German plan is achieved and German power fastened upon the world is as fatuous as the dreamers in Russia." Wilson criticized Bolshevik Russia as an enemy for aligning with Imperial Germany. But he also warned American workers not to identify with the radical revolution in Russia. "Let us show ourselves Americans by showing that we do not want to go off in separate camps or groups by ourselves, but that we want to cooperate with all other classes and all other groups in the common enterprise which is to release the spirits of the world from bondage. I would be willing to set that up as the final test of an American. That is the meaning of democracy." The president expected American workers to remain patriotic, rejecting the radical class politics of the Bolsheviks and adhering to the moderate liberal democracy of the United States. "We claim to be the greatest democratic people in the world, and democracy means first of all that we can govern ourselves. If our men have not self-control, then they are not capable of that great thing which we call democratic government."[12]

Wilson viewed the Bolsheviks as others and hoped that the Russian people would reject their radical revolution. His liberal version of self-determination denied legitimacy to these extreme Socialists or Communists. To counter their appeal for peace with the Central Powers, he announced his alternative vision of a new world order in the Fourteen Points. He sought to prevent Russia from concluding a separate peace on the Eastern Front that might allow Germany to defeat the Allies on the Western Front before the United States could send a sufficient military force under General John J. Pershing's command to help win the war. The president, however, could not stop Lenin's government from signing the Treaty of Brest-Litovsk on 3 March 1918. Even afterward, he tried to encourage the Russian people to resist both the Bolsheviks and the Germans. In a message to the Russian people on 11 March, he reiterated "the whole heart of the people of the United States is with the people of Russia in the attempt to free themselves forever from autocratic government and become the masters of their own life."[13] Throughout the war Wilson maintained his anti-German and anti-Bolshevik stance as a posture against external enemies of liberal democracy.

Counterparts to these external enemies posed internal threats in the United States, as the president perceived them. He distinguished between patriotic Americans and others who were potentially subversive or disloyal. Hyphenated Americans, he feared, might identify more with their ancestral lands than with their adopted country. German-Americans and Irish-Americans topped his list of suspects. He distrusted them far more than Anglo-Americans, who appeared simply as Americans to Wilson. Even before the United States had entered the war, he had questioned the patriotism of some foreign-born citizens as well as resident aliens. In an address on citizenship on 13 July 1916, he emphasized that loyalty means self-sacrifice. "Certain men—I have never believed a great number—born in other lands, have in recent months thought more of those lands than they have of the honor and interest of the government under which they are now living." They needed to sacrifice their old national identities to become loyal Americans, which required them to accept America's "vision of real liberty and real justice and purity of conduct."[14]

Before the Great War, the United States had experienced a massive influx of European immigrants at the same time that it was expanding its empire abroad. These immigrants brought the old world into the new, while Americans were also encountering others through imperial expansion, as with the annexation of the Philippines after the Spanish-American War of 1898.[15] Long before he became president Wilson contemplated the historical implications of these interacting developments. Writing about "The Significance of American History" in 1902, he claimed that "a virgin continent discovered in the West" had opened a place where "men out of an old world" could undertake their "work as pioneers." They brought their "old civilization" and transplanted it in the "wilderness" of the new world. "Men out of every European race, men out of Asia, men out of Africa, have crowded in, to the bewilderment alike of statesmen and historians," he observed. European immigrants in the new world had created the "new race" of Americans through "the mixture of races." Wilson viewed the creation of this new nation as a process of liberal assimilation. European nationalities—or races as he described them—became American as they acquired the cultural values and embraced the institutions that the United States had derived from its English origins. American national identity could be traced back to the Anglo-Saxons, although it was the product of history more than of biology. Wilson affirmed the idea of civic rather than racial or ethnic nationalism, even though he still believed that the core of Americanism came from the nation's British heritage. Acculturation, later called the "melting pot," had transformed European immigrants, such as the Dutch and the French, into Americans. Their new national identity, he affirmed, was as genuine as if "we kept the pure Saxon strain." He explained: "All peoples have come to dwell among us, but they have merged their individuality in a national character already formed; have been dominated, changed, absorbed." In Wilson's view, history provided a better explanation than biology or race for the enduring British legacy in the United States. Although the nation's origins could be traced back to the Anglo-Saxons, historical developments were more important than primordial roots in shaping the American identity. "Nations grow by spirit, not by blood," he avowed, "and nowhere can the significant principle of their growth be seen more clearly, upon a more fair and open page, than in the history of the United States." American history, he elaborated, was "an offshoot of European history and has all its antecedents on the other side of the sea, and yet it is so much more than a mere offshoot." He anticipated that in the twentieth century the United States would play an even larger global role. "The life of the new world grows as complex as the life of the old. A nation hitherto wholly devoted to domestic developments now finds its first tasks of the great world at large, seeking its special part and place of power. A new age has come which no man may forecast. But the past is the key to it; and the past of America lies at the center of modern history."[16]

Although early in his academic career Wilson had espoused the germ theory of history, he later embraced the civic nationalism of modern liberalism. During the 1880s, he had traced the origins of the United States back through English history to the Anglo-Saxons. But after meeting Frederick Jackson Turner at Johns Hopkins in 1889, he began to shift his focus from primordial roots to the frontier experience in the American West as the critical factor in shaping the national identity.[17] This transition in Wilson's historical thinking undergirded his confidence in liberal assimilation of even the so-called new immigrants from Southern and Eastern Europe. The historical process of orderly progress, epitomized by the frontier, could transform the newcomers into Americans. He did not join advocates, such as President Theodore Roosevelt, of a "racialized nation."[18] Less optimistic about liberal assimilation of immigrants, proponents of a racialized nation adopted a harder line on Americanization. He also resisted new restrictions on immigration. Yet Wilson obviously preferred the old immigrants from Western Europe. In *A History of the American People* (1902), he noted a change in the pattern of immigration after 1890 from "the sturdy stocks of the north of Europe" to "the lowest class of the south of Italy and men of the meaner sort out of Hungary and Poland." He added that "the Chinese were more to be desired, as workmen if not as citizens, than most of the coarse crew that came crowding in every year at the eastern ports."[19]

During the Great War, Wilson reaffirmed his belief in liberal assimilation. He reminded the Daughters of the American Revolution on 11 October 1915 that "America has not grown by the mere multiplication of the original stock." Instead, the nation had preserved the ideals of its founders by teaching their principles to subsequent generations of immigrants. "It is easy to preserve tradition with continuity of blood," he acknowledged, "but it is not so easy when that race is constantly being renewed and augmented from other sources, from stocks that did not carry or originate the same principles." Nevertheless, under proper American tutelage, they too embraced the national legacy of liberty. "So from generation to generation strangers have had to be indoctrinated with the principles of the American family, and the wonder and beauty of it all has been that the infection has been so generously easy." Thus, later immigrants from various lands became foreign-born citizens who were just as patriotic as those born in the United States. With few exceptions, they too were ready to fulfill their duties as Americans.[20]

Wilson interpreted the closing of America's western frontier in 1890 as the turning point in its history. Whereas the United States had previously concentrated on internal developments, it subsequently began to assume global responsibilities. He reminded his Omaha audience on 5 October 1916 that the war with Spain in 1898, only eight years after the frontier's closing, left the United States as the guardian of Cuba and the possessor of Puerto Rico. "And," he added, "that frontier which no man could draw upon this continent in 1890 had been flung across the sea 7,000 miles to the untrodden forests of some part of the Philippine Islands." The president believed that America's history at home prepared it for a new role in world affairs. Seeking to link his audience's local experience with America's global mission, he explained: "Nebraska was once, as I have phased it, the melting pot in which the various elements of America were fused together for the purpose of American life. Now it is our great duty to fuse the elements of America together for the purpose of the life of the world." He anticipated that the United States would help create a postwar league of nations to preserve the peace. "What disturbs the life of the whole world is the concern of the whole world," he avowed, "and it is our duty to lend the full force of this nation, moral and physical, to a league of nations which shall see to it that nobody disturbs the peace of the world without submitting his case first to the opinion of mankind."[21] From this perspective, Wilson outlined his ideas for a "peace without victory" to end the European war. He proposed that all nations should adopt the doctrine that President James Monroe had heralded in 1823, affirming that "no nation should seek to extend its polity over any other nation or people, but that every people should be left free to determine its own polity, its own way of development, unhindered, unthreatened, unafraid, the little along with the great and powerful." "These are American principles, American policies," he affirmed in his address to the Senate on 22 January 1917.[22]

After the United States entered the Great War, Wilson stressed national unity. To defeat foreign enemies, the American people needed to fulfill their duties as U.S. citizens. They should support the war effort by volunteering for military service or contributing in other ways, but if they neglected these obligations, he resolved to use the federal government's powers of coercion. The wartime experience thus contributed to the making of the modern American citizen. Under Wilson's leadership, the United States intensified the liberal assimilation or Americanization of European immigrants and their descendants. Expecting all patriots to support the

American principles that he articulated, he stifled dissent and rejected cultural pluralism.[23] In his view, the "melting pot" on the western frontier had created the prototypical Americans out of European immigrants of various nationalities. In a telegram to the Northwest Loyalty Meeting in Saint Paul, Minnesota, on 16 November 1917, he called upon all Americans to unite to win the war. "You have come together as the representatives of that Western Empire in which the sons of all sections of America and the stocks of all the nations of Europe have made the prairie and the forest the home of a new race and the temple of a new faith," the president wrote. "The time has come when that home must be protected and that faith affirmed in deeds. Sacrifice and service must come from every class, every profession, every party, every race, every creed, every section. This is not a banker's war or a farmer's war or a manufacturer's war or a laboring-man's war—it is a war for every straight-out American whether our flag be his by birth or by adoption."[24] By identifying "a new race" of Americans as including "the stocks of all the nations of Europe," Wilson reaffirmed his belief in the nation's ability to transform immigrants from the old world into citizens of the new world. Like other Americans who had expanded their understanding of "whiteness" to include Irish Catholics and the new immigrants from Southern and Eastern Europe, many of whom were Jews or Catholic or Orthodox Christians, he no longer restricted the national identity to Anglo-Saxon Protestants or Anglo-Americans. But, notably, he omitted any reference to Asian- or African-Americans. His liberal inclusiveness excluded people of color. Nonwhite Americans did not fit his ideal of U.S. citizenship. They were others.[25]

Wilson drew a sharp color line despite his apparently universal liberal rhetoric. During his presidency, the racial segregation of the Jim Crow South became the common practice in the federal government. In 1915 he watched the racist film *The Birth of a Nation* at the White House as a favor to his Johns Hopkins classmate and friend, Thomas Dixon, Jr., who had joined D.W. Griffith to make this movie about the Civil War and Reconstruction. They included Wilson's quotations from *A History of the American People* in this silent film to give credibility to their historical interpretation of the "war between the states" and the postwar reconstruction of the South. They used his words to exonerate the Ku Klux Klan, which had inflicted violence and terror to overturn the interracial governments and restore white supremacy. Whatever he might have said in private after viewing the film, the public knew that the president had seen it and had not criticized its virulently racist message. Thus, although he never publicly praised the film, he implicitly endorsed its glorification of the KKK and white supremacy. All viewers, after reading the quotations from Wilson's book between the first and second parts of the film, would have identified him with its message. Nevertheless, he refused to express any public criticism of this most popular silent movie. Deeply embedded in the text of his liberalism was the subtext of white racism. Despite his universal rhetoric, the president's idea of freedom and democracy marginalized black people.[26]

Wilson sought to unite white Americans from the North and the South but denied African-Americans equal rights as citizens. Speaking to Confederate veterans on 5 June 1917, he emphasized their place in the reunited nation. He affirmed "the great ends which God in His mysterious Providence wrought through our instrumentality, because at the heart of the men of the North and of the South there was the same love of self-government and of liberty, and now we are to be the instrument in the hands of God to see that liberty is made secure for mankind." White Americans from the North and the South, who shared a common "passion for human freedom" even when they had fought against each other, should now unite to help liberate the old world.[27]

Wilson's concept of national self-determination projected his American belief in the "melting pot" onto the peacemaking. His Fourteen Points outlined the new map of Europe and the Middle East. He thought all Europeans, if they practiced self-control like Americans, were capable of governing themselves. They could establish liberal democracy throughout the old world. When he announced the Armistice at a joint session of Congress on 11 November 1918, the president shared his vision of orderly progress toward the new world order. He urged the emerging nations to "preserve their self-control and the orderly processes of their governments." He warned that "peoples who have just come out from under the yoke of arbitrary government and who are now coming at last into their freedom will never find the treasures of liberty they are in search of if they look for them by the light of the torch. They will find that every pathway that is stained with the blood of their own brothers leads to the wilderness, not to the seat of their hope."[28] Wilson wanted viable nation-states to establish democratic governments and join the League of Nations but he greatly underestimated the problems of competing nationalities in Russia, Central Europe, and the Middle East after the collapse of the Romanov, Habsburg, Hohenzollern, and Ottoman empires. The various peoples in the lands of these former empires embraced racial or ethnic nationalism rather than Wilson's civic nationalism.[29] New nation-states, such as Poland, Czechoslovakia, and Yugoslavia, experienced ethnic conflicts within their borders as well as with their neighbors. A civil war in Russia, which the Bolsheviks eventually won, prevented it from becoming the democratic partner Wilson expected in Eastern Europe. It was not easy for him to apply American liberal principles in the old world.

Leaders of the new Weimar Republic that replaced Kaiser Wilhelm's government after the 1918 German Revolution, also held a different concept of national self-determination. They wanted the president to help them keep or acquire all lands in Central Europe that were inhabited by Germans. That was their understanding of his Fourteen Points. They were deeply disappointed, of course, when he expected them to accept territorial losses to Poland, France, Belgium, and Denmark, and when he opposed their annexation of Austria or German-speaking parts of Czechoslovakia. Wilson's belief, based on the liberal American idea of the "melting pot," that Germans outside the new borders of the Weimar Republic could assimilate into other nations made no sense from their perspective of racial or ethnic nationalism. They did not think that fellow Germans should be absorbed into Poland, France, Belgium, or Denmark, or kept apart in Austria and Czechoslovakia. When the German delegation received the peace treaty from Wilson and the Allied leaders at Versailles on 7 May 1919, and immediately demanded revisions, believing that he had betrayed his promise of the Fourteen Points, he stiffened his resolve to require them to sign the treaty anyway. Until they accepted and fulfilled the peace conditions, he agreed with the Allies that Germany should be excluded from membership in the new League of Nations. Even with a republican government, it did not qualify for this partnership of democratic nations. Still an enemy, Weimar Germany remained one of the others in Wilsonianism.[30]

People of color around the world also found the peace settlement deeply disappointing. The president's call for a new order based on self-determination and equality of nations resonated in, among other places, Egypt, India, China, and Korea. Anti-colonial nationalists appropriated his words to advocate their independence from the great powers that dominated the Paris Peace Conference. Expecting him to bolster their claims, these leaders used Wilson's rhetoric to justify their causes. They felt betrayed, however, because he never gave them the kind of support they expected. Given his Eurocentric orientation, he had not even imagined that so many peoples outside of Europe would think he was promising them self-determination any time soon. In his view, colonial peoples were not yet sufficiently civilized to qualify as nations ready for self-government. They still needed tutoring by the advanced nations. Although the president's liberal ideals were apparently universal, he did not apply them in the colonial empires of the victorious Allies. He agreed that Egypt and India should remain in the British Empire and that Japan would keep Korea and take over Germany's assets in China, notably in Shandong. Some anti-colonial nationalists, in their disillusionment with Wilsonianism, subsequently turned to Bolshevism. Lenin promised self-determination to all nations, including colonial peoples. Given Wilson's attitude toward these others, he was not ready for "the Wilsonian moment."[31]

Wilson's vision of a new world order drew a global color line. Yet, while protecting the colonial empires of the victorious Allies, he expected them to accept minimal supervision by the League of Nations under a system of mandates for their new acquisitions of the defeated empires' former possessions outside of Europe. New nations emerging from conquered empires in Europe were presumably ready for self-government. But Germany's former colonies and some peoples in the former Ottoman Empire were deemed not yet ready. For them Wilson advocated mandates that would authorize the mandatory powers, under the League's oversight, to provide tutelage for the local peoples. The various mandates affirmed a racial hierarchy. Some new nations in the former Ottoman lands, which were regarded as fairly advanced and thus closer to eligibility for self-government, would be placed in so-called "A" mandates. Other "less-developed" peoples of Germany's Pacific-island and African colonies would be assigned "B" and "C" mandates. Although Wilson's rhetoric seemed to promise an end to colonialism, the League mandates perpetuated its legacy in a new form. These peoples were still others in the racial hierarchy of his new world order.[32]

At the Peace Conference, Wilson rejected the idea of racial equality. During the drafting of the Covenant for the League of Nations, Japanese delegates introduced an amendment to affirm that "the principle of equality of nations and the just treatment of their nationals should be laid down as a fundamental basis of future relations in the world organization." British delegates vociferously opposed the amendment. In the commission that drafted the Covenant, only Wilson and a Polish delegate joined the British to criticize it. Many delegates favored the amendment. At the meeting on 11 April 1919, eleven of the seventeen delegates voted for it, but as chair of the commission, the president ruled that the amendment was defeated because the vote was not unanimous. At no other time did he require such unanimity. Japanese delegates then raised the issue at a plenary session on 28 April, but they lost again to the British and the Americans, who did not want their empires open to Japanese or other Asian immigrants. By his crucial role in defeating the Japanese racial equality amendment, Wilson, along with the British, drew a global color line. His liberal ideals, although ostensibly universal, were exclusive in practice. The full benefits of Wilsonianism were available only for white nations of the West.[33]

African-Americans wanted Wilson's ostensibly universal promise of freedom and democracy for themselves. With few exceptions, they loyally supported the war effort. But he saw their assertive claims for human or civil rights as a danger. His administration used its wartime coercive powers to investigate and control them. During the Peace Conference, he confided to Dr. Cary Grayson his fear that "the American negro returning from abroad would be our greatest medium in conveying bolshevism to America."[34] The president identified African-Americans with foreign foes of Wilsonianism, although—or because—they, like anti-colonial nationalists abroad, affirmed its evident promise of racial equality. They too learned that Wilson still excluded them. His modern liberalism at home revealed the same fundamental paradox of apparent universality and actual exclusivity that characterized Wilsonianism abroad. For him, there were many others who did not—or at least not yet—qualify for his new world order.

Despite its limitations, Wilson touted his new world order on 10 July 1919, when he submitted the Versailles Treaty to the Senate, although he acknowledged that "it was not easy to graft the new order of ideas on the old, and some of the fruits of the grafting may, I fear, for a time be bitter." To overcome the evil influences, purposes, and ambitions that had produced the "sinister designs of Germany," he heralded "the League of Nations as an indispensable instrumentality for the maintenance of the new order" in "the world of civilized men." To replace the old order, "the united power of free nations must put a stop to aggression, and the world must be given peace." The League was "the only hope of mankind. ... The stage is set, the destiny disclosed," Wilson proclaimed. "It has come about by no plan of our own conceiving, but by the hand of God who led us into this way. ... It was of this that we dreamed at our birth. America shall in truth show the way. The light streams on the path ahead, and nowhere else."[35]

Yet others still resisted Wilson's new world order and he blamed them for it. In private conversations with Secretary of State Robert Lansing, he denounced Great Britain, France, Italy, Romania, and Greece, confessing that "I am almost inclined to refuse to permit this country to be a member of the League of Nations when it is composed of such intriguers and robbers. I am disposed to throw up the whole business and get out." He condemned the old world for "the inordinate cupidity and disregard of right by all nations."[36] Nevertheless, he sought American support for the League of Nations. During his western tour in September 1919, he questioned the loyalty of its critics. "Opposition is the specialty of those who are Bolshevistically inclined," he asserted.[37] Helping to whip up the Red Scare, he claimed that "there are apostles of Lenin in our own midst."[38] Denouncing hyphenated Americans, especially German-Americans, he alleged that "the most un-American thing in the world is a hyphen."[39] Pro-German and pro-Bolshevik propagandists sought to keep the United

States out of the League and defeat this progressive reform. If they were to win the treaty fight, it would serve the interests of America's foreign enemies, Weimar Germany and Bolshevik Russia.[40] It would prevent the United States from fulfilling its providential mission to guarantee the new world order.[41] Despite his patriotic appeal against all these others, Wilson failed. Republicans, who controlled the Senate under Henry Cabot Lodge's leadership, rejected the treaty and kept the United States out of the League.[42]

Both at home and abroad, Wilsonianism generated a backlash. Although ostensibly universal, it excluded or disappointed others and they reacted negatively. African-Americans and anti-colonial nationalists felt that the president had betrayed his promise of freedom and democracy for all peoples by drawing a global color line. The Japanese, too, suffered from his rejection of racial equality. The Germans also blamed him for not supporting their nationalist claims as they had expected. Other Europeans strove to create new nation-states that would achieve their hopes for racial or ethnic self-determination, simply ignoring his preference for civic nationalism based on liberal ideals. Bolsheviks in Russia identified him as an enemy, and he held a reciprocal view of them. Even the Allies resisted his vision of a new world order and pursued their own interests. Wilson painfully perceived, although he did not acknowledge it publicly, that the old world was rejecting Wilsonianism. Ironically, like the others whom he saw as real or potential enemies and sought to exclude from his new world order, he too was eventually marginalized in the peacemaking after the Great War.

Notes

1. For various perspectives on Wilsonianism, see N. Gordon Levin, Jr., *Woodrow Wilson and World Politics: America's Response to War and Revolution* (New York: Oxford University Press, 1968); Thomas J. Knock, *To End All Wars: Woodrow Wilson and the Quest for a New World Order* (New York: Oxford University Press, 1992); Tony Smith, *America's Mission: The United States and the Worldwide Struggle for Democracy in the Twentieth Century* (Princeton, NJ: Princeton University Press, 1994); Frank Ninkovich, *The Wilsonian Century: U.S. Foreign Policy since 1900* (Chicago: University of Chicago Press, 1999); G. John Ikenberry, *After Victory: Institutions, Strategic Restraint, and the Rebuilding of Order after Major Wars* (Princeton: Princeton University Press, 2001), 117–62; Lloyd E. Ambrosius, *Wilsonianism: Woodrow Wilson and His Legacy in American Foreign Relations* (New York: Palgrave Macmillan, 2002); Alan Dawley, *Changing the World: American Progressives in War and Revolution* (Princeton: Princeton University Press, 2003); Joan Hoff, *A Faustian Foreign Policy from Woodrow Wilson to George W. Bush: Dreams of Perfectibility* (Cam-

bridge: Cambridge University Press, 2008); Lloyd E. Ambrosius, "Democracy, Peace, and World Order," in *Reconsidering Woodrow Wilson: Progressivism, Internationalism, War, and Peace*, ed. John Milton Cooper, Jr. (Washington, DC: Woodrow Wilson Center Press, 2008), 225–49; Ross A. Kennedy, *The Will to Believe: Woodrow Wilson, World War I, and America's Strategy for Peace and Security* (Kent, OH: Kent State University Press, 2009).

2. Woodrow Wilson, *The Public Papers of Woodrow Wilson: War and Peace*, ed. Ray Stannard Baker and William E. Dodd (New York: Harper & Brothers Publishers, 1927), 1: 158–59, 162.

3. Robert W. Tucker, *Woodrow Wilson and the Great War: Reconsidering America's Neutrality, 1914-1917* (Charlottesville: University of Virginia Press, 2007).

4. Wilson, *Public Papers: War and Peace*, 1: 8, 12–14.

5. Ibid., 53; Richard M. Gamble, *The War for Righteousness: Progressive Christianity, the Great War, and the Rise of the Messianic Nation* (Wilmington, DE: ISI Books, 2003).

6. Wilson, *Public Papers: War and Peace*, 1: 180–84.

7. Ibid., 257–58.

8. Ibid., 397.

9. Ibid., 61–63, 66–67.

10. Ibid., 50.

11. David S. Fogelsong, *America's Secret War Against Bolshevism: U.S. Intervention in the Russian Civil War, 1917-1920* (Chapel Hill: University of North Carolina Press, 1995); Norman E. Saul, *War and Revolution: The United States and Russia, 1914-1921* (Lawrence: University Press of Kansas, 2001); Donald E. Davis and Eugene P. Trani, *The First Cold War: The Legacy of Woodrow Wilson in U.S.-Soviet Relations* (Columbia: University of Missouri Press, 2002).

12. Wilson, *Public Papers: War and Peace*, 1: 120, 122–23.

13. Ibid., 191.

14. Wilson, *Public Papers: The New Democracy*, 2: 251–52.

15. Matthew Frye Jacobson, *Barbarian Virtues: The United States Encounters Foreign Peoples at Home and Abroad, 1876-1917* (New York: Hill & Wang, 2000); Paul A. Kramer, *The Blood of Government: Race, Empire, the United States, and the Philippines* (Chapel Hill: University of North Carolina Press, 2006).

16. Woodrow Wilson, "The Significance of American History," *Woodrow Wilson: Essential Writings and Speeches of the Scholar-President*, ed. Mario R. DeNunzio (New York: New York University Press, 2008), 212–17.

17. Lloyd E. Ambrosius, *Wilsonian Statecraft: Theory and Practice of Liberal Internationalism during World War I* (Wilmington, DE: SR Books, 1991), 3–13. See also Ronald J. Pestritto, *Woodrow Wilson and the Roots of Modern Liberalism* (Lanham, MD: Rowman & Littlefield Publishers, 2005).

18. Gary Gerstle, *American Crucible: Race and Nation in the Twentieth Century* (Princeton: Princeton University Press, 2001), 14–80; Gary Gerstle, "Race and Nation in the Thought and Politics of Woodrow Wilson," in *Reconsidering Woodrow Wilson*, 93–123.

19. Woodrow Wilson, *A History of the American People* (New York: Harper & Brothers Publishers, 1902), 5: 212–13.

20. Wilson, *Public Papers: New Democracy*, 1: 376.

21. Ibid., 2: 345, 348.

22. Ibid., 410, 414.

23. Desmond S. King, *Making Americans: Immigration, Race, and the Origins of the Diverse Democracy* (Cambridge, MA: Harvard University Press, 2000), 1–165; Christopher Capozolla, *Uncle Sam Wants You: World War I and the Making of the Modern American Citizen* (New York: Oxford University Press, 2008); Geoffrey R. Stone, *Perilous Times: Free Speech in Wartime* (New York: W. W. Norton & Company, 2004), 135–233; Geoffrey R. Stone, "Mr. Wilson's First Amendment," *Reconsidering Woodrow Wilson*, 189–224.

24. Wilson, *Public Papers: War and Peace*, 1: 127.
25. Matthew Frye Jacobson, *Whiteness of a Different Color: European Immigrants and the Alchemy of Race* (Cambridge, MA: Harvard University Press, 1998).
26. Lloyd E. Ambrosius, "Woodrow Wilson and *The Birth of a Nation*: American Democracy and International Relations," *Diplomacy and Statecraft* 18 (December 2007): 689–718. See also Glenda Sluga, *The Nation, Psychology, and International Politics, 1870-1919* (New York: Palgrave Macmillan, 2006).
27. Wilson, *Public Papers: War and Peace*, 1: 55.
28. Ibid., 301–2.
29. Aviel Roshwald, *Ethnic Nationalism and the Fall of Empires: Central Europe, Russia, and the Middle East, 1914-1923* (London: Routledge, 2001).
30. Ambrosius, *Wilsonianism*, 125–34; Lloyd E. Ambrosius, "Nationale Selbstbestimmung im Ersten und Zweiten Weltkrieg: Eine Vergleichsstudie von Wilson bis Roosevelt," in *Deutschland und die U.S.A in der Internationalen Geschichte des 20 Jahrhunderts*, ed. Manfred Berg and Philipp Gassert (Stuttgart: Franz Steiner Verlag, 2004), 237–62.
31. Erez Manela, *The Wilsonian Moment: Self-Determination and the International Origins of Anticolonial Nationalism* (New York: Oxford University Press, 2007).
32. Margaret MacMillan, *Paris 1919: Six Months That Changed the World* (New York: Random House, 2001), 98–106.
33. Paul Gordon Lauren, *Power and Prejudice: The Politics and Diplomacy of Racial Discrimination* (Boulder: Westview, 1988), 82–107; Marilyn Lake and Henry Reynolds, *Drawing the Global Colour Line: White Men's Countries and the International Challenge of Racial Equality* (Cambridge: Cambridge University Press, 2008), 284–309.
34. Woodrow Wilson, *The Papers of Woodrow Wilson*, ed. Arthur S. Link (Princeton, NJ: Princeton University Press, 1986), 55: 471; Mark Ellis, *Race, War, and Surveillance: African Americans and the United States Government during World War I* (Bloomington: Indiana University Press, 2001); Theodore Kornweibel, Jr., *"Investigating Everything": Federal Efforts to Compel Black Loyalty during World War I* (Bloomington: Indiana University Press, 2002); Jonathan Rosenberg, *How Far the Promised Land?: World Affairs and the American Civil Rights Movement from the First World War to Vietnam* (Princeton: Princeton University Press, 2006), 15–72.
35. Wilson, *Public Papers: War and Peace*, 1: 541, 545, 548, 551–52.
36. Wilson, *The Papers of Woodrow Wilson*, 62: 428–29.
37. Wilson, *Public Papers: War and Peace*, 2: 10.
38. Ibid., 108.
39. Ibid., 78.
40. Ibid., 143.
41. Ibid., 249–62.
42. Lloyd E. Ambrosius, *Woodrow Wilson and the American Diplomatic Tradition: The Treaty Fight in Perspective* (Cambridge: Cambridge University Press, 1987); John Milton Cooper, Jr., *Breaking the Heart of the World: Woodrow Wilson and the Fight for the League of Nations* (Cambridge: Cambridge University Press, 2001).

Chapter 7

The Nazis and U.S. Foreign Policy Debates
History, Lessons, and Analogies

Michaela Hoenicke Moore

Hitler and the Nazis are ubiquitous in American culture.[1] Setting aside the realm of popular culture and considering only political references, we find Nazi comparisons in American domestic political debates from the 1930s through today. In accordance with their main purpose one can distinguish between diagnostic, justificatory, and slanderous analogies evoking Hitler or Nazism. The latter category predominates in the domestic realm and includes the Tea Party's 2010 Obama-Hitler comparison. Shocking as such equations are to people who know something about the Third Reich, they are, in fact, as old as the Nazis themselves; although one could add as extenuating circumstances that in the 1930s many people did not yet fully understand what the Nazi regime was up to. The fact that living memory of World War II is now rapidly fading presents a serious new challenge and places a particular obligation on historians and teachers to renew efforts of telling "what actually happened."

The Hitler gang enjoyed its most significant afterlife in American foreign policy discourse. In the realm of international relations historical references to World War II and the German leader have been deployed mainly for diagnostic and justificatory purposes.[2] During the Cold War the most popular explanatory analogy involving Hitler was the anti-appeasement lesson drawn from the Munich Conference of 1938. But the Nazis' afterlife in American foreign policy discourse extends beyond the Cold War. Warning against inaction in 1990, President George H.W. Bush famously compared Saddam Hussein to Hitler.[3] Over the subsequent decade, the

---

Notes for this chapter begin on page 159.

Nazis and more specifically the Holocaust were evoked in order to jolt an apathetic audience into action, to mobilize Congress, and to put pressure on the president to use military force for humanitarian interventions in Bosnia, Rwanda, and Kosovo.[4] More recently, during the War on Terror the term "islamofascism" combined diagnostic with defamatory intent and aimed to identify features in political Islamism—often via the concept of totalitarianism—that allowed for an equation with Nazism and high-lighted persistent anti-Semitism in the Arab world.[5] Building on Mark Stoler's observation that American "memory of [World War II] diverged sharply from the historical reality," historians must address the complex-ity in American understanding of the Third Reich in order to contrast this wartime ambiguity with the subsequent memory and political use.[6] Much of the literature on enemy images works from a postulation of clear di-chotomies: "the national image ... is the last great stronghold of unso-phistication ... Nations are divided into 'good' and 'bad'—the enemy is all bad, one's own nation is of spotless virtue."[7] Surprisingly, this was not the case with the American wartime image of one of the starkest historical examples of an immoral and criminal state, the Third Reich. Today, the Nazis and Adolf Hitler are recognized and invoked as a universal symbol of evil and the American military effort against them as the "good war." Yet American prewar and wartime conceptions of Nazi Germany are a striking counterexample to the usual tale of vilifying the enemy, essential-izing the other, and the notion of Manichaean enemy images dominating U.S. foreign policy. The enemy image remained ambiguous and the les-sons drawn from World War II were contradictory. The contest over the meaning of Nazism and World War II continued after the war.[8]

In the foreign policy realm, however, this ambiguity was soon resolved in favor of clear lessons. Over the past six decades foreign policy elites evoked Hitler, 1930s diplomacy, and, less readily, the Holocaust, as sim-iles, often precariously detached from their actual historical significance. If an analogy to the Nazi regime is established, it serves the purpose of ruling out—even denouncing diplomacy—legitimating military interven-tion.[9] A heavily edited memory of the interwar period and World War II has been used in American foreign policy rhetoric to sanctify and enno-ble military means by vilifying isolationism and appeasement. This use of World War II does not do justice to the much more complex and profound debate or to the range of insights that have marked contemporary Ameri-can responses to the Third Reich.

The war effort against the Third Reich, however appealing as a moral touchstone for American foreign policy in the decades since 1945, was any-thing but a single-minded crusade. The Franklin Roosevelt administration and an array of mainly liberal internationalists defined Nazi ideology as antithetical to American values and Hitler's foreign policy aims as a threat to American national security and interests. But this mobilization campaign was hampered by a set of powerful racial, cultural, and ideological factors that worked in favor of the German enemy and obscured the true nature of the Nazi regime in American public perception. Some American opinion makers and wider sections of the public struggled intellectually to keep the Germans in the fold of a shared civilization due to ethnic or cultural identification. This resulted in a significant misunderstanding of Third Reich reality. For many Americans it was only in retrospect that the military campaign against the Nazis acquired the urgency and moral clarity that turned any reference to World War II into a justification for military intervention.

A closer analysis of popular, official, and elite responses to the Third Reich reveals a complex and unresolved debate.[10] This posed considerable challenges to the Roosevelt administration's domestic mobilization campaign.[11] Yet what equally deserves to be highlighted is the sincerity on the part of intellectuals and politicians to grasp the enormity of Nazi ideology and German policies—and to suggest appropriate action. The contemporary slogan "know your enemy" captured the imperative to understand Nazism properly in order to not only defeat it militarily, but to devise effective safeguards against it politically. Even beyond the widespread use of the disease metaphor for Nazism, many popular as well as political analyses of the Third Reich took the tripartite form of the patient's (Germany's) case history resulting in a (political or psychocultural) diagnosis, followed by proposed treatment (postwar plans). As one commentator explained, "The convalescence of the bled and broken world into a healthy new one will be determined largely by how its medicine-men interpret the German national character."[12] In some circles a dawning understanding arose that Germany was engaged in a break with civilization, even with humanity.[13] Today the expression "enemy of civilization" has the ring of self-righteous propaganda, but at the time this emerging realization of what the Third Reich was all about constituted an important intellectual achievement.

To most Americans the reality of the Third Reich was confusing and somewhat threatening, yet distant. Interpretations making sense of this reality and explaining what it meant for the United States varied considerably, which kept the debate open and fluid. It is useful to distinguish three levels on which the American prewar and wartime discussions on Nazism took place, namely, among government officials and politicians, among intellectuals and professionals concerned with Germany or foreign policy, and finally, among the American public at large. The latter included voters and subsequently soldiers (and their families). As the least articulate group, this was the target audience for the other groups' expository efforts.

Not in any direct correspondence to these three groups, but rather revealing overlapping and crisscrossing patterns, we can distinguish three broadly different responses to the Third Reich. Traditional political elites oriented toward Great Britain revived a World War I–derived enemy image based on a deterministic cultural understanding that limited the problem to Germany. Among journalists, refugees, and intellectuals with personal ties or intellectual affinities to that country, a very different interpretation emerged that saw in German aggression, racism, and anti-democratic populism the West's own ignored dark side. Much of the analyses by foreign correspondents, refugees, diplomats and scholars were remarkably accurate and insightful, whether they condemned Germany or found some redeeming features in "the other Germany." Finally, there was a less articulate, vaguely ethnically based goodwill toward the German people that shaped the American debate in surprising ways. It dampened any effort to mobilize the American public around a hate- or fear-filled notion of the German enemy and, at the same time, it allowed insights of the more academic discourse on Nazi Germany to enter a wider public consciousness.[14]

The previous Great War had left a complicated and tragically inverted legacy for the political class and the larger public alike as far as Germany and military intervention were concerned. From the interwar revisionist period through the early years of World War II, government officials and many Americans deliberately rejected ideas and practices of the Creel Committee (Committee on Public Information, CPI). Those included a clear-cut ethnic-ideological enemy image of the Germans as "Huns," charges of German war atrocities, and an effective government-sponsored propaganda campaign that in retrospect came to be regarded as overzealous and detrimental to democracy at home. During the 1920s and 1930s congressional investigations and popular books implied that the real threat against which Americans had to guard was not Germany, but national and international bankers, weapons manufacturers, and anti-German propaganda that had incited ethnic violence on the home front and led the country into an unnecessary war. The backlash against World War I atrocity tales had undoubtedly the most problematic and tragic consequences. Not only had German soldiers, in fact, committed war crimes against Belgian and French civilians in 1914, but the subsequent rejection of CPI-style campaigns and the injunction against the use of atrocity stories in 1942 became further obstacles to a clear understanding of the nature of the "new Germany," the centrality of its racist dystopia, and genocidal warfare.[15] Moreover, shock over the carnage of World War I and disillusionment with Wilsonianism, the crusading, missionary strand in American foreign policy aiming at making the world safe for democracy by military intervention, led in the interwar period to an unprecedented rise of pacifism and a loss of faith in war as a political means.

By contrast, the single most important group molding American popular understanding of the new Germany was an assembly of extraordinarily talented and conscientious American journalists stationed in Europe during the 1930s. Not until 1942 would the administration have something comparable to offer with its civilian and military information agencies. Between them the foreign correspondents formulated a set of enduring interpretative models regarding the nature of the Third Reich, its structure, and its regime. On the central question of German support for Hitler and later popular complicity in Nazi crimes, the journalists described ordinary Germans' behavior as ranging from sporadic acts of courage and decency to cowardice, acquiescence, occasional fanaticism, and mostly self-interested opportunism and apathy.

Edgar A. Mowrer, whose *Germany Puts the Clock Back* was published just as the Nazis came to power, explored the collusion of Germany's traditional elites with the right-wing extremists and the failure of the liberals and social democrats to defend the republic. As to the broader question why the German people offered so little resistance to the Nazis and their excesses, his colleague William L. Shirer concluded, "the majority of Germans ... are behind Hitler and believe in him."[16] Mowrer and Shirer, who later wrote scripts for the War Department's propaganda films, prepared with their prewar writings an understanding of Nazi Germany that emphasized the deeper roots of Nazism in German political culture and the broad popular support that Hitler enjoyed. By contrast, their colleague John Gunther in his widely read account *Inside Europe* (1936) focused on the Nazi leaders. Drawing on popular psychological interpretations he presented them as a simultaneously scary and entertaining freak show.[17]

The most widely read American journalist on "the German problem," Dorothy Thompson, inaugurated several of the enduring tropes in American contemporary understanding of Nazi Germany: the dictator as buffoon, the masses as the problem, the early recognition that Nazism meant war, the faith that Germany was salvageable, the concern over anti-Semitism at home, and, most importantly, the recognition that Nazism was a "disease with more than purely Germanic roots."[18] Thompson, who in the 1930s was vilified as a warmonger and later as a sympathizer of Germany, offered the most profound and comprehensive analysis of the Third Reich. Stateside, the journalists' portraits of the new Germany were reinforced by Jewish groups and leftist political and labor organizations, some with contacts to the opposition in Germany.[19] But for all their consistent coverage and remarkable insights, the journalists' reporting did not coalesce into a coherent image of Nazism that could have been easily digested into a propagandistic enemy image when the time came.

Throughout the twelve years of the Third Reich's existence, American foreign correspondents and anti-Nazi activists bemoaned the persistent gap between their own reporting and the image of Nazi Germany as it emerged on the other side of the Atlantic. Skepticism and disbelief at home counteracted the impressive American journalistic coverage of the Third Reich, in particular at four critical junctures. First, at the beginning of the Nazi revolution there were sympathetic musings whether a strong leader or a dictatorship might not—in some cases—be a better alternative to failing democracies. With regard to stories about the persecution of political opponents (mainly on the left) and Jewish citizens, there were doubts whether things were really as bad as reported. Second, toward the end of the decade, as war broke out in Europe, the "great debate" on whether the United States should get involved in this war centrally involved the question of Nazi war aims. The claim that Hitler intended to attack the Western Hemisphere and was aiming for global hegemony struck many Americans as an unrealistic exaggeration by Roosevelt and his supporters.[20] Third, in 1942, as the systematic murder of European Jews was reported in newspapers and to the Western governments, officials and the interested public alike had difficulties grasping or believing the dimensions of German organized atrocities. As Thompson wrote before the 1938 November pogrom, "I suppose we keep our sanity these days partly at the cost of our sensibilities and certainly we tend to subdue our imaginations rather than to use them."[21] Finally, from 1943 on the question of German popular responsibility and complicity gained renewed significance in the context of Allied postwar plans and Germany's potential for democratic change.

This gap is in part attributable to the fact that the critical and perceptive coverage of the Third Reich in much of the daily print media competed in the public sphere with more sympathetic voices and was further blunted by indifference. Conservative critics of the Roosevelt administration were inclined to "come to terms" with Nazi Germany and saw the real totalitarian danger as emanating from within.[22] In response to alleged liberal exaggerations and warmongering, conservative commentators "normalized" Hitler's foreign policy by characterizing it as standard European power politics and presented the Third Reich as Western civilization's last bulwark against Bolshevism. Open admiration for the German people, their pleasant decency, and their energetic industriousness, often coupled with disparaging comparisons of their European neighbors, dominated in this alternative coverage of Nazi Germany in the 1930s, especially in popular conservative magazines like *Saturday Evening Post*. Commentators of different political persuasion argued that the German government was only trying to restore the country to its rightful place among the nations and that Versailles, and possibly Wilsonianism, had caused Hitler. Along those lines the popular historian William Durant offered a subtle analysis of the current (1938) world situation. While he—in contrast to others—did not sweep Nazi brutalities under the rug, he argued that "cowardly cruelty represents not the soul of Germany but a neurotic reacting against defeat, suffering and fear [of Bolshevism]" and that going to war would only produce "another Versailles, another decade of disorder, another Hitler." In a formulation that is especially disorienting to read from a post-Vietnam, post–Iraq war perspective, Durant maintained: "We shall preserve democracy, not by fighting battles abroad to force it upon peoples that show no eagerness or aptitude for it, but by making it function more successfully than dictatorship."[23] One can see how one of the noninterventionists' strongest argument against messianic-missionary-universalist crusades was seemingly forever discredited by having been used against Nazi Germany and why isolationism was so easily turned into a slanderous term.

Cultural-ethnic goodwill toward the enemy population posed a challenge to an effective mobilization campaign. It also clouded many Americans' understanding of the true nature of the Third Reich.[24] For the most part, Americans during the 1930s and 40s thought of Germans as people "like us." The simple linguistic distinction between Nazis and Germans served to exonerate the latter for reasons of ethnic solidarity, cultural affinity, religious familiarity, or liberal scruples. A month after Germany started World War II, 66 percent of Americans polled agreed with the statement that "the German people are essentially peace-loving and kindly, but they have been unfortunate in being misled too often by ruthless and ambitious rulers." Barely 20 percent (19.6) chose the opposite assessment that "the German people have always had an irrepressible fondness for brute force and conquest which makes the country a menace to world peace so long as it is allowed to be strong enough to fight."[25] Other surveys confirmed this picture: a large majority of Americans plainly distinguished between a basically decent, possibly victimized German people and its bad leaders. This people-versus-government distinction reflected both a long cherished liberal tenet of American democracy and also accommodated ethnic preferences.[26]

In opinion studies Germany continually came out near the top when Americans were asked which other country they regarded favorably or felt close to.[27] In 1942 a massive wartime survey showed 41 percent of Americans considered Germans "to be as good as we are in all important respects." An exasperated George Gallup commented that it seemed as if "German ideas of racial superiority find their counterpart in our own theories of racial and cultural superiority."[28] More pragmatically, the poet-turned-propagandist Archibald McLeish explained to his frustrated British counterparts who worried about the German-American element in U.S. electoral politics that "it would never be possible to secure [domestic] support for a racial war against the German people."[29] Stereotypes are often thought to convey negative distortions. In the case of the Germans, however, their generally positive appraisal as "clean," "industrious," "cultured," and in general "like us" put significant limits on what a large section of the American population was willing to believe about the German public's acquiescence to Nazi rule and German atrocities. They served to whitewash the Germans. The term seems appropriate because qualities like "efficiency," "ingenuity," "modern," and "progressive" appear in prominent places both in American political documents concerned with postwar planning and throughout wartime opinion surveys. They established the "whiteness" of the Germans and hence shielded the enemy population—to a considerable degree—against the accusation of acting in a "barbaric" manner—an accusation more widespread in Europe than in the United States.

To most Americans Germany originally did not pose a threat to their country; it had not attacked the United States, and later it committed "alleged" wartime atrocities in faraway places against other peoples. The most basic definition of an enemy requires the combination of a perception of difference with a sense of fear. This truism provides an important clue as to why American wartime images of Germany were so ambiguous—many Americans thought they knew and understood Germany. Only after the war did analysts, who had found in 1943 that 54 percent of combat soldiers felt that Germans are "just like us, it's too bad we have to be fighting them," wonder: "If hatred of the enemy was a help in fighting the Japanese, [this number] raises the question as to whether identification with the enemy may not have been, on the other hand, a liability requiring counteraction in fighting the Germans."[30]

The impact of this lingering goodwill was reinforced by other trends in American public opinion. Those included apart from the partisan opposition to any policies by "that man in the White House," the liberal faith that people are inherently peaceful and democratic, and the disillusionment with military intervention in Europe. The widespread reluctance across the political spectrum to go to war again in Europe, the religiously as well as politically grounded commitment to pacifism during this interwar period, should not be dismissed in hindsight as naiveté and isolationism. In 1937, 70 percent of Americans considered entry into World War I a mistake.[31] This did not necessarily indicate indifference to events in Nazi Germany. Surveys also revealed that both the Czech crisis (Munich Confer-

ence) in 1938 and the November pogrom against German Jews of the same
year dominated ordinary Americans' perceptions of international events.
By 1939 a growing number of Americans had recognized the criminal nature of the German regime and condemned its policies—but they had not
yet been convinced that turning their citizens once more into soldiers and
sending them abroad was going to fix the "German problem."[32]

Contemporaries recognized that World War II involved stark ideological contrasts that had preoccupied intellectuals and increasingly a wider
public since the 1920s.[33] But President Roosevelt consistently deflected attempts to define the war in ideological terms—concerned that this would
only sharpen domestic divisions rather than uniting the nation behind the
war effort. As late as 1942 confidential opinion surveys identified a sizable
minority of 30 to 40 percent of Americans as holding views detrimental
to the war effort: anti-Semitic, anti-Communist, distrustful of the government or of the Allies—and ready to make peace with Nazi Germany.[34] In
spite of the president's "Germany first" strategy, fighting morale regarding the Germans remained low compared to the readiness to take on the
Pacific enemy, and government officials worried about opinion trends that
favored a negotiated peace with Germany, saw that country as a bulwark
against communism and would have preferred to transform the war into
a campaign against the Soviet ally.[35] More than half of the people in wartime surveys admitted they did not have a clear idea of what the war was
about.[36] The Army, which conducted its own systematic studies confirmed
those findings and reported that "the usual term by which disapproval of
idealistic exhortation was invoked was 'bullshit.'"[37]

The meaning of the war against Nazi Germany thus remained contested. Government officials eschewed an ideological mobilization campaign of the kind the country had seen a generation earlier. Wary of public
opinion, the president rejected the use of the leftist term "people's war"
and favored instead "survival war," trying to instill a sense of urgency to a
vague popular mood that "we had to fight because we had been attacked."
Generally, Roosevelt has been admired for his ability to translate daring
political initiatives into everyday, familiar terms. Accordingly, the Office of War Information (OWI), America's propaganda agency from 1942
on, used his speeches as a blueprint to design a campaign educating the
American people as to the "why we fight" and "the nature of the enemy."
Following the president's lead, they sidestepped political and ideological
controversies. Information officials recognized and deplored the correla-
tion between a widespread skepticism regarding war aims and a vague,
often misconceived popular image of the German enemy.

To the extent to which the OWI from 1942 on attempted to create an
ideological enemy image by defining fascism as the opposite of liberal,

pluralist democracy, it was softened by skirting over the role that German society played in the launching and maintenance of this regime. The enemy was an ideology, not a people. The OWI accommodated rather than challenged popular opinion as it was recorded in surveys: a majority of Americans continued to distinguish between Nazi leaders and the German people. Consequently, the latter emerged in OWI guidelines and output as the first victim of the Nazi enslavement of Europe.[38]

Two further aspects of the government's main civilian propaganda office deserve mention. In its very conception it was designed as a countermodel to both the Creel Committee and the type of intense and pervasive state propaganda associated with the Soviet Union and Nazi Germany. It followed instead "a strategy of truth" that the foreign correspondents and other anti-Nazi commentators had inaugurated in the 1930s.[39] The "truth" strategy was combined with another approach likewise pioneered by the journalists: "let the Nazis speak for themselves." The most prominent example for the success of this dual strategy was the OWI's handling of the German destruction of the Czech town Lidice in 1942.

But this also meant that, in line with its rejection of World War I–style propaganda, the OWI decided against the use of atrocity stories: it did not use for propaganda purposes evidence of the genocide that lay at the center of the Nazi project, the one dimension that together with the war of annihilation in the East would have brought the nature of the enemy into clear focus. Incoming information regarding the Holocaust was partly misunderstood, partly ignored, and often treated as an irritant, a potential disruption of a mobilization scheme that targeted a mainstream America that opinion polls found to be largely indifferent to the fate of Central and Eastern European Jews and refugees.[40] Political concern over domestic anti-Semitism, moreover, led U.S. government officials to misrepresent the German persecution and murder of Jews as part of two different stories. First, continuing a practice that originated with private groups in the 1930s, the government portrayed the German campaign against the Jews as part of a larger Nazi project of discrimination against all religious groups.[41] Second, OWI policy guidelines stipulated that war crimes against European Jews be folded into the Nazis' oppressive policies toward everyone, including the German people, because "open atrocities directed against … the Jews cover up the normal daily terror of National Socialism for an entire strata of the German population."[42] Here the OWI officials—against their better judgment—seemed to have been guided by public opinion polls that told them that more Americans identified with "ordinary Germans" than with Eastern European Jews.

Soon the challenge of an adequate information policy became entangled with the question of what to do about the genocide that became official and public knowledge by late 1942. Many scholars have rightly criticized parts of the British and U.S. governments for inaction, callousness, and obstruction. Yet, it is also important to remember that neither military strategies nor public calls for humanitarian interventions were a common feature at the time. Thus underlying at least some of the inaction was helplessness as summarized in a *Council on Foreign Relations* study that concluded that it was "hard to know what to do in the face of the destruction of the Jews."[43] The scholars Shlomo Aronson and Richard Breitman, moreover, have shown how very limited—and by German design: tragically perverse—rescue opportunities were.[44]

In sharp contrast to the widespread notion of the Germans as the first victims of the Nazis, a powerful counterargument emerged within the American public debate that postulated a historical trend in German militaristic aggressive behavior and laid the blame for the Third Reich squarely at the feet of the German people. This approach to the Third Reich was—pejoratively—labeled "Vansittartist" after the high-ranking British diplomat Robert Lord Vansittart.[45] The proponents of this interpretation of the Third Reich, a diverse group of influential commentators and politicians, rejected the notion of a dichotomy between Nazi leaders and an innocent captured German people as their first victims; instead they recognized much popular support for Nazi foreign policy aims, racial views, and excessive nationalism. The Vansittartists also had serious reservations about the notion of "the other Germany," that of a cultured, liberal, democratic Germany. They did not deny the existence of such Germans, but they doubted their efficacy.

Much of their depiction of Nazi Germany drew on the preexisting World War I enemy image of Imperial Germany. George F. Kennan, for example, expressed alarm at President Roosevelt's seeming inability, widely shared, Kennan feared, to grasp the essential difference between the Germany of Kaiser Wilhelm and that of Hitler. But a closer reading of both Roosevelt's statements and the Vansittartists' output reveals a very different picture: shocked by unprecedented brutality and contempt for the liberal and enlightenment principles of Western civilization, the Vansittartists emphasized how deeply embedded Nazism was in German political culture by linking it to older German traditions and previous policies. In this context, as one of their most important propaganda tools, the Vansittartists seized on the pre-Nazi German self-proclaimed myth of a special path, which originally had been positively connoted, and argued that there were indeed long and deep roots of a German cult of superiority. Journalists like Mowrer and Shirer had shaped this understanding since the 1930s; the Society for the Prevention of World War III promoted this interpretation most effectively toward the end of the war. President Roosevelt, who had recommended Vansittart's book *Black Record* to his psychological warfare coordinator, Bill Donovan—privately—shared in particular the notion that the German people were deeply implicated in the crimes of the Nazi regime.[46]

In much of the historiography the Vansittartist position has been misrepresented and maligned as an unfortunate, exaggerated enemy image promoting collective guilt of the German people and fueled by hatred and vengeance. Yet in its descriptive parts, minus some of the wartime hyperbole, this interpretation of the Third Reich was much closer to reality than the OWI propaganda and other exculpatory lines of argument such as that Hitler just sought what had been denied to the Germans a generation earlier. Rather than promoting collective guilt, the Vansittartists kept the focus on German actions, on mass murder, torture, and humiliation, on genocidal warfare and racial war aims. They argued that the Third Reich should be judged by its objectives as well as its policies and they pragmatically insisted that German society was too deeply implicated in this system to be usefully separated from the Nazis. Both through active participation but also through silent acquiescence Germans had shattered a fundamental bond of human solidarity. It is true that at times strong emotions were voiced in the Vansittartist camp, but it is difficult to imagine how this could not have been the case for people who opened their eyes to the reality of the Third Reich.

As the Vansittartists saw in Nazism only the latest manifestation of a century-old German will to conquer and subjugate, their interpretation was best suited for a cogent enemy image and was thus employed in much of the military propaganda output, like the *Why We Fight* series, directed by Frank Capra and the *Soldier's Pocket Guide to Germany*. With the decline of the OWI's domestic branch in 1943, the War Department's information campaigns came to the fore and thus helped promote the Vansittartist interpretation. Two of the most powerful American wartime propaganda films about Nazi Germany, *Here is Germany* and *Your Job in Germany* (both 1945), at the same time exemplify the Vansittartist interpretation but also reveal how positive stereotypes of the German people prevailed through the very end. In spite of its appeal as an enemy image, the Vansittartist presentation of the Third Reich remained contested and was even sharply criticized all throughout 1944.

As many Americans, including political experts and public intellectuals, were not ready to recognize the Germans of the Third Reich as the other, the Vansittartist argument evoked angry counterarguments. In magazines, radio shows, roundtables, and government offices, the "special path" interpretation of German history was passionately challenged. The most severe and frequent charge leveled against the Vansittartists was the claim that their presentation amounted to "an inverted form of Hitler's racial theories;" that the Vansittartists talked "about the Germans in almost the same fashion that Nazis talk about Jews."[47] This self-critical concern with behaving differently than the enemy was pervasive in public and official pronouncements.

The American debate over Vansittartism also yielded some of the earliest instances of comparing domestic political opponents to Nazis, here less out of concern about not acting like the enemy and rather with the intention to vilify. One of the more extreme and disturbing analogies were Republican attacks on Secretary of the Treasury Henry Morgenthau, Jr., the one cabinet member who took the incoming information on the genocide seriously and devised rescue plans. Like President Roosevelt, Morgenthau indeed embraced an interpretation of the Third Reich that recognized German culturally reinforced racism and militarism as one of the greatest challenges to a peaceful Europe. His colleague, Secretary of War Henry L. Stimson, characterized the treasury department's postwar plans for defeated Germany as "just such a crime as the Germans themselves hoped to perpetrate upon their victims … a crime against civilization itself." Others compared Morgenthau to Heinrich Himmler, the coordinator of the Holocaust, and the treasury plans to German policies of mass murder and extermination.[48] Two dimensions of these slanderous accusations are worth emphasizing: their authors apparently did not fully understand the ideology and policies of the Third Reich and their empathy went, for whatever reason, to the Germans rather than the Germans' victims.

The same feature that made the Vansittartist model so suitable for propaganda use also marked its limitations: it contained the monsters in time and space. The problem was—only—Germany. In the meantime others explored a different framework of meaning; for them the German problem had wider implications. These commentators shared with the Vansittartists an early anti-Nazi, pro-interventionist stance, but they also pondered the question what it all meant for "our civilization" beyond the necessary military defeat of Nazi Germany. The left-liberal writer and social critic Dwight Macdonald is representative of these voices in recognizing that as a consequence of the German actions, everyone now lived in a different world than before. He saw in the Third Reich evidence for a horrible transformation he believed to be characteristic of modern society in general.[49] Already in the prewar period popular American writers like the novelist Thomas Wolfe or Thompson's husband Sinclair Lewis had characterized Nazi Germany as "a terrible part of the universal heritage of man," as a perversion of modern Western politics "that could happen here," too.[50] During the war, when supposedly everything was geared toward stark contrasts between them and us, critical self-reflections on

American democracy, racism, military power, and responsibility continued to be an integral part of the political discourse on the German enemy.[51]

This group could be called the "humanist universalists" — in contradis-
tinction to those who emphasized "German peculiarities." Here a no less
clear-sighted understanding of the Third Reich invited probing analyses
of the implications of German crimes for democratic culture, mass society,
the modern state, and the modern state's military, in general; the threat
was not only external. And evil was not only to be destroyed militarily.
These contemporary analyses focused on perversions but also inherent
dangers of modern mass politics, techniques of propaganda, the connection between bureaucracy and the loss of individual responsibility. Public
intellectuals, sociologists, psychologists, and political scientists, many of
them Central European Jewish refugees, took up the question of what Nazism meant for democracy.[52] The theologian Reinhold Niebuhr discussed
the implications of the necessary military intervention against Nazi Germany for American foreign policy.[53] Throughout the war, Niebuhr warned
against the "God is on our side" attitude and the fallacy of confusing military strength with morality: "[self-righteousness] does not understand
that the evil against which we contend is only a different, and probably
a more extravagant form of the evil which is in our soul also." The challenge for people like him was that "Yesterday we had to stand against
the sentimentalists who declared that we had no right to resist Nazi tyranny because we were also guilty. Today we must resist the Pharisees who
imagine that our impending victory is the proof and the validation of our
virtue."[54] The humanist universalists were walking a tight line throughout
this war.

In this camp one group of individuals stands out for their particular
courage and high-mindedness: German-Jewish refugees, many of whom
joined the Allied war effort in civilian or military roles. This small but
in terms of their impact significant group stood at the center of the German-American confrontation and reveals the deeply personal entanglement, sometimes in heart-wrenching, close encounters; for example, when
young Jewish men, now in U.S. military uniforms, returned in 1944 to a
Germany still committed to the complete annihilation of all Jews. In their
emotional responses to the Third Reich many of the émigrés wrestled
with fear, hatred, and a desire for retribution. Yet in their actual behavior
and public writings they embodied a profoundly humanist tradition that
several of them attributed to their deep-seated commitment to the New
Deal ethos in which the war was fought.[55] Such statements seem, however,
rather a testimony to the fact that the Roosevelt administration had managed to capture liberal-humanitarian principles in much of their wartime
propaganda.[56] The German-Jewish refugee Toni Sender, a politically en-

gaged pacifist and Socialist who by 1939 advocated American entry into the war and later worked for the Roosevelt administration, had few illusions about Germany, yet argued in 1942 that if Germany was regarded as a "hopeless case" characterized by "innate barbarism," the Western world, the democracies, would have no solution for it. "Democracy is based on faith in the common man, while Fascism believes in the permanent inequality of individuals and nations. This is the choice which is before every one of us and you cannot be in both camps at the same time."[57] Like other "universalists," Sender argued forcefully that Germany would have to be defeated militarily, but that in order to win the peace the principles of a liberal democratic culture had to be articulated and implemented.

What is presented here as two distinct strands was much more intertwined in the reality of the American wartime debate. Both the Vansittartist and the universalist position were well represented in and outside the government. In the wider public debate, popular metaphors such as Nazism as a form of political gangsterism, as a conspiracy, or as a disease, or the notion of a German dual character captured in the Jekyll-Hyde image, integrated these contrasting strands.[58] Nevertheless, in several instances the wartime debate on Nazi Germany turned intensely personal, for example, at the cabinet level, between Stimson and Morgenthau in 1944, and earlier in 1942, between the journalists and friends Mowrer and Thompson. Mowrer scolded his colleague for keeping the discussion focused too much on the Germans. He argued instead that American policy should aid the people whom the Germans treated "as never civilized peoples have been treated before." "Not the Nazis, Dorothy, the Germans … People like you … are to some extent shifting the sympathy of this country from Germany's victims to Germany."[59]

Yet the positive results of these occasionally acrimonious wartime debates about Germany and American policies deserve to be highlighted. Indeed, their significance is brought out by a comparison with the subsequent mobilization campaign conducted by FDR's successor against a new threat, the Soviet Union. Historian John Fousek concluded that "the lack of fundamental debate about the nature and purposes of U.S. foreign policy after 1950 contributed to … an increasingly militarized foreign policy controlled by narrow ideological blinders that obscured fundamental international realities."[60] Similarly, many commentators have deplored the absence of any meaningful debate and contestation either within the government or among the wider public in the run-up to the U.S. invasion of Iraq in 2003.[61] By contrast the much-criticized éclat in Roosevelt's cabinet between his secretaries of war and treasury, which involved several other departments and agencies with fundamentally different policy analyses and recommendations, should be viewed more positively in its consequences. Morgenthau's insistence on demilitarization and considerable deindustrialization arose from a generally understood need to restructure Germany's very socioeconomic foundations in order to protect its neighbors and victims. Stimson's resolve to implement a program of preserving a capitalist, industrialized Germany and integrating it into a European and transatlantic framework was supported by much of the planning emanating from the State Department and other foreign policy authorities.

The fact that the disagreement about means (toward the same end) became public in 1944 helped to focus attention once more on Germany and forced officials to articulate more clearly what was at stake. The records reveal that all sides in this debate had their blind spots: Stimson and many of his colleagues from the State Department did not seem to be much disturbed by the German campaigns of annihilation; Morgenthau and his supporters, on the other hand, were not overly interested in the question of how much liberal and anti-Nazi potential there was in Germany that could serve a new beginning. The controversy brought into full daylight different interpretations and policy plans that had been in preparation for years. It resulted in a compromise worked out over the next three years reaching from the war crimes tribunals and the occupation program of the four "D"s (demilitarization, denazification, decartelization, and democratization) to the Marshall Plan. This combination of punitive restructuring and restorative rehabilitation turned out to be a success and set the stage for West Germany's internal liberalization and democratization process over the next two decades.[62]

Beyond the aggravation apparent in the Stimson-Morgenthau éclat, and in other similar clashes, the participants shared an understanding of contingency, of the inherent dilemma of imposing democracy, of the conflict between military means and political ends, between outside intervention and need for internal reform. At the highest level, the president, like many experts on the German question, believed that the depth of the political and moral catastrophe the Germans had brought about was beyond the power of American foreign policy to solve.

More generally, a consensus prevailed among Roosevelt's supporters that "you cannot kill an idea by killing the person who holds it" and that "the defeat of the enemy is not peace."[63] Political approaches would take precedence over purely military solutions. Only in the midst of German victories in 1940 did Dorothy Thompson come to the conclusion: "There seems to be no way of opposing the Supermen- by-virtue-of-steel, except to prove that the rest of us who detest the whole business will nevertheless and against our reason, tastes, and intelligence, defeat them at their own game."[64] What changed over the course of the next sixty years is that successive generations of Americans became accustomed to their country assuming the burdens of globalism and being at war. By the early twenty-first century the "whole business" of war was no longer so detestable or regarded to be in opposition to American "reason, tastes, and intelligence."[65]

The liberal interventionists' insistence that the United States had to respond to Hitler's empire with a better vision for the postwar world was realized. The American debate on Nazism informed the wartime planning for a new multilateral, cooperative international order, including an expanded and strengthened human rights agenda and government support for economic recovery and relief as a means of encouraging democratic habits. 1945 marked an internationalist and multilateralist moment in American consciousness. Calls for American leadership in setting up organizations and standards for the promotion of human rights and peaceful cooperation tapped into a newly accepted sense of the nation's international responsibility and, equally importantly, its citizens' newly gained cosmopolitan outlook.[66] Yet this triumph of internationalism also paved the way for an increasing militarization of American foreign policy in subsequent decades. An activist internationalism and a heavy reliance on military strength became defining aspects of "who we are" as Americans. As John Bodnar finds in his study of the American public memory of World War II, "the land of the free increasingly became known as the home of the brave; acts of killing and dying were transformed into heroic deeds and cherished memories."[67]

The transfer of enemy characteristics from Nazi Germany onto the other totalitarian power proved crucial in this regard. Historian Abbot Gleason describes the emotive-political importance of the concept of totalitarianism as "channel[ing] the anti-Nazi energy of the wartime period into the postwar struggle with the Soviet Union."[68] Within months after the end of World War II, formulations that had been used to describe Nazi rule and ideology were applied to the Soviet Union in internal memoranda as well as public proclamations. This time, used to describe the ideology, the master plan, and the world conquest intentions of the Soviet Union, they turned out to be more compelling and less contested than they had been as a propaganda blueprint characterizing the Third Reich. The domestic political divisions that had plagued the wartime mobilization effort—but had invigorated and deepened the national debate on Nazism and America's role in the world—were now submerged in a new sense of national purpose derived from a confrontation with a more readily recognizable enemy, Bolshevist Russia and world communism. It was anti-communism that—in conjunction with an extraordinarily propitious American situation, in terms of economic and military power—shaped the central lessons Americans drew from World War II. Among them, the Munich lesson that postulated that aggression unchecked leads to general war was the most problematic, but also the most enduring.

Notes

1. Nazis, and more recently Nazi zombies, appear in popular TV shows, tabloids, movies, books, and computer games. Gavriel D. Rosenfeld, *The World that Hitler Never Made: Alternate History and the Memory of Nazism* (New York: Cambridge, 2005).
2. The two functions—internal analysis and public legitimation—in fact overlap. Yuen Foong Khong, *Analogies at War: Korea, Munich, Dien Bien Phu, and the Vietnam Decisions of 1965* (Princeton: Princeton University Press, 1992).
3. Joseph M. Siracusa, "The Munich Analogy," in Alexander DeConde, Richard Dean Burns and Fredrick Logevall, eds., *Encyclopedia of American Foreign Policy* (New York: Scribner, 2002): 2, 443–54.
4. Alan E. Steinweis, "The Auschwitz Analogy: Holocaust Memory and American Debates over Intervention in Bosnia and Kosovo in the 1990s," *Holocaust and Genocide Studies* 19 (Fall 2005): 276–89; Alan E. Steinweis, "The Holocaust and American Culture: An Assessment of Recent Scholarship," *Holocaust and Genocide Studies* 15 (Fall 2001): 296–310.
5. George Packer, *The Assassin's Gate: America in Iraq* (New York: Farrar, Strauss and Giroux, 2005), 47–50; Norman Podhoretz, *World War IV: The Long Struggle Against Islamofascism* (New York: Doubleday, 2007).
6. Mark Stoler, "The Second World War in U.S. History and Memory," *Diplomatic History* 25 (Summer 2001): 383.
7. Kenneth Boulding, "National Images and International Systems," *Journal of Conflict Resolution* 3 (1959): 130.
8. Brian C. Etheridge, "The Desert Fox, Memory Diplomacy, and the German Question in Early Cold War America," *Diplomatic History* 32 (April 2008): 207–38; John Bodnar, *The "Good War" in American Memory* (Baltimore: Johns Hopkins University Press, 2010).
9. Robert D. Schulzinger, "Memory and Understanding U.S. Foreign Relations," *Explaining the History of American Foreign Relations*, ed. Michael J. Hogan and Thomas G. Paterson (New York: Cambridge University Press, 2004), 336–52.
10. See Michaela Hoenicke Moore, *Know Your Enemy: The American Debate on Nazism, 1933-1945* (New York: Cambridge University Press, 2010).
11. Steven Casey, *A Cautious Crusade: Franklin D. Roosevelt, American Public Opinion, and the War Against Nazi Germany* (Oxford: Oxford University Press, 2001).
12. H.M. Kallen, "What Shall We Do with Germany?" *Saturday Review of Literature* 26, 28 May 1943, 4.
13. Pierre Van Paassen, ed. *Nazism: An Assault on Civilization* (New York: Harrison Smith And Robert Haas, 1934).
14. For internal debates and differences between civilian and military propaganda on the issue of hatred of the enemy, see Hoenicke Moore, *Know Your Enemy*, 139, 157.
15. John Horne and Alan Kramer, *German Atrocities, 1914: A History of Denial* (New Haven: Yale University Press, 2001); Deborah Lipstadt, *Beyond Belief: The American Press and the Coming of the Holocaust, 1933-45* (New York: Free Press, 1986).

16. William L Shirer, *Berlin Diary: The Journal of a Foreign Correspondent, 1934-1941* (New York: Knopf, 1941), 84. Edgar A. Mowrer, *Germany Puts the Clock Back* (New York: William Morrow & Co., 1933).

17. John Gunther, *Inside Europe* (New York: Harper and Brothers, 1937).

18. "Dorothy Thompson to Tom Lamont, October 1, 1941," Box 1, Series II, *Thompson Papers*, George Arents Research Library, Syracuse University.

19. From March 1933 on cities like New York became centers of anti-Nazi protests, boycotts, and mass demonstrations. The following year a mock trial was held in Madison Square Garden by religious, political, and labor union leaders convicting the German government of crimes against civilization. The Third Reich continued to provoke horror and outrage among Americans, reaching a climax in 1938 with Hitler's demands on Czechoslovakia and the violent November pogrom and first deportations.

20. Hoenicke Moore, *Know Your Enemy*, 96–101.

21. Peter Kurth, *American Cassandra: The Life of Dorothy Thompson* (Boston: Little, Brown, 1990), 276.

22. Abbott Gleason, *Totalitarianism: The Inner History of the Cold War* (New York: Oxford University Press, 1995), 53.

23. Will Durant, "No Hymns of Hatred," *SEP*, 4 June 1938, 23, 48, 51. In general, the more sympathetic portraits of the Third Reich found credence among those who had heard good things about the new Germany from returning American travelers, businessmen, clergy, students, friends, or family members.

24. This sentiment of closeness had its roots in a generally positive appreciation of the large number of German-American communities in the United States. In mid century, Americans of German descent self-identified as the second largest ethnic group in the United States. See *Harvard Encyclopedia of American Ethnic Groups*, ed. Stephan Thernstrom (Cambridge, MA: Harvard University Press, 1980), 405. See also, Ruth Miller Elson, "Deutschland und die Deutschen in amerikanischen Schulbüchern des 19. Jahrhunderts," *Internationales Jahrbuch fuer Geschichtsunterricht* 7 (1959/60), 51–57.

25. George Gallup, *The Gallup Poll: Public Opinion, 1935-71* (New York: Random House, 1972), 1, 500.

26. "Gallup and Fortune Polls," *Public Opinion Quarterly* 4 (March 1940), 94, 96, 99.

27. Thomas A. Baily, *The Man in the Street: The Impact of American Public Opinion on Foreign Policy* (New York: Macmillan, 1948), 224; Quincy Wright, *A Study of War* (Chicago: University of Chicago Press, 1942), 1241–60.

28. While Canadians, English, Dutch, Scandinavians, and Irish were ranked above the Germans, Germany's main victims—Jews, Poles, Russians, Greeks, and others—attracted considerably lower empathy. George Gallup, "An Analysis of American Public Opinion Regarding the War," 10 September 1942, President's Personal File 4721, *FDR-Papers*, FDR-Library, Hyde Park, New York.

29. Minutes of the 5th meeting, Joint Committee on Information Policy, 10 September 1942, Box 5, Entry 1, RG 208, Federal Record Center (FRC).

30. Samuel A. Stouffer et al., *The American Soldier* (Princeton: Princeton University Press), 2, 161. For more detailed analyses of changing attitudes among American combat soldiers toward the (German) enemy, see Gerald F. Linderman, *The World within War: America's Combat Experience in World War II* (New York: Free Press, 1997), 90–142; Peter Schrijvers, *The Crash of Ruin: American Combat Soldiers in Europe during World War II* (New York: New York University Press, 1998).

31. Gallup, *Poll*, 65, 137.

32. Ibid., 112, 121, 131, 179.

33. Benjamin Leontief Alpers, *Dictators, Democracy and American Public Culture: Envisioning the Totalitarian Enemy, 1920s-1950s* (Chapel Hill: University of North Carolina Press, 2003).

34. Hoenicke Moore, *Know Your Enemy*, 110–12.
35. With notable frustration, one contemporary analyst observed that "our war aims as stated in the Atlantic Charter and the Four Freedoms were undoubtedly intended for world consumption—they have not registered a very deep imprint at home." "War Aims and Postwar Policies," April 17, 1942, Box 1849, Entry 171, RG 44, FRC; "What People Think About Peace and the Role of the U.S. in the Post-War World," 14 February 1942, Official Files 788; "An analysis of American Public Opinion," Intelligence Report No 45, 16 October 1942, Box 156, President's Secretary File, OWI, FDR-P, FDR-L.
36. "Do you know what you're fighting," *Colliers* 11 December 1943.
37. The "main reason" soldiers cited for fighting this war was "that we *had* to because we were attacked." Those who wallowed in "idealistic values and patriotism" were seen as "hypocritical." Equally troublesome to the government must have been the admission by over 40 percent of the troops to feel "very often" (11 percent) or "sometimes" (32 percent) that "this war is not worth fighting." *American Soldier* 2, 151–53.
38. Michaela Hönicke, "'Know Your Enemy': American Wartime Images of Germany, 1942/43," *Enemy Images in American History*, ed. Ragnhild Fiebig-von Hase and Ursula Lehmkuhl (Providence, RI: Berghahn, 1997), 231–78.
39. As the novelist Thomas Wolfe, a frequent traveler to Germany, insisted in 1938 "about Hitler's Germany … one must be very true … you could not meet lies and trickery with lies and trickery." Thomas Wolfe, *You Can't Go Home Again* (Garden City: Sun Dial Press, 1942), 632.
40. Hoenicke Moore, *Know Your Enemy*, 72, 153.
41. Journalists like Dorothy Thompson and Jewish groups like the Non-Sectarian-Anti-Nazi League had opted for a twofold deliberate strategy of appealing to mainstream Christian Americans by claiming that Nazi persecution of Jews was only part of a larger strategy of abolishing all religion and by camouflaging Jewish leadership in American anti-Nazi groups. Ibid., 57.
42. OWI Radio Background Material, Subject: Our Enemies: The Nazis, January 12, 1943, Philleo Nash Papers, Harry S Truman Library, Independence, Missouri.
43. Robert D. Schulzinger, *The Wise Men of Foreign Affairs: The History of the Council on Foreign Relations* (New York: Columbia University Press, 1984), 102.
44. Shlomo Aronson, *Hitler, the Allies, and the Jews* (New York: Cambridge University Press, 2004); Richard Breitman, *Official Secrets. What the Nazis Planned, What the British and Americans Knew* (New York: Hill & Wang, 1998).
45. Jörg Später, *Vansittart. Britische Debatten über Deutsche und Nazis, 1902-1945* (Göttingen: Wallstein, 2003); Lord Vansittart, *Lessons of My Life* (London: Hutchinson, 1943).
46. Hoenicke Moore, *Know Your Enemy*, 116, 256.
47. Malcolm Cowly, "Vansittartism," *The New Republic*, 25 October 1943, 586.
48. Henry L. Stimson, "Memorandum for the President, September 15, 1944," Stimson Diary [mf], Yale University Library, Reel 9, vol. 48, 84. The Morgenthau-Himmler analogy—which disturbingly echoes real Nazi propaganda—was made by Republican Senator from Indiana Homer Capehart. See Bernd Greiner, *Die Morgenthau Legende: Zur Geschichte eines umstrittenen Plans* (Hamburg: Hamburger Edition, 1995).
49. Dwight Macdonald, "The Responsibility of the Peoples," *Politics* (March and April 1945); Dwight Macdonald, The Responsibility of the Peoples (London: Victor Gollancz, 1957), 31.
50. Wolfe, *You Can't Go Home Again*, 705. The second reference is the argument of Sinclair Lewis's 1935 play with the opposite title *It Can't Happen Here*; the "universalist" interpretations seeking to place Nazism in a wider context were at the time often advanced by journalists, refugees, and intellectuals with either personal ties or intellectual affinities to Germany. Their critics were quick to point out that some of their analyses did have the (unintended) effect of exculpating the Germans.

51. While the "Vansittartists" laid the foundation for the Sonderweg thesis, the "special path" paradigm of German historiography, these alternative contemporary interpretations of the Third Reich were likewise built upon by subsequent scholarship explaining Nazism and the Holocaust in the context of modernity, Western or European history, without obfuscating the fact that it had happened in Germany. See, Zygmunt Bauman, *Modernity and the Holocaust* (Ithaca, NY: Cornell University Press, 1989); Mark Mazower, *Dark Continent: Europe's Twentieth Century* (New York: Vintage Books, 2000).

52. Martin Jay, *The Dialectic Imagination. A History of the Frankfurt School and the Institute of Social Research, 1923-1950* (Berkeley: University of California Press, 1996), 143–72; Thomas Wheatland, *The Frankfurt School in Exile* (Minneapolis: University of Minnesota, 2009), 227–63.

53. Reinhold Niebuhr, "White Man's Burden," *Christianity and Society* 6, no. 3 (Summer 1941): 3.

54. Reinhold Niebuhr, "The German Problem," *Christianity and Crisis* 3, no. 4 (1 October 1944): 2–4.

55. Hoenicke Moore, *Know Your Enemy*, 330–35; Alfons Söllner, *Zur Archäologie der Demokratie in Deutschland. Analysen von politischen Emigranten im amerikanischen Staatsdienst 1943-1949* (Frankfurt: Fischer, 1986); Petra Marquardt-Bigman, *Amerikanische Geheimdienstanalysen über Deutschland, 1942-1949* (Munich: Oldenbourg, 1995).

56. Bodnar, *The "Good War,"* 11.

57. Toni Sender, "Is Germany a Hopeless Case?," *Jewish Frontier* 9 (August 1942), 19.

58. Hoenicke Moore, *Know Your Enemy*, chapters 7, 8, and 9.

59. Ibid., 190–92, 315–18.

60. John Fousek, *To Lead the Free World: American Nationalism and the Cultural Roots of the Cold War* (Chapel Hill: University of North Carolina Press, 2000), 190.

61. Thomas Powers, "Whose Failure," *New York Times Book Review*, 2 October 2011.

62. Michaela Hönicke, "Prevent World War III: A Historiographical Appraisal of Morgenthau's Program for Germany," *The United States in Depression and War*, ed. Robert A. Garson and Stuart S. Kidd (Edinburgh: Edinburgh University Press, 1999), 155–72; Hoenicke Moore, *Know Your Enemy*, 271–92 and 345.

63. "Attachment (Stanley P. Lovell) to note by Basil O'Connor to FDR, May 31, 1941," PPF 1820, Box 5 1941, FDR-P, FDR-L; Dorothy Thompson, "Germany Must Be Salvaged," *The American Mercury* 56 (June 1943): 662.

64. Dorothy Thompson, "The Nazis [ms.], no date [1940]," Box 5, Series VII, DT Papers.

65. Andrew Bacevich, *The New American Militarism: How Americans Are Seduced by War* (New York: Oxford University Press, 2005); Michael Sherry, *In the Shadow of War: The United States since the 1930s* (New Haven: Yale University Press, 1995); Marilyn Young, "Presidential Address: 'I was thinking, as I often do these days, of war': The United States in the Twenty-First Century" *Diplomatic History* 36 (January 2012): 1–15; Mary Dudziak, *War Time: An Idea, Its History and Consequences* (New York: Oxford University Press, 2012); George Kateb, "Democracy and Untruth" *Raritan* 31 (Winter 2012), 60–88.

66. Elizabeth Borgwardt, *A New Deal for the World: America's Vision for Human Rights* (Cambridge, MA: Belknap Press of Harvard University, 2005); G. John Ikenberry, *After Victory: Institutions, Strategic Restraint and the Rebuilding of International Order after Major Wars* (Princeton: Princeton University Press, 2000), 164–214.

67. Bodnar, *The "Good War,"* 8.

68. Gleason, *Totalitarianism*, 3. See also, Les K. Adler and Thomas G. Paterson, "Red Fascism: The Merger of Nazi Germany and Soviet Russia in the American Image of Totalitarianism, 1930s-1950s," *American Historical Review* (April 1970): 1046–64.

Chapter 8

How Eleanor Roosevelt's Orientalism Othered the Palestinians

Geraldine Kidd

Eleanor Roosevelt described it as one of her most impressive experiences when, in May 1949, she watched as the blue and white flag of Israel was raised to join the array at the United Nations headquarters at Lake Success, New York.[1] The announcement of the creation of the state of Israel by Prime Minister David Ben-Gurion on 14 May 1948 had marked the formal partition of Palestinian territory. Its bifurcation meant the achievement of a pair of Eleanor Roosevelt's passionately held goals: the fulfillment of the fifty-year-old Zionist ambition, and the realization of an important UN milestone.

It also reflected the workings of a complexity of binary forces within her personally. As a celebrated humanitarian she had been elected to chair the UN's Human Rights Commission; however, by supporting the Zionist cause, she had helped to undermine the human rights of the scattered Palestinians. While advocating democracy and self-determination, she had ignored their majority rights. She appeared oblivious to the fact that by working to relieve the displaced Jews in Europe, by effecting the conditions for their passage to the new state, she had been an agent in the creation of a far greater displacement. The indigenous population of eight hundred thousand Palestinians became refugees for decades.[2] Because she perceived Israelis and Palestinians differently, this latter displacement did not evoke in her the same concern as that which she had expressed for the remnants of Hitler's Jewish victims. Unwittingly, by appropriating their cause she "encompassed" them and through this act she necessarily "othered" the Palestinians.[3]

The circumstances of Eleanor Roosevelt's reactions and interactions caused her to treat the Palestinians as inferior others, a result of her formative influences that encouraged her pro-Zionist slant. By demonstrating her access to power it is possible to uncover the types of pressures she attempted to exert in order to achieve her desired end. While her views were widely shared within mid-1940s U.S. discourse, there were also voices of dissent among her peers that revealed disharmony, but that she occluded through various justifications. When the concerns of the opposition, who predicted that unjust and enforced partition would cause catastrophe in Palestine, proved prescient, even in light of the hundreds and thousands of new Palestinian refugees, Eleanor Roosevelt remained true to her earliest convictions for the Zionist cause and exposed a blind spot that was dichotomous with her humanitarian reputation and with much of what she advocated as the necessary conditions for world peace.

Through her personal and political development Eleanor Roosevelt had formulated a clear anti-racist agenda as she fought against the discrimination of the African-Americans. From an early stage in her career she had shed the anti-Semitism that was rife within her patrician class.[4] She considered it a proud trait of her character that prompted her to intuitively approach people as individuals, no matter which larger grouping they might have been part of. "I don't lump people together, I don't think of them except as individuals whom I like or dislike," she wrote. Yet she rarely referred to the 40 million diverse inhabitants of the Middle East as anything other than "the Arabs."[5] In view of her expressed concern with individuality, this lapse in granting recognition to their heterogeneity suggests carelessness consistent with alienation, exclusion, and the creation of Palestinians as other. It is clear in her ardent support for the Zionists—which had gradually evolved as she grew to appreciate their social democratic leanings and proclivity toward progressive development—she revealed an unyielding bias against Arab Palestinian concerns.

Deeply shaken by the futile destruction wrought by two world wars, Eleanor Roosevelt had become a committed advocate of world peace and viewed the UN as the sole remaining vehicle to achieve that end. Yet as it faced its first major challenge while it considered the prospects for Palestine, she moved behind the scenes, from an early stage, to lobby the highest echelons of American power. She urged President Harry S. Truman and Secretary of State George Marshall to apply militarized force to quell Arab opposition. She acted thus as the Arab leaders were contemporaneously availing of the democratic opportunity afforded by the General Assembly to protest the planned partition of Palestine.

Nor was she acting from a position of simple ignorance. Through the critical years of Palestinian unrest, during the 1936–39 Arab Revolt and the controversial British white paper that ensued, she was ensconced in the White House as a uniquely active First Lady, dedicated to the concerns of minorities, wielding power in the most powerful nation of the world. She was positioned in an epicenter to which global communications were directed and from which they were sought. She recognized that "one cannot live in a political atmosphere ... without absorbing some rudimentary facts about politics."[6] Despite their marital schism, Eleanor Roosevelt and Franklin Delano Roosevelt (FDR) functioned efficiently as a political partnership because they had a practical need for each other and shared a common ideology.[7] FDR encouraged his state officials in the belief that he and "the missus" were a team.[8] Perforce he tolerated her frequent interventions in the business of his administration, as did his successor, Harry Truman. The Middle East was an area of particular interest to the couple and its problems were a regular topic of discussion, albeit under the premise that the region that would benefit from their joint tutelage.[9]

Eleanor Roosevelt's work within the UN provided a unique opportunity for a broad world view. As she oversaw the endeavors of the Human Rights Commission, she had been taxed to endure tedious meetings where cultural nuances and the meaning of words were meticulously dissected and practical applications were minutely analyzed by fifty-eight participating nations.[10] She had been ideally positioned to receive a thorough grounding in the complexities of the issues, concluding that "six weeks of arguing over the weight of each word put down, as well as the legal meaning of every phrase, is not so easy for me, who is somewhat impatient of the things which I do not recognize at first blush as being really important."[11] Installed, as she was for almost two years, it can be assumed that Eleanor Roosevelt was charged to consider the concepts of ethics, ethnicity, morality, and nationalism, aspects of post-colonialism, and a nascent development theory, as well as the rights attached to liberty, property, religion, law, and equality that were familiar aspects of most, but not all, American lives. This view of different cultures from an array of prisms allowed the opportunity to overcome the human tendency toward ethnocentricity and provided occasion to appreciate the innate qualities that constituted the essence of all human beings.[12] Ultimately, under her stewardship, the UN accorded recognition to "the equal and inalienable rights of all members of the human family ... without distinction of any kind such as race, color, sex, religion or politics."[13] Eleanor Roosevelt's myopic view of the Palestinians, and her reactions to them, expose that she did not adhere to the principles that she espoused.

These dichotomies—including the advocacy of rights yet their denial; the concern for democracy yet the ready neglect of its practical application; anti-racism combined with unwitting prejudices; the espousal of peace but the willingness to use force; and the deep knowledge that was expressed in obliviousness—appear most readily when they are considered in observation of her attitudes toward the Middle East. By failing to seriously consider the ramifications of her activities, she consigned the Palestinian Arabs to the status of invisible marginalized others.

It is contended that Eleanor Roosevelt had absorbed the pervasive orientalism that imbued her culture. This is an outlook that attributes certain negative racial characteristics to a whole body of people and allows the beholder to feel superior. Orientalism was integral part of her heritage, too. Her uncle Theodore Roosevelt, a former U.S. president, had acted as a guide during her formative years. As a firm believer in the hierarchy of races, he had declared that "it is impossible to expect moral and material well-being where Mohammedianism is supreme."[14] Although she was not crude—for example she did not repeat crass generalizations of exoticism and feminization—her embodiment of orientalism was nevertheless profound. Ultimately it appears that Arab concerns were so irrelevant to her that she simply ignored the Palestinians to such an extent that they were excluded from due consideration. She also frequently implied that she had little faith in Arab ability to govern democratically, to develop with the desired American-style efficiency, and to avoid clannish fighting in the interests of peace and prosperity—traits that typify Western views of the Orient.

Although Edward Said's iconic analysis *Orientalism* would demonstrate how othering and the accepted hierarchies had laid the foundations for imperial rule, there is also evidence of the beginnings of a movement away from the Darwinian view of racial hierarchies, which during the mid 1940s placed Arabs near the bottom of its pyramid.[15] It is interesting to note in Eleanor Roosevelt's papers a newspaper report of a Californian psychologist, Dr. Frenkel-Brunswik, who had attracted attention when she reported on the personality of racially prejudiced persons. Her research had demonstrated that "the racially prejudiced are insecure though externally they may exhibit confidence and even arrogance. They accuse racial groups of aggression, underlying weakness, preoccupation with sex." She opined that "these are things which the prejudiced find in themselves, but are unable to face in themselves. Therefore, they project these unpleasantries to others, usually a racial group. It is a mechanism for blaming others for one's own shortcomings."[16] This conclusion offered an opportunity for holding a reflective mirror to prejudices which were current.

An Evolving Interest in Zionism

Eleanor Roosevelt had overcome great personal adversity before she took a confident position on the world stage. Orphaned at the age of ten having endured hurt and neglect as a child of an abusive marriage, she sought approbation. She garners empathy as she recalls that "attention and admiration were the things through all my childhood which I wanted because I was made to feel so conscious of the fact that nothing about me would attract attention or bring me admiration."[17] FDR's infidelity reinforced her feelings of exclusion and encouraged an early identification with the marginalized in society. She tended to respond to individuals—her liberalism was forged out of daily experiences, out of face-to face encounters, and out of direct personal appeals to her office rather than as a result of a commitment to a particular ideology. She encouraged contact with the American public by appealing from the outset of her White House years that "I want you to write to me."[18] Thousands responded with needs of their own that she endeavored to follow up on an individual basis. Through these means Eleanor Roosevelt's public and personal life was remade by a combination of personal convictions and political context.

Family had failed her and the various exclusions she had endured heightened her need for the inclusion provided by close friendships. Many of her closest friends were Jewish-Americans.[19] Her relationships with two younger men, Joe Lash and David Gurewitsch, bore the hallmarks of unusually devoted companionship. Henry Morgenthau, secretary of the treasury, and his wife Elinor, both Jewish and neighbors from the Hudson Valley, were originally assimilationist in their aspirations. However, they were catalyzed by the inadequate U.S. response to Hitler's atrocities and evolved to a position where they wholeheartedly embraced Zionism. Eleanor Roosevelt, always unsure of her place, paralleled their evolution.[20] Another Jewish acquaintance was convinced that Eleanor Roosevelt was motivated by an acute guilt at the sustained Christian prejudices that had fueled the Holocaust—a wrong she was determined to right as she viewed their desperate plight in Europe.[21]

Her natural instinct to assist the victims of Nazi Germany had been constrained by the yoke of the administration's wartime policy.[22] When freed of these stays after FDR's death, she took an early opportunity to visit the Displaced Persons' Camps in Germany, in February 1946. It was at the Zelcheim Camp, outside Frankfurt, that she had a moment of epiphany. There, an old woman threw herself on her knees in the mud and repeated the words "Israel Israel."[23] This pitiful action left a lasting impression. That internees had been schooled by the Zionists to promulgate their cause in such ways did not apparently occur to Eleanor Roosevelt. Press reports stated that she was followed by a crowd of about four hundred Jewish internees pleading "send us back to Palestine."[24] They carried bilingual signs with messages stating "We want to go, we have to go, we must go, we will go to Palestine."[25] Though such activity bears the hallmarks of organization and preparation for this distinguished visit, Eleanor Roosevelt made no comment.

This occasion lies in stark contrast with her reaction on a visit, in 1952, to a Palestinian refugee camp. While the Jewish camps had impressed her by their efforts to keep "their hopes alive and [they] tried to make their temporary quarters into 'homes' even under the most difficult conditions … the Arab refugee camps were the least hopeful I had ever seen." Again she was met with a chorus of "We want to go home," but on this occasion she recognized that "it was a slogan, because they say it in unison."[26] She assumed that the Arab leaders, trained by the Communists, "find it to their interest to keep alive the bitter feelings using as a political weapon the demands of an unhappy people to have their wrongs righted."[27] In her different reactions to such similar situations, Eleanor Roosevelt was consonant with Senator William Fulbright's later observation that "man's" capacity for decent behavior varies directly with the perception of others as individuals with human motives and feelings whereas the capacity for barbarism is related to perceptions of an adversary in abstract terms, "as the embodiment of some evil design or ideology."[28] Despite her vast travels this had been her first visit to the Middle East. There had been few Arabs in her acquaintance—those that she belatedly experienced presented as foreign and alien. She revealed that her tendency to view the Middle Easterners as others had remained entrenched, despite the passage of the years and the tragic events that had been spawned.

In view of her vehement determination to secure the promised Jewish homeland, she was fortunate to have such a formidable ally as President Truman. His early call, in August 1945, for the issuance of one hundred thousand additional immigration certificates to Palestine for the Jewish camp survivors was also partially motivated by humanitarian considerations.[29] Prime Minister Clement Atlee availed of that opportunity to embroil the Americans in the intractable affair by suggesting a joint Anglo/American Commission of Enquiry in November 1945.[30] Eleanor Roosevelt had been well briefed on the problems in the region. Zionist leader, Dr. Chaim Weizmann, had relayed to her his story of the Balfour Declaration and of his meeting with Arab leader, Sharif Faisal, in 1918.[31] Weizmann assured her of the Emir's full acceptance of Zionist intentions. "He was very convincing," Eleanor Roosevelt later wrote, "but I have heard many arguments on the other side."[32] Nevertheless, as her commitment to Zionism grew she cited these agreements, of Balfour and Faisal, with monotonous regularity, adding that tacit American support was evidenced by congressional resolution and in presidential favor as she attempted to offset criticism of her stance.[33] She acknowledged that the Arab leaders held an interpretation that was at variance with this view but rationalized her perspective by concluding that "she had always assumed that when Lord Balfour pledged British support ... he had meant that the Jews should have their own country under their own government."[34] Since the Zionist view accorded with her own understanding, she concluded that Arab concerns were "simply one of those emotional questions about which feelings run so high that neither side can concede even the possibility of another point of view."[35] With the repetition of her beliefs, she herself appeared to become ever more convinced of the righteousness of her stance. At the same time, the Palestinian voices of protest became ever more distant as she celebrated the "extraordinary spirit" of those Zionists who had labored to make the "unpromising land ... productive."[36]

Eleanor Roosevelt was aware that her husband had explored the possibilities of population transfer of the Arab Palestinians to neighboring Arab states in order to make way for a coherent Jewish homeland.[37] When technical enquiries proved that the necessary water was elusive, she realized that "immigration to all lands must be restricted by how many people the land can support and that will be a determining factor in Palestine."[38] Zionists reacted swiftly to this statement, forwarding a Hadassah memorandum entitled *The Absorptive Capacity of Palestine* to Eleanor. It reflected the conclusions of Dr. Walter Lowdermilk, an agronomy expert, and claimed a future potential population of between 4 to 5 million for the territory.[39] The review that FDR requested of his settlement adviser, Dr. Isaiah Bowman, provided a more pragmatic response.[40] The latter advised Eleanor Roosevelt that peace would only be maintained in Palestine by the use of outside support—the larger the population the more precarious the political and military situation would be for the Anglo/American governments. He reminded her of the firm objections of the Saudi Monarch, Ibn Saud, and those of 40 million Arabs to Zionism.

Indeed she had heard FDR's graphic descriptions of his meeting with the King on board the *U.S.S. Quincy* in February 1945. It had been, he believed, the one major failure on his protracted trip to Yalta; in this instance he had sought some relief for the Jewish plight, to no avail.[41] Ibn Saud had traveled to meet the president on board the *U.S.S Murphy*. As a desert dweller, he could not countenance the confinement of a ship's cabin. He therefore spread canvas over the deck of the destroyer to create a tent and, using oriental rugs, ensured comfort on the hard surface.[42] Colleagues told of his seven-foot Nubian slaves, who roamed the ship with clanking scimitars swinging from their belts, as live sheep were slaughtered and Arabian coffee was cooked over charcoal in the gun turrets, while they served their king.[43] This cameo, juxtaposing the cold modernity of the battleship with the earthiness of the "unsophisticated" Arabs, cultivated in Eleanor Roosevelt latent prejudices and reinforced in her a sense of Arabs as others. Ralph Bunche, a UN colleague who acted as a UN mediator in Palestine during 1948, revealed a similar state of affairs. He believed these images had contributed to the almost "primitive" conception of Arabs that she had retained, and considered them to be the cause of the difficulties in discussing Palestine with her.[44] Another UN adviser, Durward Sandifer, concurred, noting that Eleanor Roosevelt had been always receptive to his advice but "there was one subject on which she was adamant and that was Palestine."[45]

The combination of primitive Arabs, deserving Jews, and Anglo/American commitments convinced Eleanor Roosevelt of the righteousness of her cause as she addressed the Women's Division of the United Jewish Appeal of New York in early 1946. She described what she had witnessed on her tour of the camps as one hundred thousand displaced Jews—"the miserable, the tortured, terrorized Jews," who, although they possessed nothing materially, did not even have the right to appeal to a government—"there was nothing to hold on to." She accepted their desire to go to Palestine as the one place where they would have a status.[46] The Palestinian status, however, did not warrant her consideration.

Her awareness of Arab weakness and American strength prompted her letter to Anglo/ American Commissioner, Dr. James McDonald, in April 1946, as she sympathized with his position in dealing with the conflict. Convinced of the justice of the Zionist ambition, she wrote, "I think we should have the courage to tell the Arabs that we intend to protect Palestine … it would only take a small air force and it would seem to keep them in order." [47] Her inclination toward a show of force was motivated by an article in *The Nation* by its editor, Freda Kirchwey, who, on a visit to Cairo, sensed a fear of Truman's plans among the Egyptians: "They knew that an uncompromising stand in Washington backed by solid promises of material help would go far to offset Arab threats."[48] Kirchwey was energized by Zionist conviction and the Nation Associates, of which Eleanor Roosevelt was a cosponsor, became an important lobbying arm for their cause.[49] Kirchwey coordinated activity with the Jewish Agency in Palestine, and answered in programmatic detail every argument against the creation of a Jewish state offered by the State Department, the oil lobby, the British, and the Arabs.

Eleanor Roosevelt received the publications and was commissioned by Kirchwey to garner further support for their campaigns.[50] One publication examined whether the Arabs could stage a revolt.[51] That the authors had their doubts is evidenced by their review of Middle Eastern society—an undeveloped, underpopulated region where slavery is recognized by law and women are bought and sold; the governments were corrupt, illiteracy was "staggering," and infant mortality levels were record-breaking. The article noted that the military prowess of the seven Arab states was so slight as to constitute "no danger whatsoever" and the authors did not believe that "the feudal overlords will give up oil and other concessions from which they garner millions of dollars a year for their personal use" by risking war. Although living standards and social relations in the Middle East "are as feudal today as they were in the days of Mohammed," the one area of exceptional difference was Palestine; its state of improvement was attributed to the "stimulus of Jewish enterprise [which] could be paralleled throughout the Arab world with the application of modern science, democratic governments and democratic social and economic conditions in the whole Middle East."[52] This report appealed to Eleanor Roosevelt: Zionist zealousness had long impressed her, and the opinions expressed accorded with her understanding of Palestinian passivity. The Arabs, she wrote, were "a nomadic people leading simple lives."[53] Because she perceived them as incapable of Western-style development, they could be readily excluded as others and deemed less worthy.

Delays in the achievement of these goals were occasioned by the various Commissions of Enquiry that took place. The protagonists' rejection of the recommendations of the Anglo/American Commission and the Morrison-Grady Report provoked a rising level of frustration in Eleanor Roosevelt.[54] Galvanized to action, she effectively used the tools that were available to her, her access to the president and to his senior officials and also her ready media access through her daily widely syndicated column, to express her concerns and to urge a proactive approach. Her writings regularly adapted the arguments of the Nation Associates.[55]

She granted that the Arab rights should be protected but appeared willing for them merely to have adequate access to the religious shrines.[56] When they protested the UN plan to appoint a committee of small nations to deliberate and decide the case, Eleanor Roosevelt expressed her distaste, remarking that she "hated to see us tremble before the Arab threats" as she wondered by "what theory the Arab leaders are so lightly flaunting defiance of the UN."[57] It appears that in her view, they did not have this right. Without this organization, she believed, small nations would live in continual uncertainty. She seemed blinded to the prolonged uncertainty that the Palestinians, as an aspiring small nation, had already endured in a situation that had all the hallmarks of further deterioration. She contended that they should have protested but then quietly accepted the UN majority decision even though it was not agreeable to them as "we must expect occasionally to have to subordinate our desires if they do not meet with the approval of the majority."[58] By so acting "they would have earned respect and sympathy throughout the world"; instead they were creating "a sense of irritation among many people."

While Arab concerns were not mere "desires," but in fact life-threatening matters, Eleanor Roosevelt herself might have become directly responsible for their further demise had her wishes been carried out. She wrote to Secretary of State George Marshall stating that the U.S. position was "very weak" because the Arabs cannot "after all cause very serious trouble from the military standpoint if we wish to use planes and tanks."[59] She also sought the shipment of U.S. arms to Palestine in order to assist the Zionists.[60] Her letters to Truman on one occasion warned him of his "need for the Jewish vote" as she urged the removal of the U.S. arms embargo, which she believed disadvantaged the Zionists and favored the Arabs. On another occasion she asked him to exert pressure on Britain to allow entry of the illegal Zionist shipments of refugees to Palestine.[61] Both men were charged to mild admonishment, in the first instance by reminding her that the democratic processes of the UN had to be upheld and that the humanitarian aspects of the problem had to be considered. Marshall explained that American shipments of arms to Palestine would facilitate acts of violence and would render still more difficult the task of maintaining law and order.[62] Truman advised that his office could not condone the illegal actions that attempted to smuggle refugees into Palestine.[63]

Eleanor Roosevelt threatened to resign from her position on the U.S. delegation to the UN on 22 March 1948 when it appeared that the United States itself would contravene the General Assembly's recommendation to partition Palestine by advocating an interim trusteeship.[64] Truman averted the potential cataclysm that her resignation would cause for his administration by appeasing her; he wrote that he would "deplore as calamitous your withdrawal from the work of the United Nations at this crucial time."[65]

A Voice of Opposition

It was not merely among elites that Eleanor Roosevelt caused a stir. Members of the public, whose opinions she had invited since 1933, availed of the opportunity to express their discontent and surprise at her attitudes. Once again Eleanor Roosevelt was provided with worthy opinions to consider. Some attempted to change her positions by pointing out instances of injustices that she apparently supported, which in their view conflicted with her espousal of rights and democracy. Other letters were from people with personal experience with the Middle East. Individual American citizens took upon themselves to represent those who were others—to argue their case—by speaking back to power.

Beatrice Patton was succinct when she wrote that she could not support any organization in which "our own delegates vote to scrap the good neighbor policy and the Four Freedoms, in order to wrest their land from a people with whom we have no quarrel and give it to the Jews to whom it does not belong."[66] Lydia Bacon's husband had lectured at the American University at Beirut for twenty-one years and had become well acquainted with Arab people and their culture.[67] She abhorred the intention, in contravention of Palestinian wishes, to partition a state as small as Vermont, particularly in view of the longevity of Palestinian residency there. She asked that if "Americans feel so badly for the Jews, why do we not give them one of our states"? Puzzled, she wondered "how can we give away another's country" as she reminded Eleanor Roosevelt of past American misdeeds toward the Native Americans, Mexicans, and African-Americans. Edna Binn added in concurrence that as "the Jews are a people who know how to operate under our profit system and private enterprise to perfection," it would not burden the United States to take its share rather than partitioning such a small country.[68]

Mr. Baracat, citing her "Godmotherly" image among oppressed peoples, found Eleanor Roosevelt's stance disturbing.[69] He suggested that she had fallen victim to "Jewish emotional appeals" and that her desire to "force the issue as settled" through the UN is "just adding fuel to the fire." He believed that "the whole thing was wrong, contrary to human rights, contrary to Christian ideals and contrary to American principles." He urged that the UN should acknowledge its "blunder" and make an honorable retreat rather than continuing with an unworkable plan "Merchant of Venice style," advising that Eleanor Roosevelt ought to take sufficient time to review the problem from all angles.

Erma Sharpe was disturbed by what she perceived as U.S.-assisted territorial aggression on the part of the Zionists. She observed that "no country in the world has screamed more or shouted louder against territorial aggression that the U.S.A."[70] She too blamed the ubiquitous propaganda of a powerful minority of Zionist Jews for the current position, but also felt that her view was supported by eminent opinion makers, such as Walter Lippmann and Joseph Alsop, who had predicted that partition could not be enforced without "dire results." Ms. Sharpe had felt compelled to write as she felt "bewildered and puzzled because heretofore you have always spoken out against injustice, intolerance and the denying of rights to any people."[71]

Others considered Arab objections to the partitioning of Palestine by attempting to imagine it through Arab eyes. They saw analogies between the partition of their territory and the putative seizure of Alaska by Canada.[72] They wondered whether the United States would acquiesce to the return of part of Manhattan Island to the American Indians.[73] Robert Bridgens wrote that "what we did to the American Indians bears a close parallel to what we are trying to do to the Arabs in Palestine."[74] Eleanor Roosevelt had demonstrated her sensitivity to racial issues when she had recently highlighted the injustices perpetrated against them by the American settlers, noting that "Now the Indian turns to the white man for justice. He asks very little—that he many retain the land allotted to him, that he may be treated as a citizen." It behooved Americans to find a way to live together amicably, she advised, as "it is white people who really are a minority" and she wondered how "our arrogance" had been tolerated for so long. That she could recognize this othering as inequitable gives credence to the view that she was unwittingly beholden to orientalism.

In her responses to this correspondence Eleanor Roosevelt provided a potted version of her view of the struggle for Palestine.[75] She took the opportunity to relay the development work that the Jews had achieved there as they turned an arid country into a "garden spot" and ridded its regions of malaria. That "the Arabs have now awakened to the fact … it seems to me that that decision has come a little too late." She dismissed the writers' concerns when she stated "it will not hurt the Arabs, in fact they will profit by it, but we do not always like what is good for us in this world." In this sentiment she displays a sense of condescension that one would only apply to an "other" who is perceived as not worthy of due respect.

In her next column she wrote of her surprise at the sudden influx of correspondence from different parts of the country that suggested that the UN decision was unfair and should be reconsidered.[76] She referred to the suggestion of donating a U.S. state and countered that "this particular suggestion is somewhat funny. That the Americans should be asked to arbitrarily displace citizens of a certain state and turn that state over to the Jews, strikes me as a suggestion to which the writer gave very little thought!" She concluded that if Palestine was considered from an economic standpoint then the Arab inability to develop the territory contrasted starkly and unfavorably with Jewish success. On the same day as this column appeared, Baddia Rashid was motivated to put pen to paper and convincingly demolished her arguments.[77] Eleanor Roosevelt's interpretation that the Arabs had taken a defiant attitude toward a "decision" of the UN is her "first misinterpretation," as the Assembly had only the authority to recommend solutions and could not enforce its deliberations by military action, Rashid argued. He pointed to the incursions against UN authority by the "flaunted defiance" of the Soviets and by the Americans themselves—yet the UN had survived. He scathingly wrote "And only because the Arab people have opposed an unwarranted 'recommendation' you are quick to conclude that the United Nations will not long survive!!" With apparent disdain he explained that he would be discouraged to realize that nations had to follow hasty and mistaken judgments with a blind determination never to retrace their footsteps. Recalling Lydia Bacon's suggestion of offering a U.S. state for the resettlement of the Jews, he had noted that Eleanor Roosevelt did not accept that the United States should "arbitrarily displace citizens," and had expressed a belief that the suggestion was given without much consideration. He contended that her continued advocacy for the Jewish people to "take over with military force if necessary the land of the Palestinians" led him to conclude that the analogy was almost identical. With evident frustration he ended with the thought that "what you are asking and demanding of the Arabs, you refuse to consider as feasible for our own country."

At the end of April 1948 Eleanor Roosevelt wrote to Adlai Stevenson, a friend and fellow politician, that she was very unhappy about American vacillation, which she blamed for "much of the Arab arrogance and violence."[78] That the correspondence of these random citizens seemed to have little impact on her views is significant, as it showed her to be out of accord with contemporary considerations of justice as expressed by her compatriots, who could identify with the Arab leaders' concerns, and who did not dismiss the Arabs as others. Yet she was simultaneously enjoying renown as an advocate of human rights.

Supporting Zion, Denying Palestine

By the spring of 1948 the world had been provided with a glimpse of the violence that was to ensue in Palestine over the coming months and years. The brutality involved in the forced evacuation of the Palestinian Arabs was contemporaneously compared with that of Nazi atrocities.[79] Although Zionist propaganda tried to persuade the observant public that the flight was the result of orders on the part of the Arab leaders, both American and British intelligence knew otherwise, as historians have since amply demonstrated.[80] The atrocities of Deir Yassin had occurred on 9 April 1948. A force of 130 Irgun-Stern dissidents attacked the village with the consent of the Jewish Agency in Palestine. There were numerous appalling reports of the murders of an estimated 250 people "by every circumstance of savagery."[81] The British Chief Secretary of the Palestinian government, Sir Hugh Gurney, noted that "as the bestialities of Deir Yassin are coming to light … Belsen pales beside them."[82]

Eleanor Roosevelt was provided with her own personal glimpse of the events through letters she received from Wadad Dabbagh, a self-described

"Arab wife and citizen of Palestine" who "begs to bring to your kind attention some real facts about her poor country."[83] She asked Eleanor Roosevelt to desist in her support of the Zionists until she visits Palestine and sees with her own eyes what injustices they are causing. "They are driving us out of our homes, depriving us of our lands, robbing us of our means of living." She described the buildings pulled down without pity on helpless families leaving the women to treat the wounds of those "who have been mutilated by the Zionists whom you seem to defend." She was sure that Eleanor Roosevelt's sympathies were based on false information.

The response she received must have been cold comfort to her, as Eleanor Roosevelt replied that "the Arabs had protested wrongly"—they should have accepted the UN recommendation for surrender of their lands.[84] To support her case she once again relied on the Balfour Declaration. She considered their defiance deserving of the censure of the rest of the world, their behavior to have been "unrealistic and stupid" and that it had led them inevitably to face the horrors of war. Undeterred, on 30 June 1948, Ms. Dabbagh wrote again.[85] Because she had read Eleanor Roosevelt's speech on the proposed Charter for Human Rights, she was encouraged to renew her plea for understanding. Recounting recent Palestinian history she demonstrated its struggle for self-determination, describing the first attempts to free itself of Ottoman control and the postwar Palestinian frustration at the Balfour Declaration to which their leaders had never acquiesced. She explained that its anniversary was a day of mourning in Palestine. That the Declaration was always the object of Arab protest had been illustrated by the insurrections of 1922, 1929, 1933, and 1936–39. The Jews, she wrote, are strangers to Palestine but are planning to take the land either by expelling the Arabs out of their homes or by exterminating them, and she listed the areas of atrocities—Deir Yassin, Haifa, Jaffa, Safad, and Tiberias.

She reminded Eleanor Roosevelt that the Arabs are not a savage people—that they had largely contributed to the cause of civilization, and had "propagated" to the world the first principles of science, culture, and justice. She finished with the plea "I am sure, dear Madame, that you can do something, and you are going to do it in the name of Justice and Human Rights which you are admirably defending and advocating." Wadad Dabbagh had provided good reason for Eleanor Roosevelt to identify with her; she showed herself to be rational, sophisticated, and educated.

Eleanor Roosevelt failed to react similarly because she apparently viewed Ms. Dabbagh as part of the Arab morass, an invisible other. Her curt reply of twenty-four words effectively stating that "there is nothing I can do" prompted another response from Ms. Dabbagh.[86] She felt the dismissal sharply but nevertheless maintained her dignity as she wrote again: "I regret to see that there is a great difference, in the meaning of those human rights, between theory and practice, and I am sorry to feel that I have bothered you in vain with my previous correspondence. I have to thank you anyway."[87] Wadad Dabbagh was correct in her understanding that the espoused human rights were not universal but apparently rested upon which part of the universe one dwelt in and the pigmentation of one's skin.

As she closely observed the early days of the war, Eleanor Roosevelt fretted over possible Arab gains as she rooted for Israeli success.[88] She resented the truce negotiations as she believed this provided the Arab leaders with opportunity for regrouping to improve their position—she particularly complained about their ability to receive arms from Britain through treaty obligations.[89] Another reader, who described himself as a longtime admirer of hers, wondered about her clear opposition to the Arabs, writing that "the fact that the Arabs are a backward Oriental people should not enter the question. We have seen the 'white man's burden' argument used as a cloak for taking advantage of backward peoples too often."[90] Although he explicitly demonstrated a current view of Arab culture and through his description relegated them to the status of an unfavored other, it is apparent that he also sensed the injustice of the status quo, yet Eleanor Roosevelt appeared to have been unmoved. In her columns she continued to express her admiration for the unity and single-minded purpose among the Jewish people and their willingness to sacrifice for the land they had created out of the desert. Aligning their endeavors with the American experience she noted that the Jewish task was "curiously reminiscent of all other pioneer movements where people have tried to establish themselves in new places and flee oppression and interference elsewhere." The vast majority of Jews in Palestine seem to have this spirit, she concluded.[91]

A September column informed Eleanor Roosevelt's readers of her meeting with a group of young people—all were members of the Israeli army—who had been brought from Israel to speak for the United Jewish Appeal.[92] She described the inadequacy of their equipment and their small numbers but how, through conviction, they had accomplished what had seemed impossible. She mused about the feelings of General George Washington's young troops as they faced the British Army, and imagined that they had held the same conviction evident in these Israeli soldiers. Pointedly, she appealed to American patriotism, when she pondered what the outcome of the American Revolution would have been had Lafayette been unable to persuade the French government to aid the colonies. She wrote that she would like to question some Arab soldiers to establish "whether they more nearly approximated the Young Hessians of our own Revolutionary War, who fought for the sake of fighting and the pecuniary returns."

Within a year of this war, there were approximately eight hundred thousand displaced Palestinian Arabs living in refugee camps in Arab countries bordering Israel. Eleanor Roosevelt was well aware of their plight because, ironically, her UN role on the Human and Social Affairs Committee made her partially responsible for alleviating their conditions. She informed the public about the report provided by Count Bernadotte, the UN mediator to Palestine, who outlined for the General Assembly the appalling circumstances.[93] She described the difficulties faced by the refugees, 30 percent of whom were children under five years of age. They were almost entirely without food and lacked medical care. Imminent threats from the spread of disease, and from the impending winter conditions, faced them and their health had been depleted by their "present starvation diet."

Despite her public utterances of concern for the Palestinian refugees, behind the scenes she engaged in certain obstruction of the speedy delivery of aid until the political considerations pertaining to agreed boundaries were adequately addressed. A telegram from Virginia Gildersleeve, dean of Barnard College, reported that American organizations cooperating in relief for Palestinian refugees "are puzzled and distressed by reports in the *New York Sun* that you have asked the Social Committee to delay consideration of this question."[94] Gildersleeve urged immediate action to mitigate the suffering of hundreds of thousands of human beings. Eleanor Roosevelt responded that consultation must take place between delegates and their governments, noting that otherwise "it is easy to vote relief when you do not have to supply it."[95] Although the Palestinian refugees were not the responsibility of the other Arab states, she believed that the U.S. Congress would delay appropriations until the Arab contribution was clarified. In her dealings with Arab representatives she had found them ill prepared: "when I got some of them together yesterday for lunch, they ... had no ideas on distribution and practically no real plans" with an implication that the Eastern "inferiors" needed the assistance of their Western "superiors." As her UN colleagues pressed her for action, and British delegate, Hector McNeil, advised that he had garnered sufficient votes for a favorable decision, she countered that while he may have the votes, "she had the dollars," as she insisted on procrastination.[96] Privately, in a letter to Bernard Baruch, another Jewish friend and an influential political adviser, she confirmed her position, stating that she was refusing to discuss anything about repatriation or removal to another area until the political question was settled.[97] Her remark—"of, course, they will have to have relief, we can not [sic] let four or five hundred thousand people die without doing something for them, but they are a part of the settlement of the political question"—conflicts with her perceived humanitarianism and gives substance to considerations of her orientalism.

During this period, Eleanor Roosevelt had read to the assembled delegates of the UN General Assembly, on 18 December 1948, the unanimously agreed Universal Declaration of Human Rights. Article 13 (2) laid out the principle that "Everyone has the right to leave any country, including his own, and to return to his country."[98] Still, Eleanor Roosevelt supported Israeli intransigence on allowing this right to the Palestinians. Controversy was sparked by the remarks of Mrs. Mark Ethridge, whose husband was an official of the Palestine Conciliation Commission. On her return to the United States in 1949, the *New York Herald Tribune* reported Mrs. Ethridge's view that it "was very unfortunate that Israel was admitted to the UN while displaced Arabs were being forced to live in the most squalid and horrible condition in the Jordan valley."[99] She believed that it was "too bad that the Jews, in building a national home, had found it expedient to throw out 910,000 persons who had been living there for 1,400 years," and deplored the Jewish disregard of the UN resolution directing them to take back the Arab refugees to Israel.

Eleanor Roosevelt devoted space in her column to defend the Israelis, musing that "it is odd" that Mrs. Ethridge did not happen to find in Israel the many communities in which the Arabs remained "happily" living with the Jews.[100] While noting that Mrs. Ethridge "intimates" that the Arabs had been driven from their homes she also wondered why they "ran away from a 'danger' which was certainly no worse than the danger they took themselves into." Her support for the status quo is demonstrated when she proffers that the opportunity for their return had passed given the "great influx" of Jewish immigrants from Cyprus and Central Europe, writing that "the Arabs probably will be better off if the funds already in hand are used to resettle them in some of the other Arab countries where there are vacant lands that need people to work them." She concluded that the *Tribune* article was "very hostile" to the new state of Israel.

Missives that reached her mailbag attempting to prod her conscience were unsuccessful. Constantine Hutchins, a reader who had spent time in Israel, bemoaned the one-sided accounts of the conditions that had been provided to the American public. Attributing blame to the Americans for their role in creating the current difficulties she, as an American citizen, felt responsible for the thousands of pathetic refugees who arrived in Hazauth "without food or clothing and in a desperate condition."[101] She noted that the UN plan had been completely disregarded by the Israeli authorities who had taken over land apportioned to the Arabs. Pointedly referring to Eleanor Roosevelt's recent column, she noted that "when we are moved by the sufferings of the Jews, we are being sympathetic, but when we begin to feel for the Arab refugees, we are hostile." She urged that recompense be made to the Palestinian Arabs for "the sad situation they are in." Eleanor

Roosevelt's response could have offered little reassurance or comfort. She wrote that Ms. Hutchins seemed "to forget that we are carrying more than half of the cost."[102] She referred to the Arabs who had not fled "at Mufti instigation" and were now living peacefully in Israel. While she had confidence that Israel would help to alleviate their situation, she argued that "the Arabs are not blameless."

A reasoned letter from Frank Sakran attempted to settle the controversy about the cause of the exodus. Because Eleanor Roosevelt had defended the Israeli position by pointing to the Arabs who remained, he chided her for ignoring the atrocities committed by the Jews at Deir Yassin particularly when Irgun leader, Menachem Begin, on a recent visit to New York had admitted that the purpose of that attack had been precisely to achieve such a clearance.[103] He noted that according to her argument "we must not believe that the Jews drove the Arabs away so long as a single Arab remains under Jewish rule." However, he wrote that the same analogy—that as long as a single Jew survived the Holocaust—could be employed to argue that Hitler had never persecuted the Jews. In his opinion, the Israeli authorities' refusal to permit the Palestinians to return to their homes proved that they drove them out in order to replace them with Jewish immigrants. He had been convinced of this as he considered the hastiness of the "great influx of Jewish immigration" that she had referred to in her column. He was particularly chagrined that the Zionists could have prevailed upon "no less a champion of democracy and human rights than yourself to defend them."[104] Eleanor Roosevelt denied her opposition to the Palestinian right of return and proffered a weak defense of her position by suggesting that on their repatriation, the refugees "would have to undergo the same hardships as the Jewish people ... and that might be more difficult for them than to resettle in an Arab area."[105]

Clearly all attempts to alter Eleanor Roosevelt's entrenched positions failed. For the rest of her life she remained committed to the success of Israel. She wrote a book, *India and the Awakening East,* after her first visit to the Middle East in 1952, when she visited the Palestinian refugee camps in Lebanon and Jordan. Her firsthand experience of conditions there appalled her but was not a cause for reflection on past events or a revision of her initial views of the other. Instead she delighted upon Israeli "progress" and encouraged its development. Their industriousness accorded with the hopes for progressive development that her culture encouraged and suited the drive of her Protestant work ethic. Conversely, Arabs, about whom she subliminally assimilated the ubiquitous stereotyping that prevailed around her, and who had threatened the realization of her goal with their unreasonable defiance, remained unfathomable aliens. To address this dilemma the avenue she had chosen was to convince herself, and attempt to convince others, of Arab unworthiness by othering them.

Notes

1. "Eleanor Roosevelt to Ms. Berg, April 25, 1950," *Eleanor Roosevelt Papers Project* (hereafter cited as ERPP), George Washington University, Serial No. 033341, from Anna Eleanor Roosevelt Papers, (hereafter cited as AERP), Franklin Delano Roosevelt Library, (hereafter cited as FDRL), Box 3358.
2. Evan M. Wilson, *Decision on Palestine: How the U.S. Came to Recognize Israel* (Stanford: Hoover Institution Press, 1979), 62; Donald Neff, *Fallen Pillars: U.S. Policy towards Palestine and Israel since 1945* (Washington, DC: Institute for Palestine Studies, 1995), 62; Benny Morris, *Righteous Victims: A History of the Zionist-Arab Conflict, 1881-2001* (New York: Vintage, 2001), 254–58.
3. Gerd Baumann and Andre Gingrich, eds., *Grammars of Identity/Alterity: A Structural Approach* (New York: Berghahn Books, 2004), 31.
4. Blanche Weisen Cook, *Eleanor Roosevelt: Volume II, The Defining Years* (New York: Penguin, 2000), 153; Michael H. Hunt, *Ideology and U.S. Foreign Policy* (New Haven: Yale University Press, 1987), 46.
5. Joseph Lash, *Eleanor: The Years Alone* (London: Andre Deutsch, 1975), 110.
6. Joseph Lash, *Eleanor and Franklin: The Story of Their Relationship Based on Eleanor Roosevelt's Private Papers* (London: Andre Deutsch, 1972), 335.
7. Blanche Weisen Cook, *Eleanor Roosevelt: Vol. 1, 1884-1933* (New York: Penguin Books, 1992), 228; Eleanor Roosevelt, *The Autobiography of Eleanor Roosevelt* (New York, Da Capo Press, 1961), 283.
8. Lash, *Eleanor and Franklin*, 335.
9. Wilson, *Decision on Palestine*, 54.
10. Mary Ann Glendon, *A World Made New: Eleanor Roosevelt and the Universal Declaration of Human Rights* (New York: Random House, 2002).
11. Eleanor Roosevelt, "My Day Column," 21 June 1948; Allida Black, ed., *The Eleanor Roosevelt Papers: Vol. I, The Human Rights Years 1945-1948* (New York: Thomson Gale, 2007), xxxix, xlv. In December 1935 Eleanor began her national daily syndicated column "My Day" which, by 1940, had a circulation equal to that of Walter Lippmann and Dorothy Thompson. She wrote more than eight thousand columns. It was carried in such papers as the *New York Post, Washington Daily News,* and *Seattle Post Intelligencer.* Memorandum from Pete Stewart, U.S. Mission to the UN to Eleanor Roosevelt, 25 August 1948, Microfilm reel 7, Slide 189, Eleanor Roosevelt Papers, United Nations Part I, Roosevelt Study Centre (RSC), Zeeland, the Netherlands; Allida M. Black, ed., *What I Hope to Leave Behind: The Essential Essays of Eleanor Roosevelt* (New York: Carlson Publishing Inc., 1995), 553, ("The Promise of Human Rights") and 559 ("Making Human Rights Come Alive").
12. Glendon, *A World Made New,* 220.
13. Black, "The Universal Declaration of Human Rights," in *What I Hope to Leave Behind,* 531.
14. Douglas Little, *American Orientalism: The United States in the Middle East since 1945* (London: IB Taurus, 2003), 15.

15. Edward W. Said, *Orientalism* (London: Penguin, 2003).
16. "Extreme Race Haters Verge on Imbalance, Survey Indicates," *Brooklyn Eagle*, 5 (September 1946) in *Eleanor Roosevelt Papers*, Box 60, FDRL.
17. Roosevelt, *The Autobiography*, 10.
18. Black, *The Eleanor Roosevelt Papers*, xxxviii.
19. Michelle Mart, "Eleanor Roosevelt, Liberalism and Israel," *Shofar: An Interdisciplinary Journal of Jewish Studies* 24, no. 3 (2006), 58–89.
20. Henry Morgenthau, "Oral History Interview, November 9, 1978," *AERP*, Box 4, FDRL, 77–81.
21. Judge Justine Polier, Oral History Interview, September 14, 1977," *AERP*, Box 4, FDRL 20. Judge Justine Polier, daughter of the leader of the American Zionist Organization, Rabbi Stephen Wise, described a significant moment with Eleanor Roosevelt when the First Lady puzzled over Jewish reluctance to seek help as the ongoing Holocaust was gradually revealed. Polier believed that her explanation of their hesitancy, which was the result of Jewish experience of prejudice from the Christian world, stirred a sense of guilt that motivated Eleanor Roosevelt to use all of her powers to remedy this lapse.
22. Cook, *Eleanor Roosevelt Volume II*, 304.
23. Eleanor Roosevelt, "Speech to the Women's Division of the United Jewish Appeal of New York," *AERP*, Speech and Article File, February 1946-September 1947, Box, 1417, FDRL.
24. Black, *Eleanor Roosevelt Papers Vol. I*, 259.
25. Ibid.
26. Black, *What I Hope to Leave Behind*, 597.
27. Lash, *Eleanor*, 137.
28. Cindy Arkelyan Lydon, "American Images of the Arabs," *Mid-East: A Middle East-North African Review* 9, no. 3 (May–June 1969): 3.
29. Wilson, *Decision on Palestine*, 62.
30. Ibid., 64.
31. Lash, *Eleanor*, 110.
32. Ibid., 111.
33. "My Day Column," May 14, 1947; March 22, 1948; "Eleanor Roosevelt to Ms. Miller, December 21, 1948," *RSC*, GC/48, Microfilm Reel 4, Slide 953.
34. "My Day Column," May 14, 1947; May 18, 1948.
35. Eleanor Roosevelt, *India and The Awakening East* (New York: Harper & Brothers Publishers, 1953), 25.
36. "My Day Column," December 30, 1948; February 13, 1948; May 27, 1948; September 14, 1948; March 1, 1948.
37. He had researched a program that would irrigate a sufficient quantity of land to permit large-scale emigration. Rabbi Dr. Chaim Simons, *A Historical Survey of Proposals to Transfer Arabs from Palestine 1895-1947* (Kiryat Arba: Gengis Khan Publishers, 1998), 150.
38. Monty N. Penkower, "Eleanor Roosevelt and the Plight of World Jewry," *Jewish Social Studies* 49, no. 2 (Spring 1987): 133.
39. Walter C. Lowdermilk, *Palestine Land of Promise* (London: Victor Gollanz, 1946), 160.
40. Penkower, "Eleanor Roosevelt and the Plight of World Jewry," 133.
41. Roosevelt, *An Autobiography*, 275.
42. Ibid., 274; Colonel William A. Eddy, *FDR Meets Ibn Saud* (New York: American Friends of the Middle East, 1954), 22.
43. Ibid., 28.
44. Lash, *Eleanor*, 137.
45. Durward Sandifer, "Oral History Interview, April 27, 1979," *AERP*, Box 5, FDRL, 17.
46. "My Day Column," 7 November 1945; Roosevelt, "Speech to the Women's Division of the United Jewish Appeal of New York."

47. Black, *Eleanor Roosevelt Papers*, 344; "Eleanor Roosevelt to Dr. James Mc Donald, April 28, 1946," *AERP*, Box 3256, FDRL.
48. Black, *Eleanor Roosevelt*, 346; Freda Kirchwey, "Palestine and Bevin," *The Nation*, 22 June 1946, 738; "My Day Column," 22 June 1946.
49. Ronald and Ailis Radosh, "Righteous Among Editors: When the Left Loved Israel," *World Affairs Journal* (Summer 2008), (http://www.worldaffairsjournal.org/article/righteous-among-editors-when-left-loved-israel).
50. "Freda Kirchwey to Eleanor Roosevelt," *ERPP*, GWU, Serial Nos. 006347 and 006346c, from AERP, GC 45/52, Box 3315, FDRL.
51. "Could the Arabs Stage a Revolt Against the UN, October 1947," ERGC 1945-1952, Microfilm Reel 15, Slide 686, RSC.
52. Ibid., Slide 689.
53. "My Day Column," 18 August 1946.
54. Wilson, *Decision on Palestine*, 94; "My Day Column," 19 August 1946.
55. "My Day Column," 14 May 1947. Her attitude toward the Arabs was likely shaded by her expressed view that they are not using their "oil to develop their own countries"; she noted that "all they do is sell it and only a few people profit."
56. Ibid.
57. "My Day Column," 28 February 1948.
58. "My Day Column," 15 May 1947.
59. "Eleanor Roosevelt to Secretary of State George Marshall, May 26, 1947," *AERP*, Box 1579 FDRL.
60. "Eleanor Roosevelt to Secretary of State George Marshall, February 1948," *AERP*, Box 1579, FDRL.
61. "Eleanor Roosevelt to Harry S. Truman, n.d., *HSTP*, Official File, Box 773, Msc., June/August 1947, HSTL.
62. "Secretary of State George Marshall to Eleanor Roosevelt, February 16, 1948, *RSC*, Microfilm Reel 5, Slide 619.
63. "Harry S. Truman to Eleanor Roosevelt, August 23, 1947," *ERPP*, GWU, Serial No. 044120, from *HSTP*, Chion Files Blues, Box 293, ER, HSTL.
64. "Eleanor Roosevelt to Harry S. Truman, March 22, 1948," *ERPP*, GWU, Serial No. 609221B, from *AERP*, FDRL.
65. "Harry S Truman to Eleanor Roosevelt, March 24, 1948," *HSTP*, PSF, Box 322, ER, Folio 2, HSTL.
66. "Beatrice Patton to Eleanor Roosevelt, December 14, 1947," *RSC*, Microfilm Reel 16, Slide 495.
67. "Lydia Bacon to Eleanor Roosevelt, February 24, 1948," *RSC*, Microfilm Reel 1, Slide 200.
68. "Edna Binn to Eleanor Roosevelt, October 14, 1947," *RSC*, Microfilm 10, Slide 380.
69. "Mr. Baracat to Eleanor Roosevelt, March 2, 1948," *EERP*, GWU, Serial no. 015743, from AERP, GC 45/52, Box 3256, FDRL.
70. "Erma Sharpe to Eleanor Roosevelt, March 29, 1948," *AERP*, Box Palestine, FDRL.
71. Ibid.
72. "HR Holand to Eleanor Roosevelt, March 4, 1948," *AERP*, Topical Files, Palestine Letters, Box 4645, FDRL.
73. "Erma Sharpe to Eleanor Roosevelt," *AERP*, FDRL.
74. "Robert Bridgens to Eleanor Roosevelt, n.d.," *AERP*, Topical Files, Palestine Letters, Box 4645, FDRL.
75. "Eleanor Roosevelt to Ms. Binn, October 24, 1947," *RSC*, Microfilm Reel 10, Slide 378; "Eleanor Roosevelt to Ms. Bacon, February 27, 1948," *RSC*, Microfilm Reel 1, Slide 198; "Eleanor Roosevelt to Mr. Holand, December 29, 1947," *RSC*, Microfilm Reel 16, Slide 494.

76. "My Day Column," 1–2 March 1948.
77. "Baddia Rashid to Eleanor Roosevelt, March 1, 1948," *AERP*, Topical Files, Palestine Letters, Box 4645, FDRL.
78. Black, *Eleanor Roosevelt Papers*, 798.
79. Norman Rose, *A Senseless Squalid War: Voices from Palestine, 1945-1948* (London: The Bodley Head, 2009), 194.
80. Avi Shlaim, *The Iron Wall: Israel and the Arab World* (London: Penguin Books, 2000); Wilson, *Decision on Palestine*; Norman Rose, *A Squalid Senseless War*.
81. Rose, *A Senseless Squalid War*, 193.
82. Ibid., 194.
83. "Wadad Dabbagh to Eleanor Roosevelt, n.d.," *RSC*, Microfilm Reel 2, Slide 380.
84. "Eleanor Roosevelt to Wadad Dabbagh, May 13, 1948," *RSC*, Microfilm Reel 2, Slide 378.
85. "Wadad Dabbagh to Eleanor Roosevelt, June 30, 1948," *RSC*, Microfilm Reel 2, Slide 385.
86. "Eleanor Roosevelt to Wadad Dabbagh, n.d.," *RSC*, Microfilm Reel 2, Slide 384.
87. "Wadad Dabbagh to Eleanor Roosevelt, August 11, 1948," *RSC*, Microfilm Reel 2, Slide 383.
88. "My Day Column," 18 April 1948; 27 May 1948; 17 July 1948.
89. "My Day Column," 29 May 1948; 5 June 1948; 10 June 1948.
90. "W. Whitton to Eleanor Roosevelt, May 19, 1948," *ERPP*, GWU Serial No, 038635 from AERP, Box 3390, FDRL.
91. "My Day Column," 27 May 1948.
92. "My Day Column," 14 September 1948.
93. "My Day Column," 25 October 1948.
94. "Dean Virginia Gildersleeve to Eleanor Roosevelt, n.d.," *RSC*, UN Part I, Microfilm Reel 6, Slide 866.
95. "Eleanor Roosevelt from Virginia Gildersleeve, October 27, 1948," *RSC*, UN Part I, Microfilm Reel, Slide 868.
96. Porter McKeever, "Oral History Interview, May 24, 1979," *AERP*, Box 3, FDRL, 6.
97. "Eleanor Roosevelt to Bernard Baruch, October 19, 1948," *ERPP*, GWU, Serial No. 027120, Bernard Baruch Papers, Mudd Manuscript Library, Princeton University, Box 1181, Folder 122, Roosevelt, Mrs FD.
98. Black, *What I Hope to Leave Behind*, 533.
99. *New York Herald Tribune*, *RSC*, GC 48, Microfilm Reel 22, Slide 551.
100. "My Day Column," 7 April 1949.
101. "Constantine Hutchins to Eleanor Roosevelt, April 12, 1949," *RSC*, GC 1948, Microfilm Reel 19, Slide 333.
102. "Eleanor Roosevelt to Constantine Hutchins, n.d.," *RSC*, GC 1948, Microfilm Reel 19, Slide 340.
103. "Frank Sakran to Eleanor Roosevelt, April 13, 1948," *RSC*, GC 1948, Microfilm Reel 28, Slide 486.
104. Ibid., Slide 487.
105. Ibid., Slide 485.

Chapter 9

Necessary Constructions
The Other in the Cold War and After

David Ryan

After the shock of 9/11 there was little surprise or questioning expressed regarding the binary construction that President Bush deployed. That night, he recorded in his diary: "The Pearl Harbor of the 21st century took place today." Over the subsequent days he would repeat such formulae, which wove through his immediate reactions. The use of these words, combined with "infamy," resonated throughout U.S. culture; the references, the sentiment, the intentions were obvious. In November 2001 he invoked the Holocaust, and by January 2002 the infamous "Axis of Evil" speech overlooked actualities in favor of a rhetorical gambit he knew many Americans would indulge. The binary formula of the Cold War was effectively, if somewhat crudely, grafted onto the "Good War" of World War II. John Dower suggests, "The president and his speechwriters lost few opportunities to cast the new crisis in the mold of the old war."[1]

Such constructions and worldviews have permeated the discourse on U.S. foreign policy, culture and cultural artifact, literature, travel writing, popular magazines, poetry, missionary writing, and political rhetoric.[2] Its attraction is mediated by the role of ideology in bridging "the gap between things as they are and as one would have them be," as Clifford Geertz suggests. In the prevailing absence of a stable national identity, the binary constructions have been prevalent and buttressed the definition of a U.S. identity, a nation defined in opposition, rather than indigenously constituted. The transformations and multiplicity of the indigenous have frequently led authors to suggest that U.S. identity has emerged from a set of values and yet the construction of these values—liberty, democracy, self-determination, individualism—stand in contradiction to much of the

American experience: servitude, empire, expansionism, and exclusive political, social, and economic practice. If a unifying identity eluded early
U.S. history, for those who preferred such essential constructions, mul-
ticulturalism challenged their quest, especially after the 1960s. Ideology
facilitated the bridge between the epistemological world view and the ontological actualities; it facilitated the discourse of "fearing and denouncing, reverencing and reviling, all of which then sometimes gets coded
into a discourse which looks as though it is describing the way things
actually are."[3] It is equally important to recognize the fallacies associated
with these world views and to account for the costs both to the United
States and to the numerous peoples engaged by its power throughout its
history. It is also important to note the sophisticated analysis and understandings of foreign policy issues in the internal record and among more
realistic diplomats or those attuned to the region and cultural sensitivities
of the nations within which they work. Yet frequently there is a compulsion to present a world view in simplistic terms; these constructions have
little bearing on the situation they propose to engage and describe. They
represent more the epistemological basis of U.S. political culture rather
than the idiosyncratic aspects of any given situation; they are drawn from
and draw on a cultural mind-set attuned to receive such constructions at
times of seeming crisis. So, for instance, the extent to which the Cold War
construction and the fallacies associated with the domino theory led the
United States into the Vietnam War with extraordinary costs for the Vietnamese population and significant costs for the United States cannot be
underestimated. Fabian Hilfrich argues that such rhetorical constructions
frequently combine a geographical premise and a psychological injunction that moves and conflates the local and the particular to the regional
and then onto the universal.[4] If, at a less intense level, the Reagan administration's characterization of the Sandinistas in Nicaragua still derived
from the same discursive threads of the Cold War, dominoes and earlier
ideological traditions, it also seemed oblivious to the lessons of the years
after the Vietnam War. More importantly, these tendencies did not originate with the bipolar constructions of the Cold War but move back in time
through to U.S. declarations of independence and the diplomatic corollary found in the Monroe Doctrine.[5] As many studies have argued, they
permeate U.S. culture. They are not confined to the United States, but the
relevance and pertinence of an idea when attached to considerable power
cannot be underestimated. And here power must be considered broadly
to include the conventional powers associated with the diplomatic, military, political, and economic realms, but these must be coupled with the
powers to narrate, to propagate and perpetuate ideological visions, to
propound public diplomacy, and to create and enhance "spheres of dis-

course." Or what Michel Foucault has identified as a "regime of truth": "the types of discourse it accepts and makes function as true." The mechanisms involved in making these statements seem true, how they are sanctioned, and the "status of those who are charged with saying what counts as true."[6]

Despite the often acrimonious political construction of "clash regimes" that emerge through significant debate and contestation, there appears to be a tendency to settle on a relatively simple formula that can be expounded, be settled, and reverberate through a multiplicity of repetitious exercises conducted not only by state agencies but through the various fields of cultural production, the media, political and cultural discourse, and academic disciplines.[7] The concentration here will be on elite discourse to examine the construction and consequences of the "clash regimes" associated with the Truman Doctrine and its derivatives: the Reagan Doctrine, the "Clash of Civilizations," and the post-9/11 discourse. In each of these areas and discursive mentalities, the power of the presidency and its associated "power to speak" cannot be discounted.[8] For Foucault, exercising power endlessly shaped and created knowledge, which in turn induced certain effects on power. Institutions, industries, and individuals associated with the defense apparatus or foreign policy-making institutes have in recent decades privileged the national security discourse, premised as it is on a threat perceived or represented. Moreover, the *national* implies both a spatial zone and a popular if not democratic consensus, whereas *security* conjures up a state of anxiety and fear, a boundary, a people, and an *other*.[9]

Such regimes of truth might temporarily serve the particular administration, they might facilitate the passage of a particular bill or an objective; they might enhance a particular aspect of U.S. identity, and sometimes they might serve to motivate and mobilize a population; the advantages of these largely domestic deliberations and deceptions are outweighed by the costs associated with the impact of policies misguided by Cold War mentalities, by Vietnam era illusions of dominos, by the cartographic fallacies of the Sandinistas sweeping toward Texas, by the metaphor of a Hitler on the Euphrates or Islamism at the proverbial gates. Such constructions ultimately trap the political actors and limit the latitude of debate, especially when imbued with the urgency of a national security issue, a sense of resolve, and an imperative to act against others who become clearly defined. But in the construction of such definitions, the particulars of the enemy, or those innocent encompassed by the definition, are disregarded. The costs to others have been enormous.[10] The costs and the implications for U.S. identity and foreign policy have been considerable.[11] By shunning the complexity involved in so many of the U.S. encounters, the footing upon which engagement occurs is frequently erroneous and fraught with unintended consequences. Moreover, the attractions of the clash regimes serve the needs of narratives associated with U.S. identity and power in world affairs and that of the presidency within the United States. That is, the centrifugal and disparate forces involved in world affairs are to some extent tamed and contained by the regime of truth, which allows the administration to avoid enquiry into and an understanding of the issues and interests of others that seek to challenge the prevailing order by attributing the dangers to some greater other, around which U.S. security discourse is defined. At times, key protagonists or opponents, struggling with their own identity, frequently claim to represent more than what they do and perpetuate the clash regime; Osama bin Laden invoked the civilizational clash in October 2001.[12]

A Grim and Uncompromising Picture

Despite the frequent and sometimes bitter historiographical debates on the origins of the Cold War and U.S. foreign policy, it is still culturally axiomatic that the United States as part of a farsighted strategy resisted the aggression and expansionism of the Soviet Union. Such narratives permeate various cultural products and expressions.[13] The epistemological structure of the Cold War was repeated endlessly in President Reagan's rhetoric, despite the countervailing ontological evidence. Of course by that stage the Soviet invasion of Afghanistan was grafted onto the cultural discourse that shaped U.S. Cold War culture.

Yet it is important to recognize that much of the internal U.S. analysis of the late 1940s did not see the Soviet Union as a direct military threat to the United States. The State Department's Policy Planning Staff's first study, PPS 1 of May 1947, indicated bluntly that the PPS "does not see communist activities as the root cause of the difficulties of western Europe." Earlier U.S. Joint Intelligence Staff in 1945 argued that the Soviets would avoid confrontation for between five years and a decade. David Campbell further cites the CIA to the effect that the Soviets did not seek the conquering of Western Europe, preferring political and economic hegemonic strategies. By 1950, George Kennan, earlier head of the PPS, pointed out that the Soviets did not intend to attack the West. Finally, through the Korean War ending in 1953, U.S. diplomats in Moscow reported that the Soviets did not seek global conflict.[14]

Two things remain problematical. First, despite this knowledge and the historiographical elaborations, orthodoxy and some postrevisionist derivatives and variations of orthodox realism in international relations have served to secure the epistemological basis for Soviet expansionism.[15] Such interpretations remain culturally plausible in the early twenty-first century. Second, despite this knowledge and the ambiguity of interpretation on the Soviet Union, depicting it as an other remained politically attractive and ultimately convincing.

Moreover, it is an irony of the period and the history of the Cold War that the bipolar constructions remained so pervasive despite the huge upheavals and transformations of those years. The loss of the bipolar configuration of power was ultimately recognized by the U.S. national security advisor to President Richard Nixon, Henry Kissinger. Or, more to the point, it was articulated after the failed Vietnam experience and the need for a more realist U.S. foreign policy; one that presumably departed not only from the open-ended liberal internationalism of the Democratic Party and presidencies, but also from some of their fantasies.[16] By the late 1960s Kissinger seemed to advance this observation without any sense of epistemological doubt. Moreover, he probably thought it a true representation of the ontological fact. Yet the Cold War period was also characterized by the displacement of numerous European empires, by the necessarily concurrent establishment of numerous new states through the decolonization process, and by the rapid growth in world population and a rapid growth in absolute global wealth accompanied by the relative impoverishment of many in the South.[17] It is no wonder that the challenges to the United States, Europe, and the Soviet Union were multiple. It is wondrous that despite this backdrop (foreground for many) that the narrative remained as strong as it did.

In some senses, perhaps, it is not that surprising. The conclusion of World War II left Europe divided, roughly where the Allied forces of the strange alliance met and, with the retreat of European powers, left two universal ideologies contending with each other. The real achievement of U.S. discourse was ultimately to further reduce this conflict to an issue concerning U.S. security, when in fact it might have been and was sometimes interpreted as a challenge to the aspirations for hegemony in the primarily political and economic spheres; Washington enjoyed the "preponderance of power" identified by Melvyn Leffler, yet the ideologies associated with its political and economic power were less secure. Nationalists from disparate parts of the world, having shed their European colonial ties, challenged the United States. It might have been the Vietnamese and Ho Chi Minh in Southeast Asia, Jacobo Árbenz and Fidel Castro in Central America and the Caribbean, Jawaharlal Nehru and Gamal Abdel Nasser in India and Egypt, but the blunt instrument epitomized by John Foster Dulles drew them into the Cold War binary. Obviously that then limited a cultural engagement and understanding of Vietnamese nationalism, of inter-American animosity dating from the early nineteenth century, or of the aspiration for nonalignment as Cold War political imperatives threatened to subvert national interests in New Delhi or Cairo. While the formal ideologies of the United States and the Soviet Union contended with each other, informal ideologies in the U.S. sphere of influence and discourse conflated the positive attributes of the myths of its diplomacy with the national security discourse and ultimately the need to protect the American way of life.[18] If the first proposition on national security was somewhat farfetched, the protection of the U.S. way of life through U.S. integration with Western Europe and a fiscal diplomacy to buttress its economy was anything but. For the same diplomats who disparaged the direct Soviet threat also recognized that they thrived on the chaos, disorder, and economic displacement that characterized the postwar European entity.

Yet the United States had undergone rapid demobilization, and there was still a Republican inclination toward isolationism and certainly a fiscal reticence especially by some Republican senators to bail out the Europeans. The Truman administration was not at liberty to push too directly for the U.S. defense of Europe unless there was a strategic security issue in it for the United States. They could not push the Europeans too hard either on the issue of decolonization despite its theoretical ideological offense to the United States. Moreover, the colonial world, albeit in transition, provided the U.S. with access to colonial economies through European markets and connections. Marshall Aid not only permeated the European economies, but also reached out to some peripheral areas. Importantly, through the politics of seeming prosperity, it simultaneously served to dampen the Socialist alternatives in some European areas.[19]

The Soviet threat was the preferred vehicle to mobilize and justify U.S. intervention and integration into European affairs at the origins of the Cold War. By 1950 the language of NSC 68 was put together by a committee headed by Paul Nitze, then head of the PPS after the departure of George Kennan. The document followed the Soviet explosion of their atomic bomb and the fall of China to communism in 1949. The document, widely regarded as a blueprint for the U.S. Cold War strategy, grafted its agenda onto the "fundamental purpose of the United States" pitting the free world against a society now associated with slavery and fascism in the form of a new Red menace. The binary construction of the Cold War was enhanced through such depictions that had been rehearsed throughout the decades preceding the construction of the Iron Curtain.[20] The constructions of us versus them advanced consensus at the cost of nuance and complexity. For Clifford Geertz, the ideology was: "Dualistic, opposing the pure 'we' to the evil 'they,' proclaiming that he who is not with me is against me. It is alienate in that it distrusts, attacks, and works to undermine established political institutions. It is doctrinaire in that it claims complete and exclusive possession of political truth and abhors compromise. It is totalistic in that it aims to order the whole of social and cultural life in the image of its ideals, futuristic in that it works toward a utopian culmination of history in which such an ordering will be realized."[21] For Emily Rosenberg "NSC 68 ... employs a familiar technique of militant nationalism: trying to forge a national consensus through the creation of a symbolic 'other,'" seemingly in opposition to U.S. traditions and power.[22] The document advanced three propositions to ensure its fundamental purpose. The first identified the "determination to maintain the essential elements of individual freedom ... our determination to create conditions under which our free and democratic system can live and prosper; and our determination to fight if necessary to defend our way of life."[23] Though the document was classified as secret, NSC 59/1, implemented by Edward Barratt, assistant secretary of state for public affairs, initiated the Campaign for Truth that disseminated the message through a range of media and exhibitions. Michael Kammen describes the cultural responses as "cohesive and patterned like a carefully designed fabric."[24]

The pattern in the fabric had such appeal because Truman's speech was immediately likened to Franklin D. Roosevelt's "Quarantine" speech of 1937 with the added metaphor of containment advanced by George Kennan.[25] In 1947 Kennan had come to welcome the Soviet challenge, though he also recognized that it was largely political, not military. He wrote in the infamous "X article" published in *Foreign Affairs* that: "surely there was never a fairer test of national quality than this." The observer of U.S.-Soviet relations would "find no cause for complaint in the Kremlin's challenge to American society." He believed that the challenge would require the entire nation to pull together and accept the "responsibilities of moral and political leadership that history plainly intended them to bear."[26]

Yet despite the timing of this writing there was disagreement between Kennan and the administration. Of course Kennan's "long telegram" had provided the initial intellectual basis for containment, though its influence was not exclusive and other tributaries enhanced the flow of the ideas. Famously, he identified in the Soviet Union "a political force committed fanatically to the belief that with the U.S. there can be no *modus vivendi*, that it is desirable and necessary that the internal harmony of our society be disrupted, our traditional way of life destroyed, the international authority of our state be broken if Soviet power is to be secure." Kennan's analysis understood that their position was based not on any "objective analysis of the situation beyond Russia's borders," but derived from "basic inner Russian necessities." Moreover, the prospects of a Soviet invasion of Western Europe were "highly unlikely."[27] Decades later he characterized the telegram, akin to a "primer for school children," further, "a grim and uncompromising picture [that] aroused a strain of emotional and self-righteous anti-Sovietism, which in later years I will wish I had not aroused."[28]

Still, a year later Truman, in the most prominent public articulation of containment, advanced what became known as his doctrine. Though the Soviets were not explicitly identified, there was little mystery on the object of his remarks. The crucial point though is that in waging this piece of public theater to wrest some $400 million from Congress in aid of the regimes in Greece and Turkey, he not only enhanced the Manichaean outlook, but posited that there were only two ways of life in world history and that peoples had to face this defining choice. One was characterized by all the positive attributes of an orthodox reading of U.S. history (oblivious to alternative readings and interpretations, let alone the prevalence of racial separation) and the other by an orthodox reading of the Soviet Union.

The formulation was necessary because U.S. policy makers had recognized and responded to the early stages of the collapse of the British Empire. They recognized the need for U.S. integration into the European economy for both political and economic reasons. Yet given the reluctance of some Republicans, the situation had to be presented in stark terms; as Senator Arthur Vandenberg had advised administration officials, it was necessary to "scare hell" out of the American people.[29]

The actualities of the separate situations in Greece and Turkey were largely glossed over. The administration was well aware that Stalin was not the source of supply and support for the disparate Greek opposition groups loosely united in the Greek National Liberation Front. Truman's language injected a crusading spirit that would vitiate U.S. foreign policy for the next two decades, and resurface in the early Reagan years. It lay at the foundations of the so-called Cold War consensus centered on the binary conflict between the West and the East.[30]

If to some extent Europe had been the object of the other in the Monroe Doctrine of 1823, the new West now incorporated at least half of it. The concept had to paint over and incorporate transatlantic disagreements, alliances with European colonial powers, and the integration of certain Third World states. All of this relied on the three approaches to alterity. The othering of the Soviet Union was an imperative strategy that facilitated the hierarchy of alterity that fit European colonialism within the matrix as a lower order other, one whose differences could ultimately be accommodated. The others from the new independent states would be treated and regarded in different ways. As a generalization, U.S. orientalism seemed far more prevalent toward countries dominated by nationalism or socialism or those that maintained certain affinities to Moscow. Whereas those more inclined toward the new West could be accommodated in the universalizing mission of U.S. integration: political, economic, ideological, and cultural. They would "develop out" of their differences through modernization. Particular traditions would erode and evolve toward a more universal modernity.

Still the U.S. pursuit of leadership ran up against European agendas and their suspicion of an overbearing American influence. Moreover, there was resistance from the left in the U.S. Democratic Party and the isolationist Republican right. The new Western identity was threatened by significant internal confusion. European powers still maintained colonial empires. That fact had to be squared with U.S. identity. The Soviets were weak and withdrawn. The European left was still attractive. Such complexity hindered social mobilization. How could the United States support European colonial powers? How could they overcome resistance to a greater U.S. global agenda? How could Washington overcome the resistance of the European left? The Cold War narrative had to be raised above the particularities and inconsistencies in the transatlantic relationship. The concept of the West was indispensable to mobilize Congress with their fiscal prerogatives. The Western Hemisphere, once that geographical and ideological territory west of the Atlantic, now transcended the ocean in the new West. The expanded West would encompass these colonial powers and maintain the narrative of freedom and self-determination. Such metaphorical discordance could only be accommodated through references to the Soviet threat. What other device could facilitate U.S. integration into Europe?[31]

The metaphor of the West, the new West, encompassing colonial Europe while simultaneously projecting that colonial identity onto the Soviets, re-created and perpetuated the identity and notion of U.S. benevolence. The dominant histories and more importantly U.S. collective memory advanced a benign meta-narrative of the U.S. diplomatic experience. The American "empire" was removed from U.S. history and consciousness, or dismissed as an aberration. The United States was until recently still missing from the realm of postcolonial studies, though its real cultural power flourished during this period. This absence has reproduced an American exceptionalism from without. The histories of U.S. westward expansion and that of European colonialism are treated as separate phenomena, thus preserving the narrative of American exceptionalism, which is applied to the concept of the West.[32]

The politics of identity and its projection became paramount because of the lingering skepticism of the United States within Europe. That the skepticism rested more at the elite levels in European society made the role and propagation of U.S. culture even more important. But the political, economic, and cultural projection of the United States into Europe cannot be separated. The influence of the concept of the West, offered by Truman and echoed culturally, represented the lowest common denominator between the U.S. and Europe. The imperial extension of U.S. culture and politics was denied, while simultaneously Soviet imperial policies were highlighted. As Amy Kaplan argues, "if the vehemence and persistence with which something is denied mark its importance and even formative power, the characterization of a nation's ideological opponents reveals as much about that nation's self-conception as it does about its enemies."[33] The dichotomies created in the long telegram, the Truman Doctrine, and the X article, and through the cultural dissemination of the content of NSC 68, represent the reduction of the identities of the Soviet Union and the West. Perhaps obviously, the complexities could not be admitted because ultimately there was a fundamental contradiction in the Cold War West. As David Gress argues, "to enroll such contradictory ideas in a common front required that the distinctions be ignored or elided."[34]

The conception of the West had to be advanced at several levels for long-term ideological acceptance. Politically, the narratives were well advanced by the early 1950s. The metaphors generated were of utmost importance and derived their powers through the all-encompassing concept of the West. Economically, the West was largely substantiated in the consolidation of the Marshall Plan, NATO provided the security umbrella, and the USIA disseminated the narrative. Only now, the United States was wedded to a West that also had access to a multitude of colonial areas.

There was urgency to the political message. Any doubts about containment were dispelled with analogies of Munich and appeasement. Munich and the word containment, the Iron Curtain, and the metaphor of the West all conjured up mental images of a geographical threat and an ideological unity; they were frequently deployed in Moscow too. The geographical content of U.S. diplomatic and cultural language buttressed the ideological messages.[35] Images of a divided Europe mapped out the essential differences; the neat geographical demarcations reinforced the binary vision and ideological construction of the West. Politically, economically, and culturally, the Americans were the principal cartographers. They implicitly constructed the "paths, or channels along which a person regularly travels," the "landmarks or signs to which he refers for self-location," and the orientation of others.[36]

The consequences were dire. For Michael Hunt, Congress was overshadowed and "the public left in the dark, and a cult of national security has flourished." The trends undermined the U.S. system of checks and balances, "restricted the flow of information, impeded intelligent debate, and diminished the electoral accountability of policymakers—all serious blows to the workings of a democratic political system."[37] Similar arguments were levied by Fredrik Logevall in his study of the Johnson administration's *Choosing War* in Vietnam; one might also suggest that the paucity of debate after 9/11 paved the path to Iraq.[38]

Truman's speech and the subsequent policy mind-set and cultural disposition to read the world through such lenses caused innumerable problems. The doctrine was enunciated in response to a particular and regional problem, yet it was articulated in terms of a universal crusade. Given the political alignment and the interests *within* Washington, the limits of policy and power could not be articulated. The mobilization of domestic opinion and congressional support in this case required the referencing and creation of an all-encompassing Soviet identity and set of objectives. Such inclinations caused difficulties not just in this region but also in readings of U.S. nationalism and nationalist aspirations throughout the Cold War. For Theodore Draper writing in the 1980s, the "mixture of a universal doctrine with limited means of action created a dangerous mixture of illusion and reality which we have yet to rid ourselves of."[39] The universalization of policy and its implications required the universalization of the Soviet threat. Moreover, once the threat had been made all pervasive, the temptation to respond stretched U.S. commitments and credibility to the breaking point during the 1960s. That it survived the 1980s resulted largely from the fact that the Reagan administration's policies on Central America did not face any real threat, but were conjured from the same cultural illusions and discourse, once again set within a Cold War frame.

Drawing A Line

By May 1985 the Reagan administration declared a national emergency in the United States because the Sandinistas posed "an unusual and extraordinary threat" to U.S. foreign policy. At that point the administration had been freed from the constraints of the 1984 electoral campaign, in which they did not want to appear too bellicose given that polling data on Central America and more particularly on Nicaragua suggested doubts about the gist of the Reagan narrative.[40] It was not that the public did not support the Reagan policies on other regional conflicts, especially in Afghanistan, which had been the object of direct Soviet intervention. It was more that the administration's claims on Nicaragua, Soviet and Cuban assistance to the Sandinistas, and U.S. militarism seemed inappropriate. To many Americans, less than a decade out of the Vietnam War, the Reagan policies in the region threatened to bring on another quagmire and the associated losses of people, power, and prestige. A sufficient number of Americans wanted nothing to do with the policies. The Reagan administration's stories on Nicaragua, Cuba, and the Soviet Union lacked credibility.

It started early and is best depicted in the wording of advice Reagan received on the campaign trail in 1980. The administration was divided by loosely defined pragmatists and ideologues who informed policy and the Reagan vision in different ways. Despite frequent inclination toward moderation, even in Central America, the rhetoric and associated acrimonious cultural discourse was informed more frequently by the ideologues. In 1980 the Committee of Santa Fe released a policy guidance document that indicated "survival demands a new U.S. foreign policy. America must seize the initiative or perish. For World War III is almost over." "The crisis," it asserted, "is metaphysical" because the United States' inability or unwillingness to protect its basic values after the Vietnam War had contributed to a "nadir of indecision and impotence." According to this influential group, many of which found employment in the administration months later, the Soviets had penetrated the Western Hemisphere, and Cuban aid throughout the isthmus generated huge problems and "in turn presents great opportunities for both Cuba and the Soviet Union in Mexico with its oil and Panama with its canal."[41] In 1980 this was not really about the strength of the Cubans or the Soviets in Central America. It had more to do with the lingering influence of the loss in the Vietnam War.

Despite the nationalistic and indigenous characteristics of the Sandinista revolution, it was imperative for the administration to depict the troubles in Nicaragua in Cold War terms and terminology.[42] Various public diplomacy campaigns were launched early in 1981. The secretary of state, Alexander Haig, infamously drew a line in El Salvador over which depictions of the advance of communism would not cross. Of course the FMLN, the Salvadoran coalition of rebel movements, was indigenous and significantly independent, yet securing San Salvador and its brutal and fragile regime was deemed imperative in the face of Sandinista export of weapons, the Cuban export of revolution, and the Soviet violation of the Monroe Doctrine. The Reagan requests for funding for the anti-Sandinista *contras* were based on the argument of interdiction of the weapons supply to the Salvadoran rebels. Yet it was well known at the time and subsequently extensively documented that the obvious and real intention was to overthrow the regime in Managua. However, the administration fight for funding on Capitol Hill was always fraught with problems and the U.S. public remained opposed to the initiatives largely because by the end of 1981 they believed that Reagan would lead them into another (Central American) Vietnam.

The frustrations that the administration experienced in terms of funding and congressional and public support eventually led the president to deliver a speech on the importance of Central America. In the absence of a consensus on the regional aspects of the situation, Reagan moved to secure the Cold War narrative, depicting the Sandinistas and all regional opposition as a part of the same issue. "We have a vital interest, a moral duty, and a solemn responsibility," he told the Congressional audience in April 1983. By this stage it was not just a question of U.S. division and internal opposition; Latin American and West European allies largely opposed Reagan's interpretation of the situation and his policies. The rhetorical deployment represented an extraordinary display of orientalism. It was imperative to the administration that legislators and wider audiences understood the geostrategic implications of the region. Reagan identified the physical threat to the Sea Lanes of Communication running through the Caribbean, depicting Central America as adjacent to "our lifeline to the outside world." He invoked the Nazi interests in the region during World War II and the ongoing Soviet interests. If they recognized the importance of the region, shouldn't the United States? He quoted extensively from the Truman Doctrine again, depicting a bipolar world in which choices were important.[43]

A part of the explanation relates to the Reagan outlook on the world, the relatively straightforward Manichaean depiction of regional opponents of the United States set within his global vision of U.S. power and opposition to a Soviet-centered system. Another part of the explanation relates to the balance of power between groups of ideologues and pragmatists within the administration. In the earlier years the ideologues held sway, though the pragmatists did what they could to limit the damage.[44] It is instructive that after the transition to the George H.W. Bush administration in 1989, the State Department and National Security Council did what it could to remove Central America from the forefront of the U.S. foreign policy agenda. Indeed secret negotiations with the Sandinistas were conducted on normalizing relations before they were ousted from power at the ballot box.[45] Another part of the explanation rests with the U.S. attempt, filtered through the Reagan vision and composition of his administration, to bolster its power in the wake of the Vietnam War and to restore the foreign policy consensus that was popularly depicted around the Cold War framework and the Soviet threat. In such discourse and thinking, "there are no grey areas, no complexities, no historicized understandings, no doubts about the self, and no qualms about the nature of the response," Campbell writes on a similar depiction.[46]

Central America was ontologically and geostrategically unimportant by the 1980s; yet epistemologically it represented the crux between power and identity for some in the Reagan administration. Given the guiding beliefs, the ideology, and the depictions, and given also that the administration removed the regional experts that served as U.S. ambassadors to the isthmian countries and replaced them with Vietnam era diplomats, there was little doubt that the situation would be depicted in an accepted conceptual form, despite the U.S. intelligence and diplomatic reporting from other agencies and foreign service officers. In that sense the orientalist depiction of the Sandinistas as the other, aligned directly through Havana and Moscow, was considered critical to winning U.S. and Congressional support for the faltering policies. Further, once the threat had been aligned to a rhetorical commitment to the *contras* there was no backing away from the situation after the withdrawal from Vietnam until the 1989 change of administration in Washington.

In the absence of any ontological threat in the region to the United States, the wording connected to the 1985 national emergency is instructive. The threat to the foreign policy of the United States was more related to the inability of the administration to construct a consensus in this policy and of the nation to unite around a common purpose after the Vietnam War. Significantly, the actual export of weapons had ended in 1981; the Cuban presence remained, but was not decisive. The Soviet provision of weapons increased in tandem to the militarization of the region across the years 1981 to 1984, but crucially the Soviet weapons were largely defensive in nature. U.S. or U.S.-backed offensives had not only been anticipated, but should one occur, it was indicated that the Sandinistas would be able to inflict sufficient damage to stay the public support for the intervention.[47]

Imaginary Fault Lines

If the Reagan administration's depiction of the Central American crisis represented one of the last (yet strident) gasps of the Cold War construction, just as the Soviet Union was corroding and then collapsing internally, there was a nervous sense of indirection in the early years of the Bush administration. The secretary of state, James Baker, clearly recognized the end of an era and the fact that the United States had no more signposts to guide its foreign policy. The strategic review of the spring of 1989 produced no more than a steady-as-she-goes policy buttressed by a firmer grip on realism and U.S. interests characterized at the time as "status quo plus." Articulated in 1988 and published in 1989, the former head of the Policy Planning Staff, Francis Fukuyama, advanced the End of History thesis centered on the certainty and triumph of an advancing liberal democratic capitalism. Yet this formula for a universal homogenous state, the terminus of history, lacked the appeal of the more strenuous aspects of U.S. policy popularized almost a century earlier by Theodore Roosevelt.

Other and more particular theses were advanced, but the Samuel Huntington thesis on the Clash of Civilizations had a far wider appeal and resonance in the cultural discourse. Its resonance related not just to its timing, but to the desire to find direction and purpose, to craft a new identity, or to craft a new enemy other around which the positive aspects of U.S. identity could be grafted. The thesis resonated through the institutions and individuals habituated to the Cold War discourse and decades of enculturation into the national security discourse.

Huntington's thesis advanced the idea that the fundamental source of conflict would move from the ideological and economic to the cultural sphere in the future. Bluntly stated, it would exist between the civilizations identified by the author. "The fault lines between civilizations will be the battle lines of the future."[48] The article provided an Olympian geopolitical view of the past centuries of conflict, up through the Cold War. As that conflict drew to an end it was, Huntington argued, replaced by the cultural division between "Europe ... and Western Christianity, on the one hand, and Orthodox Christianity and Islam, on the other." Coinciding with the war in Bosnia, the article, first produced in the journal *Foreign Affairs*, included a graphic of a new line running down through Europe, slightly to the right of the Iron Curtain, depicting the division between the Habsburg and Ottoman empires. All the attendant values and myths associated with such depictions resonate with this division. Gearóid Ó Tuathail has amply demonstrated that such thinking, though unavoidably textual, "it nevertheless promotes a special way of thinking that arranges different actors, elements and locations simultaneously on a global chessboard." The combination of the geographical (worldwide) and the conceptual (comprehensive and total) "appears more visual than verbal, more objective and detached than subjective and ideological."[49] Certainly the emergent discourse on the clash between the West and Islam resonated throughout the period, grafted as it was onto the tail of the Gulf War, but also the more widespread discourse since 1979 as well as the Iranian revolution and Reagan's and other Western media depictions of Islamic terrorism. The orientalism associated with the reductions to the "West against the rest" thus depicted a world view of "a Western 'here' (the United States and Europe) and a Rest 'over there' (all lands beyond these regions) but more profoundly a clash between an 'us' ... and a 'them.'"[50]

Ultimately the thesis created another bipolar depiction of the world that also resonated later, in the days after 9/11. The challenge from these different cultures ensured that history could not end and cautioned against any U.S. complacency relating to defense and national security issues. Just because the Soviet threat had receded—no, imploded ("receded" reinforces the spatial imagery of the threat)—that was no reason not to think about revolutionary Islamism, terrorism, or the combination thereof. The focus on such externalized other, preferably depicted as a unified entity, facilitated the articulation of the positive aspects of U.S. identity and legitimated or at least excused the ongoing U.S. support and funding for a range of authoritarian regimes, which would not experience pressure until 2011. The presentation of a challenge by a seemingly simple, monolithic external force seemed essential in U.S. cultural discourse. The pity is that rarely did such a unified entity exist; certainly not during the Cold War, not even in the guise of the Islamist threat. An even greater pity is that once the discourse acquired credibility through repetition and reverberation by individuals and institutions, policy makers would then use that frame of reference to advance particular objectives.

Ultimately the relationship between language, discourse, and power needs to be considered. Why stop the domino in Vietnam? Because ultimately it would threaten the West and its possessions, challenging its power and the centrality of the narratives that it advances. Similarly, the new clash regime, buttressed by the graphic and cultural echoes, implied that defense or containment was required at the frontier or the fault line. Said writes: "Thus to build a conceptual framework around the notion of us-versus-them is in effect to pretend that the principal consideration is epistemological and natural—our civilization is known and accepted, theirs is different and strange—whereas in fact the framework separating us from them is belligerent, constructed, and situational."[51]

Though the Clinton administration rejected the thesis it remained culturally relevant in the contexts of the Bosnian War, the post–Gulf War and Cold War era. It applied similarly erroneous logic that had been applied in the early Cold War years, leading to numerous instances of misinterpretation in regional conflicts from Korea to Vietnam and Central America that resulted in millions of fatalities.[52] Moreover, homogenizing the macro-level identity of the other implied also a unified and coherent West. This thesis ignored the intra-civilizational conflict and the lack of shared objectives by groups within the cultures.[53] For Edward Said, Huntington had extended two ideas put forward by Bernard Lewis in his "Roots of Muslim Rage," an article first published in the *Atlantic Monthly*. First, there was the notion that civilizations were both monolithic and homogenous. And second, he develops his overarching argument on the assumption that there is an "unchanging character of the duality between 'us' and 'them.'"[54]

While derivatives of this regime of truth circulated throughout Western media, invoking a range of academic retort, the cultural effect remained. The article generated more discussion than any other article in *Foreign Affairs* since the publication of the X article in 1947. It made an extraordinary mark, according to Melani McAlister; Huntington revived the classical orientalist understanding of the world; his thesis moves beyond the East and the West because simultaneously he identifies seven, possibly eight, civilizations *and* reduces the likely clash to the West and the rest. As in classical orientalism, the civilizations of which he talks are seemingly unchanging, "facing each other along clean lines of belief and value."[55] These constructed images often have very little bearing on reality and the ontological particulars of given situations and spaces. Nevertheless, Arshin Adib-Moghaddam argues, "The reason why it was possible for Huntington and others to replant this idea in the twentieth century and for their argument to gain such prominence is exactly because it was nurtured within this regime of truth that has been located in those real and imagined early encounters. The clash regime is nourished and sustained by this circulation of myths and their institutionalisation."[56]

Fred Halliday clearly demonstrated in numerous writings that such truth regimes had very little to do with the "facts of international relations." The concept of a threat ascribed to Islamism is simply invalid, which he demonstrates by deconstructing the language of politicians in both realms and revealing the internal incoherence of the so-called civilizations. Sure these regimes testify to well-defined differences, but Halliday also argues that much of these arguments are taken from secular realms and applied to contemporary needs.[57]

Framing Depictions

"Why do they hate us?" George W. Bush asked after 9/11. His explanation moved to advance the orientalist discourse that would be necessary to precede the impending clash. "They hate what we see right here in this chamber—a democratically elected government. Their leaders are self-appointed. They hate our freedoms—our freedom of religion, our freedom of speech, our freedom to vote and assemble and disagree with each other."[58] There was no mention of U.S. power, position, or influence in the Middle East and elsewhere. There was no mention of the U.S. support for a range of anti-democratic and undemocratic regimes throughout the Middle East and during the Cold War world. There was no mention of decades of U.S. involvement in the region: its support for the Saudi Arabian ruling family, the U.S. military presence on the peninsula, or the still resonant U.S.-assisted overthrow of Mohammad Mosaddegh in Iran and its subsequent support for the Shah from 1953 to 1979. There was no mention of the U.S. support for Saddam Hussein prior to 1990. There was no mention of the Gulf War and U.S. opposition after 1991. Douglas Little

controversially argued that even though Bin Laden's occidentalism provided a mirror image of U.S. orientalism, "the attack on the World Trade
center was also a product of the unintended consequences of five decades
of U.S. policy in the Middle East." He was referring not just to the enmity
of Bin Laden or al Qaeda, but also of Ayatollah Khomeini; had the United
States had a modicum of tolerance "for the devil of revolutionary nationalism after 1945," it might have averted the extremism of the confrontation
in the late twentieth and early twenty-first centuries.[59] Lewis Lapham, the
editor of *Harpers*, argued that nothing could excuse the actions of 9/11,
"but neither can we excuse our own arrogance behind the scenes of shock
and disbelief. Enthralled by an old script, we didn't see the planes coming
because we didn't think we had to look."[60] Yet David Clark, an advisor
to the British foreign secretary, argued that in the longer term the United
States would have to reflect on the lessons of this terrible attack. He stated
the attacks "took place within a political context that we ourselves have
helped to shape. Something rotten has happened to relations between the
West and the rest. In many parts of the developing world a deep sense of
alienation has begun to manifest itself in a hatred of the industrialized
countries and the U.S. in particular."[61] Certainly in the decade since 9/11,
little of this sort of reflection is evident in the upper echelons of the United
States. Bush embellished the old script. There was no need to question
U.S. history or foreign policy. The United States, he told his audience at
the National Cathedral days after the attacks, would fight the enemies of
human freedom. Moreover, he told his audience in Congress, that "this is
not … just America's fight. And what is at stake is not just America's freedom. This is the world's fight. This is civilization's fight. This is the fight of
all who believe in progress and pluralism, tolerance and freedom."[62] This
was the deployment of the rhetorical framework, removed from history,
the situation, and the context. Here were the words that would no doubt
comfort and uplift his audience and obscure inquiry. It would obviously
be difficult to advance criticism of the U.S. president under such circumstances, but these words, so divorced from various interpretations of U.S.
history and foreign policy, conjured yet another version of the orientalist
gaze. They were only possible because, as Adib-Moghaddam explains,
no regime of truth "could function without the empirical inference of an
archive. The power of the clash regime emanates from the salience of its
constitutive discourses which are 'thickened' via innumerable narratives
situated within that socially engineered constellation."[63]

Bush's orientalist construction of the enemy that the United States faced
led to innumerable definitional and policy complications. The rhetorical
framework advanced that well-worn essential U.S. meta-narrative associated with all the benign aspects of its national mythology, but one that is

repeated endlessly and without so much as an ironic smirk in U.S. culture. Second, despite objections to the contrary, the framework that emerged in the weeks after 9/11 was essentially orientalist. The other that was created in the U.S. public discourse did not only allow the early and easy conflation of al Qaeda with the Taliban, leading to the U.S. intervention of October 2001, from which Obama has spent years trying to figure out how to leave with political credibility intact—but later the conflation of the "terrorists and the tyrants" also purported the links and in part the justification to invade Iraq in 2003; the secular Saddam Hussein was in league with the Islamists.[64] The tragedy is that the frame and context of 9/11 was so strong that little sophisticated political debate in the United States took place on the merits of invasion before Iraq was engaged. Bush even drew associations with the meta-narrative of U.S. opponents when he argued that "We have seen their kind before. They are the heirs of all the murderous ideologies of the 20th Century ... they follow in the path of fascism, and Nazism, and totalitarianism." Finally, Bush echoed the defining choice in history that President Truman offered his audience in 1947, as he asserted that states were either with the United States or with the terrorists.[65]

It was not just the enormity of the events of 9/11 that Bush framed in a particular way. He defined the United States as freedom's home and defender. He conjured an image of a unified nation: "Americans from every walk of life unite in our resolve." The unity was in part premised on a received other. It was not just the discourse after 9/11 in the U.S. media; this simply echoed decades, if not two centuries, of U.S. discourse. It was the intellectual predisposition of the leadership and the media to follow suit. This was the archive, the constellation, the inclination to talk and to see through these prisms. Even before 9/11 and the presidency Bush tried to identify an indefinite yet certain enemy: "when I was coming up, with what was a dangerous world, we knew exactly who they were. It was us versus them, and it was clear who the them were. Today we're not so sure who the they are, but we know they're there."[66] In the wake of the 9/11 attacks such rhetoric was received with even more credibility.

Here was just the latest manifestation in a long tradition that reached back to the earliest parts of U.S. history, but of course was also much broader than that. Arshin Adib-Moghaddam suggests that throughout history there have been sufficient individuals advancing these constructions, which are well endowed and institutionally entrenched, and that they have propagated such ideas and formalized them through "exclusionary definitions of self and other." Moreover, such discourse works precisely because it echoes in a society fed through various disciplines on "clash-conducive memories ..."[67]

Notes

1. Bob Woodward, *Plan of Attack* (New York: Simon and Schuster, 2004), 24; George W. Bush, *Decision Points* (London: Virgin Books, 2010), 126–49; John W. Dower, *Cultures of War: Pearl Harbor/Hiroshima/9-11/Iraq* (New York: W. W. Norton, 2010), 10.
2. Malini Johar Schueller, *U.S. Orientalisms: Race, Nation, and Gender in Literature, 1790-1890* (Ann Arbor: University of Michigan Press, 1998).
3. Clifford Geertz, *The Interpretation of Cultures* (London: Fontana, 1993), 204–05; Terry Eagleton, *Ideology: An Introduction* (London: Verso, 1991), 15, 18–19.
4. Fabian Hilfrich, "Visions of the Asian Periphery: Vietnam (1964-1968) and the Philippines (1898-1900)," in *America, the Vietnam War, and the World*, ed. Andreas W. Daum, Lloyd C. Gardner, and Wilfried Mausbach (Cambridge: Cambridge University Press, 2003), 53–54, 57.
5. David Ryan, *US Foreign Policy in World History* (London: Routledge, 2000), 1–54.
6. Michel Foucault, cited by Arshin Adib-Moghaddam, *A Metahistory of the Clash of Civilisations: Us and Them Beyond Orientalism* (London: Hurst and Company, 2011), 5–6.
7. See for instance Pierre Bourdieu, *The Field of Cultural Production: Essays on Art and Literature* (Cambridge: Polity, 1993), 106–07.
8. The term is analyzed by William K. Muir in "Ronald Reagan: The Primacy of Rhetoric," in *Leadership in the Modern Presidency*, ed. Fred I. Greenstein (Cambridge, MA: Harvard University Press, 1988).
9. Gearóid Ó Tauthail, "Thinking Critically about Geopolitics," in *The Geopolitical Reader*, ed. Simon Dalby and Paul Routledge (London: Routledge, 1998), 3–4. See also Michel Foucault, *The Archaeology of Knowledge* (London: Routledge, 1989); Michael Foucault, *The Courage of Truth: The Government of Self and Others II*, Lectures at the Collège de France, 1983–1984, ed. Frédéric Gros (London: Palgrave, 2012); Walter Hixon, *The Myth of American Diplomacy: National Identity and U.S. Foreign Policy* (New Haven: Yale University Press, 2008).
10. John Tirman, *The Deaths of Others: The Fate of Civilians in America's Wars* (Oxford: Oxford University Press, 2011); Ted Honderich, *After the Terror* (Edinburgh: Edinburgh University Press, 2002).
11. Ryan, *US Foreign Policy in World History*.
12. Osama bin Laden, "Terror for Terror," in *Messages to the World: The Statements of Osama Bin Laden*, ed. Bruce Lawrence (London: Verso, 2005), 124; Gilbert Achcar, *The Clash of Barbarisms: September 11 and the Making of the New World Disorder* (New York: Monthly Review Press, 202); Tariq Ali, *The Clash of Fundamentalisms: Crusades, Jihads and Modernity* (London: Verso, 2002).
13. David Ryan, "Mapping Containment," in *Cold War Culture*, ed. Douglas Field (Manchester: Manchester University Press, 2004); Scott Lucas, *Freedom's War: The US Crusade against the Soviet Union 1945-56* (New York: New York University Press, 1999); David W. Noble, "The Reconstruction of Progress: Charles Beard, Richard Hofstadter and Postwar Historical Thought," in *Recasting America: Culture and Politics in the Age of Cold War*, ed. Lary May (Chicago: The University of Chicago Press, 1989), 74; Rob Kroes, "American Empire and Cultural Imperialism: A View from the Receiving End," *Diplomatic History* 23, no. 3 (Summer 1999): 465; Christian G. Appy, ed., *Cold War Constructions: The Political Culture of the United States Imperialism, 1945-1966* (Amherst: University of Massachusetts Press, 2000); Walter L. Hixon, *Parting the Curtain: Propaganda, Culture and the Cold War, 1945-1961* (London: Macmillan, 1997); Michael Kammen, *Mystic Chords of Memory: The Transformation of Tradition in American Culture* (New York: Vintage Books, 1993), 574; Michael J. Hogan, *A Cross of Iron: Harry S. Truman and the Origins of the National Security State, 1945-1954* (Cambridge: Cambridge University Press, 1998), 17–18; Jessica C.E. Gienow-Hecht, "Shame on U.S.? Academics, Cultural Transfer, and the

Cold War—A Critical Review," *Diplomatic History* 24, no. 3 (Summer 2000): 467–69; Alan K. Henrikson, "Mental Maps," in *Explaining the History of American Foreign Relations*, ed. Michael J. Hogan and Thomas G. Paterson (Cambridge: Cambridge University Press, 1992), 177–78, 189.

14. David Campbell, *Writing Security: United States Foreign Policy and the Politics of Identity* (Minneapolis: University of Minnesota Press, 1992), 27–28.

15. Ibid., 21–23.

16. Henry Kissinger, "Memorandum from the President's Assistant for National Security Affairs to President Nixon, Analysis of Changes in International Politics since World War II and Their Implications for Our Basic Assumptions about U.S. Foreign Policy, October 20, 1969," Document 41 in *Foreign Relations of the United States, 1969-1976*, vol. 1, Foundations of Foreign Policy, 1969-1972 (Washington, DC, 2003), 123–39.

17. Eric Hobsbawm, *Age of Extremes: The Short Twentieth Century, 1914-1991* (London: Michael Joseph, 1994).

18. Hixon, *The Myth of American Diplomacy*; Ryan, *US Foreign Policy in World History*; Melvyn P. Leffler, *The Specter of Communism: The United States and the Origins of the Cold War, 1917-1953* (New York: Hill & Wang, 1994), 38, 62.

19. Thomas G. Paterson, *On Every Front: The Making and Unmaking of the Cold War*, rev. ed. (New York: W. W. Norton, 1992), 106; Ryan, *US Foreign Policy and World History*, 119.

20. Patrick Wright, *Iron Curtain: From Stage to Cold War* (Oxford: Oxford University Press, 2007).

21. Geertz, *Interpretation of Cultures*, 198.

22. Emily Rosenberg in *American Cold War Strategy: Interpreting NSC 68*, ed. Ernest R. May (Boston: Bedford Books, 1993), 161–62.

23. Campbell, *Writing Security*, 25.

24. Kammen, *Mystic Chords of Memory*, 572; David Ryan, "Mapping Containment: The Cultural Construction of the Cold War," in *American Cold War Culture*, ed. Douglas Field (Edinburgh: Edinburgh University Press, 2005), 62.

25. Robert L. Ivie, "Fire, Flood, and Red Fever: Motivating Metaphors of Global Emergency in the Truman Doctrine Speech," *Presidential Studies Quarterly* 29, no. 3 (September 1999), 570.

26. X [George Kennan], "The Sources of Soviet Conduct," *Foreign Affairs* 25 (July 1947), 582.

27. John Lewis Gaddis, *Strategies of Containment: A Critical Appraisal of Postwar American National Security Policy* (Oxford: Oxford University Press, 1982), 49–50; John Lewis Gaddis, *The United States and the Origins of the Cold War 1941-1947* (New York: Columbia University Press, 1972), 322.

28. Ryan, *US Foreign Policy and World History*, 121–22.

29. Walter LaFeber, *America, Russia and the Cold War, 1945-1990* (New York: McGraw-Hill, 1991), 53.

30. Richard A. Melanson, *American Foreign Policy since the Vietnam War: The Search for Consensus from Richard Nixon to George W. Bush* (London: M.E. Sharpe, 2005), 3–17.

31. Ryan, "Mapping Containment," 50–65; Christopher Shannon, *A World Made Safe for Differences: Cold War Intellectuals and the Politics of Identity* (Lanham: Rowman and Littlefield, 2001), 13; Christian G. Appy, ed., *Cold War Constructions: The Political Culture of the United States Imperialism, 1945-1966* (Amherst: University of Massachusetts Press, 2000); David Gress, *From Plato to NATO: The Idea of the West and Its Opponents* (New York: The Free Press, 1998), 410, 415.

32. Amy Kaplan, "'Left Alone with America': The Absence of Empire in the Study of American Culture," in *Cultures of United States Imperialism*, ed. Amy Kaplan and Donald E. Pease (Durham, NC: Duke University Press, 1993), 17. In addition, the point is that interests transcend identity. If one concludes that the United States is an empire, different in form from the European empires, but nonetheless an empire, then the coherence of

the West need not be considered so awkward. The difficulty arises on how to square the narrative dichotomies that had earlier been developed in U.S. culture.

33. Kaplan, "Left Alone with America," 13.

34. Gress, *From Plato to NATO*, 418, 431.

35. See the chapter by Marco Mariano in this volume.

36. Henrikson, "Mental Maps," 177–78, 189.

37. Michael Hunt, *Ideology and U.S. Foreign Policy* (New Haven: Yale University Press, 1987), 178.

38. Fredrik Logevall, *Choosing War: The Lost Chance for Peace and the Escalation of War in Vietnam* (Berkeley: University of California Press, 1999), 412–13; David Ryan, *Frustrated Empire: US Foreign Policy, 9/11 to Iraq* (London: Pluto, 2007).

39. Theodore Draper, *A Present of Things Past: Selected Essays* (New York: Hill & Wang, 1990), 73–75.

40. William M. LeoGrande, *Central America and the Polls: A Study of U.S. Public Opinion Polls and U.S. Foreign Policy Towards El Salvador and Nicaragua under the Reagan Administration* (Washington, DC: Washington Office on Latin America, March 1987), 41–42; Richard Sobel, *The Impact of Public Opinion on U.S. Foreign Policy since Vietnam: Constraining the Colossus* (New York: Oxford University Press, 2001), 99–140.

41. The Committee of Santa Fe (L. Francis Bouchey, Roger Fontaine, David C. Jordan, Lt. General Gordon Sumner, and Lewis Tambs), *A New Inter-American Policy for the Eighties* (Washington, DC: Council for Inter-American Security, 1980), 1, 3, 46, 52.

42. Elizabeth Dore and John Weeks, *The Red and the Black: The Sandinistas and the Nicaraguan Revolution* (London: Institute of Latin American Studies, 1992).

43. Ronald Reagan, "Central America: Defending Our Vital Interests, Address before a Joint Session of Congress, April 27, 1983," *Department of State Bulletin* 83, no. 2075 (June 1983), 1–5; see also *New York Times*, 28 April 1983.

44. David Ryan, "The Peripheral Centre: Nicaragua in US Policy and Imagination at the End of the Cold War from the 'Strategic Rear' to the 'Backburner,'" in *US Foreign Policy and the Periphery*, ed. Bevan Sewell and Maria Ryan (forthcoming).

45. William M. LeoGrande, "From Reagan to Bush: The Transition in U.S. Policy towards Central America," *Journal of Latin American Studies* 22, no. 3 (October 1990): 605.

46. Campbell, *Writing Security*, 97.

47. David Ryan, *US-Sandinista Diplomatic Relations: Voice of Intolerance* (London: Macmillan, 1995), 13–35.

48. Samuel P. Huntington, "The Clash of Civilizations?," *Foreign Affairs* 72, no. 3 (Summer 1993): 22.

49. Gearóid Ó Tauthail, "Thinking Critically about Geopolitics," *The Geopolitical Reader* (London: Routledge, 1998), 1.

50. Ibid., 110.

51. Edward Said, "The Clash of Definitions," in *Reflections on Exile and Other Literary and Cultural Essays* (London: Granta, 2000), 577.

52. John Tirman, *The Death of Others: The Fate of Civilians in America's Wars* (Oxford: Oxford University Press, 2011).

53. Richard E. Rubenstein and Jarle Crocker, "Challenging Huntington," *Foreign Policy* 96 (1994): 113–28; Edward Said, *The Politics of Dispossession: The Struggle for Palestinian Self-Determination 1969-1994* (London: Chatto and Windus, 1994), 384–92.

54. Said, "The Clash of Definitions," 572.

55. Melani McAlister, *Epic Encounters: Culture, Media, and U.S. Interests in the Middle East, 1945-2000* (Berkeley: University of California Press, 2001), 269.

56. Arshin Adib-Moghaddam, *A Metahistory of the Clash of Civilizations: Us and Them Beyond Orientalism* (London: Hurst, 2011), 41.

57. Fred Halliday, "Islam and the West: Cultural Conflict and International Relations," in *Two Hours that Shook the World: September 11, 2001: Causes and Consequences* (London: Saqi, 2002), 193–211.

58. George W. Bush, "Address to a Joint Session of Congress and the American People, September 20, 2001." Selected Speeches of President George W. Bush, 2001–2008, White House Archives, http://georgewbush-whitehouse.archives.gov/infocus/bushrecord/do cuments/Selected_Speeches_George_W_Bush.pdf.

59. Douglas Little, *American Orientalism: The United States and the Middle East since 1945* (London: I.B. Tauris, 2002), 316–17.

60. Lewis Lapham, *Theater of War* (New York: The New Press, 2002), 150.

61. David Clark, "Mr. Blair Must be Prepared to Stand up to President Bush," *Independent* (London), 14 September 2001.

62. George W. Bush, "Remarks at the National Day of Prayer and Remembrance, The National Cathedral, September 14, 2001." Selected Speeches of President George W. Bush, 2001–2008, White House Archives, http://georgewbush-whitehouse.archives.gov/info cus/bushrecord/documents/Selected_Speeches_George_W_Bush.pdf.

63. Adib-Moghaddam, *A Metahistory of the Clash of Civilizations*, 37–38.

64. Ryan, *Frustrated Empire*, 36–52.

65. George W. Bush, "Address to the Joint Session of Congress and the American People, September 20, 2001." Selected Speeches of President George W. Bush, 2001–2008, White House Archives, http://georgewbush-whitehouse.archives.gov/infocus/bushrecord/do cuments/Selected_Speeches_George_W_Bush.pdf.

66. Sandra Silberstein, *War of Words: Language, Politics and 9/11* (London: Routledge, 2002), 4–9; Frances Fitzgerald, "George Bush and the World," *New York Review of Books* 49, no. 14 (26 September 2002), 84.

67. Adib-Moghaddam, *A Metahistory of the Clash of Civilizations*, 267.

Chapter 10

Obliterating Distance
The Vietnam War Photography
of Philip Jones Griffiths

Liam Kennedy

The geopolitical imperatives of the American worldview—an "exceptional" conjunction of democratic and imperial impulses—have long
promoted assumptions and rationalized perceptions about liberal governance and military intervention. This worldview is supported by a "politics of visual abstraction" within which "people are represented and rationalized as types and symbols"—as others, to be framed and defined
in terms of U.S. national interest.[1] As such, it promotes a moral economy
that is fueled by abstract principles of liberal humanitarianism, individual
freedom, and democratic participation. Focused on the representation of
distant others, this moral economy defines categories of human need and
harm, and constitutes caring and suffering subjects through conventions
of representation in diverse forms of media.

Documentary photography, and especially photojournalism, plays
an important role in providing the iconography of this moral economy:
through its use of generic tropes and formal conventions it fashions scenes
and scenarios, and composes bodies and landscapes, in ways that foreground issues of human relations and address the scope of ethical concern
in international relations. A complex interplay of formal conventions and
ethical considerations characterizes the production, display, and reception
of photojournalistic images of war and conflict, more particularly when
these images, as they so often do, focus on bodies that are subjugated and/
or in pain. The imagery can function to demonize and dehumanize, rationalizing perceptions of the enemy or aggressor, but it can also function to

humanize, rationalizing perceptions of the friend or victim. It is the focus on the human that is the locus of a range of affective responses to such imagery, from horror to pity. And so, photojournalistic imagery of war and conflict both valorizes and parses humanity; it reminds us both of our common humanity and that our sense of what it means to be human is at issue under conditions of war and conflict, but it also screens what counts as human.

Photojournalism bears a complex relationship to the visual production of national identity and of foreign policy; it both contributes to and questions the militarization of vision, the dehumanization of others, and the abstraction of international issues. It can and does function to support a geopolitical way of seeing that "sees" no contradiction between American humanitarianism and the violent treatment of others. Yet the photojournalistic image can also allow us to glimpse beyond the rationality of perception that binds value and security in the American world view, to apprehend and question the relations of power and knowledge that structure it.[2]

Coverage of the Vietnam War is often cited as photojournalism's last great historical moment of record and relevance. During the war photojournalists moved into a more adversarial relationship with the military as they questioned the management of the war, and in the work of many photographers the tensions held within the conjunction of democratic and imperial impulses in the American world view began to visually erupt. At the same time, this imagery was very much shaped by the political economy of its making. A great deal of it focused on spot news and dramatic action, prerequisites to meet the demand and deadlines from the daily and weekly papers and magazines. This material was not without aesthetic or documentary merit; rather these were tailored to the representation of distinctive forms of combat activities and terrains, and the technologies of movement and violence. The result over time was that the published imagery repeatedly presented similar scenarios, motifs, tropes, and points of view: helicopters taking off or landing; troops springing from helicopters and fanning out on foot; troops on patrol through paddy fields and wading across rivers. The helicopter became a key icon in this imagery, with point-of-view shots of terrain from helicopters being common. Indeed, the cameras rendered the helicopter (on which the photographers were very often dependent for their own movements and war coverage) the ubiquitous motif of the war, one adapted by cinema at the war's end. The result was an increasingly stylized and often distanced perspective on the war, finding its *mise-en-scéne* in the framing of American men and machinery against inhospitable terrain.

The absence of the North Vietnamese in so much of this photography was a fitting visual reflection of a war of insurgency, with no clearly defined front line or enemy. Yet, they were not simply invisible; rather, like the South Vietnamese, they were rendered in distinctive ways in particular contexts and in relation to the overall direction of the war as perceived by American media. For example, in the late 1960s and early 1970s, there appeared a spate of photo-stories on child victims of the war. One of the most famous was the work of *Life* photographer Larry Burrows. In 1968 he photographed Nguyen Thi Tron, a twelve-year-old South Vietnamese girl who had lost a leg following an attack by a U.S. helicopter in a free-fire zone. Burrows befriended Tron and documented her recovery as she learned to use an artificial leg and readjust to home and village life. A photo-story focused on Tron was published in *Life* on 8 November 1968, with text by Don Moser that focused on the move toward peace in Vietnam. Tron was not the first poster child of injured innocence during wartime, but she was the most famous instance in the Vietnam War, not least because of the profile Burrows's piece in *Life* could provide. The *Life* story used her images and story to not only conjure compassion among readers (the images prompted some readers to send donations of aid for Tron and her family) but also to suggest the war was taking a new direction, moving toward peaceful resolution. As such, Tron's painful rehabilitation stands in for the national rebuilding now required of the country.[3]

This representation of the foreign other as passive victim has a long history, its meanings shaped by the ideological conditions of visuality surrounding the making, distribution, and consumption of the imagery. In late 1968, in the wake of the Tet Offensive, this imagery in *Life* magazine both announces and deflects growing domestic unease about the meaning and impact of the war. It promotes compassion as a commensurate response to this moment, but also glosses disillusion and any deeper questioning of the meaning or impact of the war. This is more starkly apparent with fresh images of Tron published over a year later in *Life*, on 12 December 1969, showing her surrounded by dolls and stuffed animals sent by American readers. These images were published one week after *Life* published images of the My Lai Massacre and in this context they function to sentimentalize the violence done to Vietnamese civilians by U.S. forces, reassuring American readers that the United States acts responsibly, with humanitarian intent.

The Burrows' images remind us that the human is a "differential norm" in visual representations of war and conflict and that the representation of the other can be framed to evoke a variety of affective and ideological responses.[4] The work of the photographer can cut against the more conventional forms of framing the otherness of the place and the people.

Vietnam Inc.

Philip Jones Griffiths was not disillusioned by the war in Vietnam, he was a skeptic before he arrived to cover the conflict and he very deliberately set about producing a body of work that boldly illustrates and indicts the destructive military and cultural presence of the United States in Southeast Asia. Griffiths was a particularly uncompromising example of the "concerned photographer," an idealist who eschews objectivity in favor of reporting truth and illuminating injustice. While he denies political motives or partisanship, he readily acknowledges a driving moral passion, an empathy with the "have-nots," shaped by his Welsh rural upbringing and his photographic apprenticeship documenting postwar Britain. Of his moral impetus, he says, "Journalism is about obliterating distances, bringing far away things closer [to] home and impressing it on people's senses. You excite your humanity every time you take a photo; lose your humanity and you stop being able to judge, to know, to see."[5] His Vietnam photography does indeed obliterate distance by taking the viewer into the cultures of the Vietnamese and the Americans. It is a form of in-depth journalism that focuses on the "why?" of the event, on causes and contexts, and so moves well beyond the military frame to focus on cultural difference and conflict. With no outlets for such imagery among the mainstream American media, Griffiths put together his book *Vietnam Inc.* (1971), a benchmark of war reporting, and an influential marker of the authorial role of the concerned photographer.

Growing up in rural Wales, Griffiths was fascinated by news photography at an early age and inspired by the great picture magazines of the postwar period, especially *Picture Post*. Although trained as a pharmacist he freelanced for *The Manchester Guardian* and other British papers and magazines, documenting social changes across Britain in the 1950s. In the early 1960s, when the appearance of Sunday supplements greatly enhanced the market for photojournalism, his career developed. He joined the staff of *The Observer* early in 1962 and later that year had a major scoop published when he photographed a hitherto unseen feature of the war in Algeria between French forces and the Front de Liberation Nationale (FLN). He trekked into the Atlas Mountains with FLN soldiers and became the first photographer to document the camp de regroupement programme, the brutal French administration of remote villages. Griffiths would observe, in much more detail, the efforts of U.S. forces to control a colonized population in Vietnam.

Traveling extensively in the mid 1960s to cover conflicts across the world, Griffiths decided he wanted to focus his energies on one substantial project rather than racing to cover many for short periods of time. In

1966, the same year he joined Magnum as an associate, he "decided the important thing to do was to get passionate about something, and you didn't have to be a genius in '66 to work out that there was something very important happening in Vietnam."[6] His approach was methodical. He read widely on the history and culture of Vietnam and on the origins of its recent wars. Once in the country he traveled across South Vietnam, visiting every province, and familiarized himself with the cultures of the Vietnamese. Although he often traveled with the American military, he was not a central member of the media packs and had limited contact with other photographers; he worked quietly and unobtrusively, for the most part living with South Vietnamese at little expense.[7] Financing was his biggest headache. Although he planned to publish a book he also needed to publish images to bring in enough funds to remain in Vietnam, but the leading newspapers and magazines only rarely published his work—he was repeatedly told his photographs were too harrowing. Later he would suggest Magnum had not done enough to try to sell his images, a charge in line with his self-aggrandizing commentaries on press coverage of the war: "In general, 95 per cent of the press was in favour of the war; 4.999 per cent was in favour of the war but not in favour of the way it was being fought. And then there was me and two Frenchmen."[8]

Griffiths claims he had an immediate affinity with the Vietnamese, likening them to the rural Welsh in terms of community bonds, resourcefulness, and canny defiance of colonists. However romanticized this view may have been, it did draw him close to Vietnamese civilians as his key source of information and perspective and certainly afforded him a very different perspective on the war from that of most journalists. As he learned more about the country and its people he not only questioned the American narratives about the war and its progress, he grew angry about the absurdity of the disjunction between these narratives and the realities he observed: "The things we were being told [about the war] didn't make any sense. So I travelled the length of the country for my own personal selfish reasons, to put together the jigsaw puzzle, and to produce a historical document. I wasn't the person working for the news agencies to make sure there was a picture on the front of the *New York Times* every morning. I worked differently."[9] Working differently meant many things. First, as indicated, it meant working apart from the established media and military frameworks, even as he took advantage of American military transport and befriended U.S. soldiers. It also meant looking for the "why?" of the war where few others were looking. Griffiths notes: "Some of the best combat photography in the war came from the battles that took place at the end of 1967 … but the pictures are meaningless, because the battles were meaningless."[10] This may be read as a harsh judgment of the work of

Burrows and many others, but it is also a characteristic statement of Griffiths's certitude and method. In other words, his photography rarely follows the event, nor does it indicate a sense of formlessness or incoherence about the war, even as metaphor. Rather, his imagery is marked by his sense of clarity about what is being depicted within the viewfinder—his sense they are historical documents.

The war *is* meaningful, Griffiths believed, and the places to look for this meaning were at the points of cultural contact between the Vietnamese and Americans and at the points of imperial myopia in the activities of the Americans. In the introduction to *Vietnam Inc.,* he writes: "I contend that Vietnam is the goldfish bowl where the values of Americans and Vietnamese can be observed, studied, and because of their contrasting nature, more easily appraised."[11] His approach to this work of observation and to putting together his book is suggestive of a social scientist in its rigor and critical method. *Vietnam Inc.* advances a form of cultural critique that operates through demystification, illuminating tensions and contradictions in the American world view. For Griffiths, a critical role of photography is to reveal what is normatively hidden: "The Vietnamese say that looking and understanding is much more important than caring about the surface. The Americans were completely blind to the subtleties of the Vietnamese language and the fascinating structure of Vietnamese society. All of the elements drew me to the country and strengthened my will to stay on, but what ultimately made me addicted to the place was the desire to find out what was really going on, after peeling away layers and layer of untruths."[12]

The key dialectic of his work is that of blindness and insight, and an urge to demystify—to peel away the layers and reveal truths—is evident in individual photographs and in the layout of the book as a whole.

A simple but effective example is a photograph Jones Griffiths spent several days trying to produce. It depicts a busy street scene in Saigon. People are looking in different directions and our eyes are pulled across the scene looking for the locus of meaning, the point of the image. Then we see it, just off-center, the young girl artfully picking the pocket of the large GI who is peering elsewhere, distracted. The image is suggestively composed. It is not a snapshot. Griffiths had waited for days on a first-floor balcony of the Hotel Royale across the street from this scene, and also photographed several similar scenes—four of them appear on one page of *Vietnam Inc.* The methodical preparation was typical of his work, shaped as it was to reveal something he already knew but was rarely visible to Western eyes. This sense of illicit or subversive viewing is replicated in the image. The attempted robbery of the GI is but one point of urban spectacle within the scene—we note the act is being observed by one or more of the people around him. In his caption, Griffiths observes that pickpockets were tolerated by the Saigon public: "Hatred of the Americans was such that no Vietnamese would ever warn one if his wallet was about to be taken. Many people could be seen surreptitiously admiring pickpockets' prowess."[13] For Griffiths, the act of pickpocketing American soldiers clearly symbolizes the more general Vietnamese activities of duping and undermining the colonizer.

This demystifying of the relations between Vietnamese and Americans is the organizing basis of *Vietnam Inc.* The book is made up of over 250 black-and-white photographs, supported by blocks of informative text and spare, often acerbic captions. It opens with a glossary, and the author wryly explains: "A book about the Vietnam War is bound, unfortunately, to need an extensive glossary to guide the reader through the fog of Orwellian 'newspeak' that the United States employs in an attempt to disguise its activities."[14] By drawing immediate attention to what he terms the "lexical war," Griffiths indicates his book aims to reveal what the fog of war has so far concealed. Throughout, he is attentive in his text as well as the images to political and military rhetoric, and particularly questions the meanings of American discourses of liberation, modernity, and freedom as applied to the U.S. mission in Vietnam. The one-page introduction succinctly presents Griffiths's view that the war in Vietnam is a war "for the minds of men," and that "America is trying to sell a doctrine to the Vietnamese," that of "Americanism." As such, he views the war as a conflict of values and finds horror in the doctrinal myopia of the U.S., its "misplaced confidence in the universal goodness of American values."[15]

The image filling the page opposite the introduction depicts a GI with a young Vietnamese girl on his knee. Both stare intently into the camera. The GI is unshaven and sunken-eyed; his gaze solemn, perhaps even sullen. The girl's clothes are sullied and she presses her hands together between her legs. As he leans forward, she leans into herself. They are frozen together but it is difficult to interpret their relationship. Elsewhere in the book, Griffiths notes that GIs liked to befriend and be photographed with children, an attempt to identify with some form of innocence in the theater of war. That may be happening here—the soldier's wedding ring may hint at an identity other than that of soldier. However, their implacable togetherness, however composed, in the context of the Introduction, suggests they are both victims of forces beyond their control and comprehension.

The book is divided into thematic sections. The first, "The Vietnamese Village," illustrates what Griffiths sees as the essential values of the Vietnamese—wisdom, harmony, and community—tied to the village environment and its culture. In particular, he draws attention to the importance of rice growing as a staple not only of diet but also of communal rituals. One image shows a child sitting on a buffalo, which threshes the rice by walking over it; another shows peasants working the fields; and another shows the graves of the dead in rice fields, where "their sprits will pass through the soil into the rice, so that their soul will be inherited by their descendants when the rice is eaten."[16] For the most part, the imagery imputes a sense of a harmonious rural society, with only allusions to the threat of American despoliation—a reference to an absent mother, for example, gone to work for the Americans. The final image of the sequence is jarring by contrast. A two-page spread, uncaptioned, it depicts what appears to be the dead body of a Vietnamese male, his upper torso visible in the top right of the image, a gun on the ground to the left, and what appears to be the shadow of an American soldier taking up the center and foreground of the photograph. For all the graphic directness of his image making, Griffiths does employ symbolism on occasion. The text in this section asserts what the imagery implies: "what American policy has attempted to do is to obliterate the village as a social unit. This, ostensibly, is to deny cover to the guerrillas, but, in reality, the purpose is to reconstruct Vietnamese society in the image of the United States."[17]

The next two sections—"Why We're There" and "The Communication Gap"—begin to show the distance between the Vietnamese and the Americans, a motif that runs through the book. Children figure prominently as they are generally in closer, less aggressive proximity to the soldiers. In one image we see a Marine hugging a child as the mother looks on anxiously, in another a child curiously feels the facial hair of a GI, and in another a GI offers a cigarette to a peasant girl in a field. In many of the images there is a sense of corruption surrounding the presence of the GIs. At a "Car Wash" young girls surround a GI to sell goods and themselves. All the while, Griffiths argues in his text, the children smile and accommodate to take advantage of the soldiers.

There are several images of prisoners, composed so that the prisoner is at the center of the image and accentuating their vulnerability. One of these compositions is famed as one of the finest combat images of the war; it shows GIs giving water to a VC fighter who had fought for three days with a severe stomach wound that had him place his intestines in a bowl and strap it to his body. The GIs admired his bravery and Griffiths honors this in his sympathetic composition.[18]

The communication gap is rendered more violent in the imagery depicting the frustrations of Americans searching for enemy combatants in rural areas. Griffiths records the growing resentment of the U.S. soldiers as they take frightened civilian villagers from their homes and call in bombings to or burn the villages. One image, taken on a search and destroy operation with a unit of the Americal Division in 1967, shows a woman cradling a child overseen by an American soldier. The caption reads "Mother and child shortly before being killed … this woman's husband, together with the other men left in the village had been killed a few moments earlier because he was hiding in a tunnel. After blowing up all tunnels and bunkers where people could take refuge, GI's withdrew and called in artillery fire on the defenseless inhabitants."[19] The soldier's odd stance is one of detachment, and likely also of resentment as we learn from the caption—the pieta of mother and child draws no sympathy, no sense of concern—this event occurred about six months before the massacre at My Lai (carried out by Americal soldiers) and implies that the murderous resentment among the soldiers was already apparent. Powerful as the image is, it relies on Griffiths caption to fully contextualize what we see. Elsewhere, he has observed, "I think the problem with photography is that you can decontextualize it. What does a picture of a wounded body or a mother clasping her wounded child mean? Why is it happening? I want to know that."[20]

The next two sections—"Search and Destroy" and "Relocation"—document the forced relocation of several thousand rural people in the Bantangan peninsula to the model village of Song Tra. This shocking dislocation from ancestral lands was rationalized by American strategists as "forced-draft urbanization and modernization, which rapidly brings the country in question out of the phase in which rural revolutionary movements can hope to generate sufficient strength to come to power."[21] Griffiths shows it to be a wretched destruction of a society and its ways of life. He portrays the burning of villages and the forced trek to Song Tra, where peasants are housed in internment camps, surrounded by barbed wire and signs announcing their "freedom." The degradations of the peasants are evidenced in incongruous scenes—one image shows peasant children looking at copies of *Playboy* magazine, distributed by a Psy-Ops officer who forgot to order "indigenous reading material."[22]

The next sections—"Our Vietnamese Friends" and "The Battle for the Cities"—document the degradations of the newly urbanized populace in the large cities, particularly Saigon, and the urban battles that ensued in the wake of the Tet Offensive in early 1968. By 1968 over three million people resided in Saigon, a city built for a tenth that number, many moved there forcibly or as refugees from dangerous or destroyed communities. Griffiths shows us a "mass of resentful people," many of them refugees, homeless people, and beggars, living in wretched conditions.[23] Graveyards are used as makeshift shelters and latrines, a desecration of these spaces. Several images depict commercial signage advertising American goods, ironically juxtaposed with imagery of destitution. These sections also provide more conventional war imagery in the depiction of the results of the massive aerial destruction of Ben Tre following the Tet Offensive and the battle for Hue, one of the most prolonged combat operations of the war. As usual, Griffiths's focus is on the civilian victims.

The fullest sequence of imagery in these sections documents the Vietcong attacks on Saigon in 1968 and the confusion this caused among the American soldiers and the Vietnamese citizenry, both unaccustomed to being attacked in this urban center. GIs look scared and bewildered as they take cover when their own artillery fire is misdirected and kills two of their number. There are several images of dead or wounded civilians on the streets. In one, a woman in bloodied clothes lies on a stretcher in the foreground while above her a soldier kneels and looks into the distance, and behind them people hurry past with their goods. It is a suggestive tableau, indicating the impotence of the soldiery to protect civilians or deter looting. Overall the imagery connotes confusion and loss of control as the city breaks apart and homes are reduced to rubble. The sequence ends with a powerful two-page spread image that shows a woman at center walking to camera carrying many belongings—including stoves, pots, and bowls—across her shoulders. On each side of her soldiers walk in the opposite direction, carrying their own accouterments—guns, backpacks, ammunition belts. They pass silently, not looking at each other. The road is churned mud and they are surrounded by the debris of bombing on all sides. It is as though two worlds have walked right past each other. To be sure, the woman is a civilian victim, but she has her belongings and appears to move purposefully, holding what remains of her world together—an individual compressed into limited space—her belongings a metonymy of her shattered world.

In the final section—"Pacification"—Griffiths focuses on the effects of the renewed battle for hearts and minds following the upheavals of 1968 and the further decline of social order in the cities. He later notes that after Tet "great disillusionment set in" among the South Vietnamese in urban centers, and he "found it a very interesting time photographing the discontent and turmoil in the urban enclaves."[24] Images of garbage dumps, of elderly people living in institutions rather than with families, and of young prostitutes on the streets combine to connote the breakdown of a traditional order. The sequence focused on prostitution is particularly disturbing, depicting girls as young as twelve with American soldiers. An image of Vietnamese women seated in and grouped around an American military truck reads: "The women of Vietnam. In a society where they are traditionally revered for their poise and purity, women have been effectively dehumanised. They sit outside American bars waiting to enter to serve the soldiers as everything from laundry maid to prostitute."[25] At the center of the sequence is a controversial image showing two male navy

SEALS on a bed with a Vietnamese woman at the U.S. naval base in Nha Be in 1970. One of the men is leaning over the prostrate woman who is lying on a rug with her dress pulled back to her midriff, while the other soldier crawls toward them on the floor. The woman's head is turned away from the soldier whose face is lowered toward her, mouth open. It is impossible to tell if the woman is laughing or screaming and the image can be and has been read as a depiction of rape. Griffiths is more sanguine in his (later) comments: "The girl is not a hooker—well, she may have been a hooker, she's certainly not an innocent farm girl—but she was there dancing for the troops, and these chaps got a little out of hand."[26]

Throughout this section Griffiths notes the fast developments in what he terms "automated war," or the use of computers and of long-range devices to conduct war. He mocks the absurdities of the use of computers to evaluate the degree of pacification of Vietnamese hamlets. In one image, four military operators stare at a computer printing. The caption reads: "The computer that 'proves' the war is being won. ... Optimistic results on the 'my-wife-is-not-trying-to-poison-me-therefore-she-loves-me' pattern are reliably produced each and every month."[27] However, he also soberly comments on the emergence of a new warfare that reduces ground troops and utilizes electronic technologies, automatic fire control, and aircraft carriers. There are several images of personnel on an aircraft carrier. One caption notes, "The sailors and the pilots on board have never been to Vietnam. They have never seen the faces of their victims, the Vietnamese people."[28] The following image is of four seriously wounded victims of anti-personnel bombs, laid side by side on stretchers, all of them "classed 'terminal' and sent home to die."[29] There follow several pages juxtaposing images of Vietnamese amputees and victims of napalm bombing, interspersed with images of the American bombs.

The penultimate image in the book is one of the most famous images of the war. It shows a Vietnamese woman holding her hands up to her fully bandaged head. The woman has a tag attached to her arm that reads "VNC FEMALE," meaning Vietnamese civilian.[30]

The image has often been reproduced to represent the effects of napalm, but the tag actually states "Extensive high velocity wound to the left forehead and left eye." It is not surprising that it should be misinterpreted in this way as the symbolism of the image is rich and it has iconic qualities that transcend its moment of production. At the very least, it stands as an image of dehumanization and so condemns the impact of the war on civilians. The tag accentuates this diminishment of the individual to a cipher in the administration of the war, while the cancellation of her identity can refer to the more general invisibility of civilians in the consciousness and lines of sight of the American military, media, and public.

Conclusion

It is the realities and visibility of the victims' lives that Griffiths most forcefully dedicates himself to documenting in *Vietnam Inc.* and in his following visual studies of postwar Vietnam. With *Vietnam Inc.* he produced an incendiary documentation of the war that took many by surprise and disturbed the field of photojournalism irrevocably. There was much that was startlingly fresh and audacious about the book. It moved the camera away from the American soldier to concentrate on the Vietnamese and to document the effects of combat seen through the eyes of civilian victims. The iconic images of the war in American public memory are images of victims of U.S. or U.S.-sanctioned violence. Griffiths provides a detailed, in-depth illustration of the consequences of this violence, not snapshots but carefully composed and sequenced condemnations of the impact of the United States on Vietnamese culture and society.

In doing so he also took an innovative step in positing the role of the photojournalist as an author. This is evident in his eschewal of objectivity in favor of working with a clear vision and a determination to interrogate the "why?" of the event. In this sense he took on the role of the photographer as witness already imputed in the Magnum tradition and radicalized it by producing a more engaged, interventionist photography than his predecessors. He also demonstrated the authorial role of the photojournalist by producing his work on his own terms and publishing it accordingly. He published little of his Vietnam imagery in established news media but turned this to his advantage by transcending the agendas and frames of mainstream media.

It is impossible to measure the impact of the book on public opinion about the war, though many claim it was significant. Noam Chomsky later wrote: "If anybody in Washington had read that book, we wouldn't have had these wars in Iraq and Afghanistan."[31] It received some very strong reviews in the very publications Griffiths had difficulty publishing his images in a few years before. In part this was due to timing, as more graphic material began to appear in the aftermath of the My Lai imagery, but also because his work provided one of the few coherent visual perspectives on the core years of the war. A glowing review in *Time* magazine described the book as "the best work of photo-reportage of war ever published. ... The book sets entirely new standards for critical judgment of the medium of photo-reportage." The *New York Times* described it as "The closest we are ever going to come to a definitive photo-journalistic essay on the war."[32]

In 1971 Griffiths joined Magnum as a full member. He was unable to return to Vietnam despite efforts to do so on an assignment for *Life* in 1972. Refused entry to the country, he was informed that President Thieu had personally demanded he be banned from entry, reportedly saying: "There are many people I don't want to see back in my country, but I can assure you that Mr. Griffiths' name is at the top of the list."[33] Griffiths did return to Vietnam, however, more than twenty times after 1980, when he first returned, to extensively photograph the legacies of the war and painful reconstruction of the society. Over that period he built a large body of work that he finally published in the form of two books, *Agent Orange* (2003) and *Vietnam at Peace* (2005). Together, they are important documents of the ongoing effects of the war and the reconstruction of a traumatized society. In the spirit of *Vietnam Inc.*, they hold up a critical mirror to U.S. foreign policy.

Notes

1. Thaddeus Oliver, "Techniques of Abstraction," *Millennium: Journal of International Studies* 30, no. 3 (December 2001), 555–70.
2. Liam Kennedy, "Securing Vision: Photography and U.S. Foreign Policy," *Media, Culture and Society* 30, no. 3 (May 2008), 279–94.
3. Liam Kennedy, "'A Compassionate Vision': Larry Burrows' Vietnam War Photography," *Photography and Culture* 4, no. 2 (July 2011), 179–94.
4. Judith Butler, *Frames of War: When is Life Grievable?* (London: Verso, 2009).
5. Amol Rajan, "Philip Jones Griffiths: The Welshman with the 'Lazy Eye,'" *The Independent*, 21 January 2008 (http://www.independent.co.uk/news/media/philip-jones-griffiths-the-welshman-with-the-lazy-eye-771515.html).
6. Graham Harrison, "Philip Jones Griffiths," *Photo Histories*, 2008 (http://www.photohistories.com/interviews/23/philip-jones-griffiths?pg=all).
7. When *Vietnam Inc.* was published, many of the media correspondents who covered Vietnam expressed surprise as very few had any idea what Griffiths had been preparing.
8. Peter Howe, "The Dauntless Spirit: Philip Jones Griffiths: 1936-2008," *The Digital Journalist*, April 2008 (http://digitaljournalist.org/issue0804/the-dauntless-spirit-philip-jones-griffiths-1936-2008.html).
9. Donald R. Wilson, "Philip Jones Griffiths Dies in London," National Press Photographers Association (http://www.nppa.org/news_and_events/news/2008/03/griffiths).
10. Howe, "The Dauntless Spirit."
11. Philip Jones Griffiths, *Vietnam Inc.* (London: Phaidon Press, 2001), 4.
12. Russell Miller, *Magnum: Fifty Years at the Front Line of History* (London: Pimlico, 1997), 213–14.
13. Griffiths, *Vietnam Inc.*, 174.
14. Ibid., 3.
15. Ibid., 4.
16. Ibid., 19.
17. Ibid., 13.
18. The scene was reconstituted in *Apocalypse Now*, a film that utilizes Griffiths's imagery.
19. Griffiths, *Vietnam Inc.*, 59.

20. Howe, "The Dauntless Spirit."
21. Griffiths, *Vietnam Inc.*, 77.
22. Ibid., 90.
23. Ibid., 106.
24. Miller, *Magnum*, 214.
25. Griffiths, *Vietnam Inc.*, 180.
26. Howe, "The Dauntless Spirit."
27. Griffiths, *Vietnam Inc.*, 164–65.
28. Ibid., 197.
29. Griffiths, *Vietnam Inc.*, 198–99.
30. Griffiths later observed this was an unusual designation as "the rule in Vietnam was that anybody who had been wounded was VCS, a Vietcong suspect." He surmises that the medic who made out the tag was anti-war. Howe, "The Dauntless Spirit."
31. Amanda Hopkinson, "Philip Jones Griffiths," *The Guardian*, 24 March 2008 (http://www .guardian.co.uk/artanddesign/2008/mar/24/photography.usa).
32. Both citations appear on the cover of the 2001 edition of *Vietnam Inc.*
33. Howe, "The Dauntless Spirit."

Chapter 11

Remnants of Empire
Civilization, Torture, and Racism
in the War on Terrorism

Arshin Adib-Moghaddam

Wars are not fought in a cultural vacuum. They are not sterile; they do not occur under laboratory conditions. Wars are polluted by cultural artifacts, sets of norms, institutions, and ideology. It is this normative context that establishes the trenches according to which friend and enemy are distinguished. In the "war on terror," begun in Afghanistan in 2001 and spread to Iraq in 2003, this fundamental distinction between "us" and "them," civilization and barbarity, has determined the way the war has been fought, legitimized, and sold to a skeptical public. From the outset, George W. Bush was clear about the civilizational mission that his administration espoused when he proclaimed in 2004 that the "rise of a free and self-governing Iraq will deny terrorists a base of operation" and that it will constitute a "decisive blow to terrorism at the heart of its power, and a victory for the security of America and the civilized world." Former British Prime Minister Tony Blair used similarly divisive language to reiterate the missionary aspect of the war in his address to the House of Commons in the buildup to the war in Afghanistan in 2001: "Our beliefs are the very opposite of the fanatics. We believe in reason, democracy and tolerance. These beliefs are the foundation of our civilised world. They are enduring, they have served us well and as history has shown we have been prepared to fight, when necessary to defend them. But the fanatics should know: we hold these beliefs every bit as strongly as they hold theirs. Now is the time to show it."[1] In this way the political case for war was made. The enemy was depicted as the barbarian other that could not be reasoned with. Richard Jackson has conceptualized this language

---

Notes for this chapter begin on page 232.

quite rightly as "identitarian," or essential in order to establish the "identities of the 'good guys' and the 'bad guys'" to make the "national story
of America's war understandable to the wider public."[2] As such, Bush and
Blair positioned themselves within a long tradition of "western" leaders
who tried to legitimize war through the discourse of civilization. Linking
that hegemonic discourse to the torture at the Abu Ghraib prison complex
in Baghdad shows how the particular form of sexualized torture of Iraqi
inmates was dependent on—and signified by—a civilizational discourse
permeated by racist depictions of Arabs and Muslims. The torture at Abu
Ghraib was not a coincidence or a freak accident. The individuals who
committed the atrocities against the detainees were not isolated. The type
of torture implemented was premised on cultural attitudes toward Arabs
and Muslims. Hence they must be analyzed as a part of a larger constellation, a system of thought that I have elsewhere called the clash regime.[3]

Tortures of War

The trials against Charles Graner, Jr., and his girlfriend Lynndie England
were designed to convey the message that the torture at Abu Ghraib was
isolated, the act of a few deranged individuals. Yet to assume that torture
that employs signs and symbols that are considered offensive, repugnant,
threatening, dishonorable, and subjugating by another culture can ever
be considered unsystematic or arbitrary borders on naiveté or misplaced
political correctness. In fact, the findings of U.S. Army Major General Antonio M. Taguba, who investigated the Abu Ghraib case, make it clear that
there was method in the madness. In his report dated March 2004, Taguba
found that "between October and December 2003 at the Abu Ghraib Confinement Facility (BCCF) numerous incidents of sadistic, blatant, and
wanton criminal abuses were inflicted on several detainees," that he clas-
sifies as "systemic and illegal abuse," perpetrated by "several members of
the military police guard force."[4] More specifically, the "abuse" included:

> Punching, slapping, and kicking detainees; jumping on their naked feet ... Forc-
> ibly arranging detainees in various sexually explicit positions for photograph-
> ing ... Forcing naked male detainees to wear women's underwear ... Forcing
> groups of male detainees to masturbate themselves while being photographed
> and videotaped ... Arranging naked male detainees in a pile and then jumping
> on them ... Positioning a naked detainee on a MRE Box, with a sandbag on his
> head, and attaching wires to his fingers, toes, and penis to stimulate electric
> torture ... Placing a dog chain or strap around a naked detainee's neck and
> having a female soldier pose for a picture ... A male MP guard having sex with
> a female detainee ... Taking photographs of dead Iraqi detainees.[5]

General Taguba would say later that the United States "violated the tenets of the Geneva Convention. We violated our own principles and we
violated the core of our military values ... even today ... those civilian
and military leaders responsible should be held accountable."[6] The International Committee of the Red Cross (ICRC) came to similar conclusions.
Avoiding the term "torture," it stated in a report in February 2004 that
"physical and psychological *coercion* used by the interrogators appeared
to be part of the standard operating procedures by military intelligence
personnel to obtain confessions and extract information."[7] Another report
filed by former U.S. secretary of defense and ex-director of the CIA, James
Schlesinger, was equally adamant to avoid the term "torture," classifying
the events as "brutality and purposeless sadism ... The pictured *abuses*,"
the report claims, "were not part of authorized interrogations nor were
they even directed at intelligence targets."[8]

A similar emphasis on the term "abuse" rather than "torture" can be
discerned from the Fay-Jones Report that states that "clearly *abuses* occurred at the prison at Abu Ghraib which were committed by a small
group of morally corrupt soldiers and civilians."[9] The same report describes how detainees "were forced to crawl on their stomachs and were
handcuffed together [and] act as though they were having sex."[10] It also
presents the case of DETAINEE-08, who was beaten "for half an hour ...
with a chair until it broke, hit in the chest, kicked, and choked until he lost
consciousness. On other occasions," it is further stated, "DETAINEE-08
recalled that CPL Graner would throw his food into the toilet and say 'go
take it and eat it.'"[11] Even the case of DETAINEE-07, who was made to
"bark like a dog, being forced to crawl on his stomach while MPs spit and
urinated on him, and being struck causing unconsciousness," is classified
as abuse rather than torture.[12]

There were, of course, very straightforward measures to rationalize
and thus diminish what happened at Abu Ghraib. The Mikolashek Report
submitted in July 2004 describes the different "legitimate" interrogation
approaches that can be employed by U.S. government personnel during
interrogations. These range from the Fear-Up Approach, according to
which the "interrogator behaves in an overpowering manner with a loud
and threatening voice," to the Pride and Ego–Down Approach, which is
"based on the source's sense of personal worth. Any source who shows
any real or imagined inferiority or weakness about himself, loyalty to his
organization, or [who was] captured under embarrassing circumstances,"
it is explained, "can be easily broken with this approach technique."[13] Having set the legal boundaries between "torture," "abuse," and legitimate
"interrogation techniques," the report comes to the conclusion that "despite the demands of the current operating environment against an enemy

who does not abide by the Geneva Conventions, our commanders have adjusted to the reality of the battlefield and, are effectively conducting detainee operations while ensuring the humane treatment of detainees."[14]

I am not concerned here with explaining legally why what happened in Iraq amounts to systematic torture. This is something that has been done by others more qualified to do so than I am, namely, the American Bar Association in their report to their House of Delegates submitted in August 2004.[15] What is rather more important to show is that the discourse of the war on terror was charged with narratives of civilizational superiority in the mainstream that transmuted into racism among influential strata of society that operate at the margins of the political establishment in the United States, but who have enough political power to influence the discourse about the enemy other. The legitimation of the Iraq war in 2003 as a part of the war on terror is quite central here. In effect it represented Iraq as an ally of bin Laden and al Qaeda. Many citizens of the United States were made to believe (and did so) that Saddam Hussein was behind the terror attacks on 9/11, which explains why U.S. soldiers marked some of their bombs with messages such as "with love from Ground Zero," or "in the name of the New York Fire Department." That the link between al Qaeda and Iraq was invented was rather obvious to most serious observers of the Iraqi-Baathist state. Yet it took the U.S. Defense Department four years to establish what most of us knew, that is, that Hussein's regime was not directly cooperating with al Qaeda before the invasion. Ironically, the report's release came on the same day that Vice President Cheney, appearing on a radio program, repeated his allegation that al Qaeda was operating inside Iraq "before we ever launched" the war, under the direction of Abu Musab al-Zarqawi, who was killed in June 2006. The report, in a recently declassified section, indicated that it was Douglas Feith, then U.S. undersecretary of defense, who asserted in a briefing given to Cheney's chief of staff in September 2002 that the relationship between Iraq and al Qaeda was "mature" and "symbiotic," marked by shared interests, and evidenced by cooperation across ten categories, including training, financing, and logistics.[16]

In this way Iraqis were labeled terrorists, in order to maximize U.S. power before, during, and after the invasion, to make it easier for U.S. soldiers "to pull the trigger." The war on terror reinvigorated a particular form of "bio-power" that was not medieval, but entirely modern, systematic, and planned. While interrogators were advised "not to leave marks on the body" of the victims, psychological torture was condoned almost under scientific conditions. A report, by the British medical journal *The Lancet*, established in August 2004 that U.S. military doctors and medics were "complicit" in the torture of Iraqi detainees and faked death certificates to try to cover up homicides. "The medical system collaborated with designing and implementing psychologically and physically coercive interrogations," writes the author, University of Minnesota professor Steven Miles. "Army officials stated that a physician and a psychiatrist helped design, approve, and monitor interrogations." A similar system was administered by doctors at the Guantanamo Bay prison complex, where "medical doctors and mental health personnel assigned to the U.S. Department of Defense neglected and/or concealed medical evidence of intentional harm."[17]

Undoubtedly then, the torture at Abu Ghraib (and Guantanamo Bay) was not arbitrary. Rather, torture and science worked hand in hand. Abu Ghraib stands for a rationalized form of punishment premised on procedures that turned cultural values of Arabs and Muslims into forms of systematic psychological and physical torment: the taboo of public homosexual acts explains why naked men were forced to pile up, bend over, and masturbate; the taboo of dogs that are considered unclean by some orthodox Muslims and notions of male honor explains why dog chains were placed around the neck of naked detainees and why female soldiers posed with them for pictures that were disseminated as trophies among soldiers; knowledge about the sacredness of the Quran and the prophet Muhammad explains why the book was flushed down the toilet in front of detainees and why some of them were forced to curse Allah and Muhammad; and an understanding that music can be used to cause psychological torment explains why heavy metal was played for hours and augmented by strobe lights in order to prevent inmates at Guantanamo Bay from sleeping. All of this hints to a cultural system of torture in the war on terror, not arbitrary acts of irrational hatred that also occurred occasionally within this system.

Imperial Ideology and Racism

Wars are dependent on notions of "us" and "them." In the war on terror the ideology delivering these categories has been loosely termed neoconservatism, an unashamedly imperial ideology espoused by influential strategists and decision makers in Washington, DC. Mainstream neoconservatism is premised on the idea that the United States is an exceptional country that needs to deliver its civilizational message to all corners of the world, especially after the demise of communism. As Irving Kristol put it: "After two decades during which 'imperial decline' and 'imperial overstretch' were the academic and journalistic watchwords, the United States emerges as uniquely powerful."[18] Other writers agree and designate the

United States the "world's only superpower" that combines "pre-eminent military power, global technological leadership, and the world's largest economy."[19] As the National Security Strategy of 2002 declares, the country holds "unprecedented—and unequalled—strength and influence in the world. Sustained by faith in the principles of liberty, and the value of a free society, this position comes with unparalleled responsibilities, obligations, and opportunity."[20] It mandates an expansionary foreign policy as the country reserves the right to act unilaterally without the support of the United Nations or even its allies. As such, neoconservatism combines belief in material power with a missionary trust in the United States' superior moral values.

On the margins of the neoconservative, current imperial theory is impregnated with Islamophobic attitudes. A quick look through the pages of David Frum and Richard Perle's angry book *An End to Evil: How to Win the War against Terror* exemplifies this. Whereas Ledeen has been influential as a consultant surrounding the White House and as an armchair ideologist endowed with "Freedom Chairs" at the American Enterprise Institute and the Foundation for Defense of Democracies, Frum and Perle are more directly immersed in politics. The former served as a special assistant to George W. Bush and coined the phrase "axis of evil," designating Iraq, Iran, and North Korea and identifying these countries as central theaters for the war on terror. Richard Perle served for the Reagan administration as an assistant secretary of defense and worked on the Defense Board Advisory Committee between 1987 and 2004. He was chairman of the Board during the immediate buildup to the invasion of Iraq from 2001 to 2003.

Frum and Perle's book is both a manifesto for imperial war making and an indictment of the timidity of political discourse in the United States. They point out the real enemy of the United States is Islam. "We sometimes wonder," they write, "how the war on terror escaped being called the war on You-know-who ... all the available evidence indicates that militant Islam commands wide support, and even wider sympathy, amongst Muslims worldwide, including Muslim minorities in the West."[21] Consequently, all Muslims must be considered dangerous, untrustworthy, and prone to brutality. They have to be policed, confined, supervised, and bullied into submission, if necessary through violence. "A world at peace; a world governed by law; a world in which all people are free to find their own destinies," the authors argue, "[t]hat dream has not yet come true, it will not come true soon, but if it ever does come true, it will be brought into being by American armed might" that should be exercised primarily in the Muslim worlds.[22] So overtly divisive is this contemporary trend in U.S. politics that it has been compared to a new kind of anti-Semitism that substitutes violence against Jews with the subjugation of Muslims. "Once it was another set of Semites who could not be trusted, whose primary loyalties lay elsewhere, who needed to be given a clear message about what was expected of them," Anne Norton writes. "Once, at the end of the nineteenth century, it was the Jewish anarchist and the Jewish communist who were portrayed as agents of global terror. Now it is Muslims who are involved in shadowy global conspiracies, Muslims who have 'fellow travellers.'" In that sense she argues that "the old language of anti-Semitism has found another target."[23] The former U.S. National Security Advisor Zbigniew Brzezinski had a comparable take on the link between Islamophobia and anti-Semitism:

> Government at every level has stimulated the paranoia. Consider, for example, the electronic billboards over interstate highways urging motorists to 'Report Suspicious Activity' (drivers in turbans?). Some mass media have made their own contribution. The cable channels and some print media have found that horror scenarios attract audiences, while terror 'experts' as 'consultants' provide authenticity for the apocalyptic visions fed to the American public. Hence the proliferation of programs with bearded 'terrorists' as the central villains. ... Hence the TV serials and films in which the evil characters have recognizable Arab features, sometimes highlighted by religious gestures, that exploit public anxiety and stimulate Islamophobia. Arab facial stereotypes, particularly in newspaper cartoons, have at times been rendered in a manner sadly reminiscent of the Nazi anti-Semitic campaigns. Lately, even some college student organizations have become involved in such propagation, apparently oblivious to the menacing connection between the stimulation of racial and religious hatreds and the unleashing of the unprecedented crimes of the Holocaust.[24]

It was Seymour Hersh, the investigative journalist of *The New Yorker*, who made the link between neoconservative ideology and racism explicit. Hersh revealed that the attitude that "Arabs are particularly vulnerable to sexual humiliation became a talking point among pro-war Washington conservatives in the months before the March 2003 invasion of Iraq."[25] Hersh argued further that U.S. neoconservatives learned of such vulnerability from a book entitled *The Arab Mind* authored by the Israeli cultural anthropologist Raphael Patai in 1973. The following paragraph gives an impression about the mode of argumentation throughout Patai's book: "As far as the traditional Arab sex mores can be observed without penetrating into the secrets of the bedchamber, the impression is gained that they are the product of severe repressions. The avoidances observed in public between men and women, the existence of two separate societies, male and female, each with its own customs, language, and religious obligation, and many other factors indicate, even, even to the psychologically untrained observer, behaviour patterns developed in response to early repression."[26] Patai then moves on to discuss Arab child-rearing practices, and the sexual hospitality of various Arab tribes in the nineteenth century whose men wore "loincloth and walk about without any covering on the head," and whose women wore "no clothing above the waist."[27] Surprisingly (or maybe not), according to an academic quoted by Hersh, this book became "the bible of the neo-cons on Arab behaviour." Hence, in the discussions of the "neo-cons," two themes emerged: "one, that Arabs only understand force and, two, that the biggest weakness of Arabs is shame and humiliation." In turn, such ideas about the way Arabs can be broken found their way into the so called the Pride and Ego–Down Approach, a particularly subjugating form of psychological torture "legitimately" exerted by U.S. interrogators in order to break their detainees:

> The government consultant said that there may have been a serious goal, in the beginning, behind the sexual humiliation and the posed photographs. It was thought that some prisoners would do anything—including spying on their associates—to avoid dissemination of the shameful photos to family and friends. The government consultant said, "I was told that the purpose of the photographs was to create an army of informants, people you could insert back in the population." The idea was that they would be motivated by fear of exposure, and gather information about pending insurgency action, the consultant said. If so, it wasn't effective; the insurgency continued to grow.[28]

I am conscious that one has to be very careful with sources that remain unnamed, especially when they are cited by journalists. But I have decided to use this material because in this specific case there is enough independent evidence to support the type of racist attitude I am alluding to, for instance in this account of Brigadier General Janis L. Karpinski given during an interview conducted at Camp Doha on 15 February 2004:

> It became sport. ... [E]ven saying this makes me feel sick to my stomach, but, they were enjoying what they were doing and the MPs who saw this opportunity—seized the opportunity. ... I would imagine ... it went something like this—in the DFAC or when they were sitting around the Internet Café. 'Oh yeah, you should see what we do to the prisoners sometime.' 'Can I come over and watch?' 'Oh yeah. How about Thursday.' And because we had a clerk over there who was thoroughly enjoying all of this sport, and the pictures anyway, and she was the girlfriend of the guy who was one of the kingpins in this. We had a guy from the maintenance who must have been one of the invited participants and—these are bad people. That was the first time I knew that they would do such a thing as to bring a dog handler in there to use for interrogation.[29]

Even more insidious examples include incidents when detainees were referred to as "Jihad Jerry," "Gus," "Shitboy," "one of the three wise men," or when they were told to "curse" Islam.[30] Moreover, at Abu Ghraib, loyalty to Islam was turned into an expedient vehicle to extract "critical intelligence" from detainees through psychological torture. In a Memorandum, dated 20 November 2003, a "request for exception to CJTF [Combined Joint Taskforce]-7 Interrogation and Counter Resistance Policy" was made (essentially, a measure to extend the legal boundaries for interrogation). The subject in this particular case was a Syrian male and an "admitted foreign fighter who came to commit Jihad against Coalition Forces in Iraq" and who was "captured in an attempted IED attack in Baghdad."[31] The detainee is thought to be "at the point where he is resigned to the hope that Allah will see him through this episode in his life, therefore he feels no need to speak with interrogators." He thus has to be "put in a position where he will feel that the only option to get out of jail is to speak with interrogators."[32] To that end:

> [i]interrogators will reinforce the fact that we have attempted to help him time and time again and that they are now putting it in Allah's hands. Interrogators will at maximum throw tables, chairs, invade his personal space and continuously yell at the detainee. Interrogators will not physically touch or harm the detainee ... If the detainee has not broken yet, interrogators will move into the segregation phase of the approach. ... During transportation, the Fear up Harsh approach will be continued, highlighting the Allah factor. ... MP working dogs will be present and barking during this phase. Detainee will be strip searched by guards with the empty sandbag over his head for the safety of himself, prison guards, interrogators and other prisoners. Interrogators will wait outside the room while detainee is strip searched. Interrogators will watch from a distance while detainee is placed in the segregation cell. Detainee will be put on the adjusted sleep schedule ... for 72 hours. Interrogations will be conducted continuously during this 72 hour period. The approaches which will be used during this phase will include, fear up harsh, pride and ego down, silence and loud music. Stress positions will also be used in accordance with CJTF-7 IROE in order to intensify this approach.[33]

This passage links up with many arguments I have made thus far: the technical language provides an example for the type of scientific torture I have mentioned at the beginning of this section and the constant reference to "the Allah factor" further elaborates on the type of culturally coded racism that is at stake here. Consciously, through the myth of Iraqi complicity in 9/11, and unconsciously, through the constant vilification of Islamic culture in the international media, the war on terror was charged with racism against Iraqis, Afghans, Arabs, and Muslims. As one U.S. soldier put it: "I think part of the problem is the blatant racism against the Arabs. When you have an enemy you kind of have to demonize them a little bit like that in order to make yourself capable of pulling a trigger."[34] "Predisposition + opportunity," General Taguba establishes later "= criminal behavior." U.S. soldiers were suddenly "immersed in the Islamic culture, a culture that many were encountering for a first time. Clearly there are major differences in worship and beliefs, and there is the association of Muslims with terrorism." Consequently, all of these "causes exaggerate differences and create misperceptions that can lead to fear or devaluation of a people."[35]

A New Form of Bio-Politics

Abu Ghraib exemplifies that today politics is enacted in systematic practices that target the body. But these micro-practices are embedded and enveloped by a larger, cultural regime of truth. The war on terror was "bio-political" in the "micro" sense because it was meant to discipline and punish its targets all the way down to their consciousness and it was bio-political from a "macro" perspective because it was charged with racist narratives that gained impetus in the aftermath of the terrorist attacks on the United States in September 2001. This racist momentum, galvanized by a less primitive discourse of civilizational superiority among the political mainstream, was very functional to process the war and to administer and abet the torture regime that sustained it. In the war on terror, bio-power, defined by Foucault as the systematic control and subjugation of a population for the purpose of discipline and punishment, was meant to break the humanity of the inmates and the torturer; it was meant to cause regression from something the Iranian revolutionary thinker Ali Shariati termed *insaniyat* or "humaneness," the disruption of the common humanity of us and them and the innumerable linkages that this inescapable dialectic reveals.[36] This seems to indicate that today bio-power is by far more destructive than Foucault imagined.

The progression in the force of bio-power becomes apparent when we consider Foucault's history of the disappearance of torture as a public spectacle in eighteenth-century Europe and America. "By the end of the eighteenth and the beginning of the nineteenth century," Foucault argues, "the gloomy festival of punishment was dying out, though here and there it flickered momentarily into life."[37] In France the *amende honorable* was finally abolished in 1830. Another practice of public punishment and ridicule, the pillory, was abolished in France in 1789 and in England in 1837. In most countries of Western Europe and the United States official public executions preceded by torture had almost entirely been abolished by the middle of the nineteenth century. "One no longer touched the body," Foucault writes:

> If it is still necessary for the law to reach and manipulate the body of the convict, it will be at a distance, in the proper way, according to strict rules, and

with a much 'higher' aim … Today a doctor must watch over those condemned to death [Foucault wrote before the death penalty was abolished in France] … thus juxtaposing himself as the agent of welfare, as the alleviator of pain, with the official whose task it is to end life. … A utopia of judicial reticence: take away life, but prevent the patient from feeling it; deprive the prisoner of all rights, but do not inflict pain; impose penalties free of all pain.[38]

This rationalization of punishment was central to the system of torture at Abu Ghraib (and Guantanamo Bay, too). It explains why Shaker Aamer, who is one of the last remaining British inmates at Guantanamo Bay at the time of writing and who has been held there without a trial for over a decade now, begged to be "tortured the old way" and why he complained that "here they destroy people mentally and physically without leaving marks."[39] But Foucault's Eurocentric empirical material did not allow him to assess how this kind of bio-power was exported to the non-"western" world, how bio-power traveled and revealed itself beyond Europe and the United States. One cannot understand the changes in power (and resistance) from the ancien regime and its notions of royal sovereignty to the (post)modern bio-political state without an understanding of how bio-power reveals itself on a global scale. If anything, I have tried to indicate that analyzing the case of Abu Ghraib (and that of Guantanamo Bay) with an open mind is a good start to appreciate how modern technologies and imperial ideology have merged in order to deliver a bio-political regime that targets the humanity of its subjects with terrifying consequences for the non-western world. However incomplete and eclectic the war on terror is, it stands for the globalization of this kind, of a terrifying bio-political regime. As such, it has added to the legacy of civilizational wars, systematic violence against the other, and scientific racism that have underpinned the various scenes and tragedies of western modernity.

Notes

1. "Full Text of Blair's Speech to the Commons," *The Guardian*, 14 September 2001 (http://www.guardian.co.uk/politics/2001/sep/14/houseofcommons.uk1).
2. Richard Jackson, *Writing the War on Terrorism: Language, Politics and Counter-Terrorism* (Manchester: Manchester University Press, 2005), 59.
3. See, Arshin Adib-Moghaddam, *A Metahistory of the Clash of Civilisations: Us and Them Beyond Orientalism* (London/New York: Hurst/Oxford University Press, 2011) and Arshin Adib-Moghaddam, *On the Arab revolts and the Iranian revolution: Power and resistance today* (London: Bloomsbury, 2013).

4. "The Taguba Report," in *The Torture Papers*, ed. Karen J. Greenberg and Joshua L. Dratel (Cambridge: Cambridge University Press, 2005), 416 (also available at http://news .findlaw.com); see also Mark Danner, *Torture and Truth* (London: Granta, 2004); Jennifer K. Harbury, *Truth, Torture and the American Way* (Boston: Beacon Press, 2005).
5. "Taguba Report," 416.
6. Seymour Hersh, "The General's Report," *The New Yorker*, 25 June 2007 (http://www .newyorker.com/reporting/2007/06/25/070625fa_fact_hersh).
7. "The ICRC Report: Report of the International Committee of the Red Cross (ICRC) on the Treatment by the Coalition Forces of Prisoners of War and Other Protected Persons by the Geneva Conventions in Iraq During Arrest, Internment and Interrogation, February 2004," in *The Torture Papers*, ed. Greenberg and Dratel, 393 [emphasis added] (also available at http://www.globalsecurity.org/military/library/report/2004/icrc_report_ iraq_feb2004.htm).
8. "The Schlesinger Report, Final Report of the Independent Panel to Review DoD Detention Operations, August 2004," in *The Torture Papers*, ed. Greenberg and Dratel, 909 [emphasis added].
9. "The Fay-Jones Report: Investigation of Intelligence Activities at Abu Ghraib, August 2004," *The Torture Papers*, ed. Greenberg and Dratel, 989 [emphasis added].
10. Ibid., 1074.
11. Ibid., 1075.
12. Ibid., 1076.
13. "The Mikolashek Report, July 21, 2004," in *The Torture Papers*, ed. Greenberg and Dratel, 851, 853–54.
14. Ibid., 635.
15. Greenberg and Dratel, eds., *The Torture Papers*, 1132–64.
16. Jeffrey R. Smith, "Hussein's Pre-war Ties with al-Qaeda Discounted: Pentagon Report Says Contacts Were Limited," *The Washington Post*, 6 April 2007 (http://www.washing tonpost.com/wp-dyn/content/article/2007/04/05/AR2007040502263.html).
17. "Medical Complicity in Torture at Guantánamo Bay: Evidence Is the First Step Toward Justice," *PloS Med* 8, no. 4 (2011), 1–2.
18. Irving Kristol, "The Neoconservative Persuasion," in *Neoconservatism*, ed. Irwin Stelzer (London: Atlantic, 2004), 36–37.
19. Donald Kagan, Gary Schmitt, and Thomas Donnelly, "Rebuilding America's Defenses: Strategy, Forces and Resources for a New Century," in *The Project for the New American Century* (September 2000).
20. "The National Security Strategy of the United States of America, September 2002" (http://www.whitehouse.gov/nsc/nss.pdf).
21. David Frum and Richard Perle, *An End to Evil: How to Win the War on Terror* (New York: Ballantine Books, 2004), 34–35.
22. Ibid., 239.
23. Anne Norton, *Leo Strauss and the Politics of American Empire* (London: Yale University Press, 2004), 212.
24. Zbigniew Brzezinski, "Terrorized by 'War on Terror': How a Three-word Mantra Has Undermined America," *The Washington Post*, 25 March 2007.
25. Seymour M. Hersh, "The Gray Zone: How a Secret Pentagon Program came to Abu Ghraib," *The New Yorker*, 24 May 2004.
26. Raphael Patai, *The Arab Mind* (New York: Charles Scribner's Sons, 1983), 128.
27. Ibid., 133–34.
28. Hersh, "The Gray Zone"; Trish Schuh, "Racism and Religious Desecration as U.S. Policy: Islamophobia a Retrospective," *Counterpunch*, 6/7 May 2006.
29. "The Taguba Report (Annex)," in *The Torture Papers*, ed. Greenberg and Dratel, 530–31.
30. Ibid., 472, 504, 522, 524.

31. Ibid., 466.
32. Ibid., 466.
33. Ibid., 467.
34. "No Blood, No Foul: Soldiers Accounts of Detainee Abuse in Iraq," *Human Rights Watch,* 18, no. 3 (July 2006), 34.
35. "The Taguba Report," in *The Torture Papers,* ed. Greenberg and Dratel, 449.
36. Ali Shariati, "Humanity and Islam," in *Liberal Islam: A Sourcebook,* ed. Charles Kuzman (Oxford: Oxford University Press, 1998), 188–89.
37. Michel Foucault, *Discipline and Punish: The Birth of the Prison* (London: Penguin, 1991), 8.
38. Ibid., 11.
39. "Ten years after his arrival in Guantanamo Bay, British resident Shaker Aamer remains held under the harshest conditions." *Reprieve,* 14 February 2012 (http://www.reprieve .org.uk/press/2012_02_14_shaker_ten_years/).

Contributors

Arshin Adib-Moghaddam is Professor of Global Thought and Comparative Philosophies and Chair of the Centre for Iranian Studies at SOAS, University of London. He is the author of several books including *A Metahistory of the Clash of Civilisations: Us and Them Beyond Orientalism* (2011) and *On the Arab Revolts and the Iranian Revolution: Power and Resistance Today* (2013). Cambridge educated, he was the first Jarvis Doctorow Fellow in International Relations and Peace Studies at St. Edmund Hall and the Department of Politics and International Relations at University of Oxford. His writings have been translated into many languages and he is a frequent contributor to leading newspapers and TV channels around the world.

Lloyd Ambrosius is the Samuel Clark Waugh Distinguished Professor of International Relations and Professor of History at the University of Nebraska–Lincoln. He is the author of *Woodrow Wilson and the American Diplomatic Tradition: The Treaty Fight in Perspective* (1987) and *Wilsonianism: Woodrow Wilson and His Legacy in American Foreign Relations* (2002). He was the Mary Ball Washington Professor of American History at University College, Dublin, Ireland, and a Fulbright Professor twice in Germany, at the University of Cologne and the University of Heidelberg. He specializes in the history of U.S. foreign relations and the history of the American presidency.

Michael Patrick Cullinane is Senior Lecturer of U.S. History at Northumbria University, Newcastle. He is the author of *Liberty and American Anti-Imperialism* and numerous articles on diplomatic history in the Gilded Age and Progressive era. He is currently researching a monograph on the legacy of Theodore Roosevelt through pop culture, sites of memorialization, and political co-option.

Jack P. Greene is Andrew W. Mellon Professor in the Humanities, Emeritus at Johns Hopkins University and invited Research Scholar at the John Carter Brown Library at Brown University. He is one of the world's most prolific writers on colonial British and revolutionary America. His recent books include *The Constitutional Origins of the American Revolution* (2011), *Evaluating Empire and Confronting Colonialism in Eighteenth Century Britain* (2013), *Creating the British Atlantic: Essays on Transplantation, Adaptation, and Continuity* (2013), and *The Intellectual Construction of America: Exceptionalism and Identity* (1993).

Walter L. Hixson is Distinguished Professor of History at the University of Akron. He is the author of *American Settler Colonialism: A History* (2013); *The Myth of American Diplomacy: National Identity and U.S. Foreign Policy* (2008); and *Parting the Curtain: Propaganda, Culture and the Cold War, 1945-1961* (1997).

Michaela Hoenicke Moore is Associate Professor in History at the University of Iowa. She is the author of *Know Your Enemy: The American Debate on Nazism, 1933-1945* (2010), which won the 2010 Myrna F. Bernath Book Award awarded by the Society for Historians of American Foreign Relations (SHAFR) and is currently working on a study of American patriotism and U.S. foreign policy debates since World War II.

Kristin Hoganson is Professor of History at the University of Illinois at Urbana-Champaign and an expert on the history of globalization, cultures of imperialism, and the United States in world context. Her recent books include *Consumers' Imperium: The Global Production of American Domesticity, 1865-1920* (2007) and *Fighting for American Manhood: How Gender Politics Provoked the Spanish-American War and Philippine-American War* (1998). Both have challenged the way scholars look at U.S. foreign policy.

Liam Kennedy is Professor of American Studies and Director of the Clinton Institute at University College Dublin. He has diverse research interests and teaching experiences, spanning the fields of American urban studies, visual culture, globalization, and transatlantic relations. He is the author of *Susan Sontag: Mind as Passion* (1995) and *Race and Urban Space in American Culture* (2000), and is currently researching a monograph on photography and international conflict as well as preparing two edited books—on urban photography, and on cultural diplomacy and U.S. foreign policy.

Geraldine Kidd is a Ph.D. candidate at University College Cork, Ireland. Her dissertation examines the orientalist impulse of Eleanor Roosevelt in relation to Palestine. Her research is an investigation of both identity and alterity and dissects a regular subject of scholarly intrigue from a remarkable new angle.

Marco Mariano is Assistant Professor of Contemporary History at University of Eastern Piedmont, Vercelli. His research examines Euro-American relations since World War II, inter-American relations, modern Atlantic history, and the history of postwar U.S. liberalism. His latest publications include *L'America nell'"occidente". Storia della dottrina Monroe, 1823-1963* (2013), as author, and *Defining the Atlantic Community: Culture, Intellectuals and Policies in the Mid-Twentieth Century* (2010), as editor.

David Ryan is Professor and Chair of Modern History at University College Cork, Ireland. He has published extensively on contemporary history and U.S. foreign policy, concentrating on the interventions in the post-Vietnam era, including Central America, Angola, Vietnam, and the Middle East, among other places. His publications include: *US-Sandinista Diplomatic Relations* (1995), *US Foreign Policy in World History* (2000), and *Frustrated Empire* (2007). He has co-edited *The United States and Decolonization* (2000), *Vietnam in Iraq* (2007), and *America and Iraq* (2009).

Selected Bibliography

Adib-Moghaddam, Arshin. *A Metahistory of the Clash of Civilisations: Us and Them Beyond Orientalism.* London: Hurst & Company, 2011.

Ali, Tariq. *The Clash of Fundamentalisms: Crusades, Jihads and Modernity.* London: Verso, 2002.

Alpers, Benjamin Leontief. *Dictators, Democracy, and American Public Culture Envisioning the Totalitarian Enemy, 1920s-1950s.* Chapel Hill: University of North Carolina Press, 2003.

Baumann, Gerd, and Andre Gingrich, eds. *Grammars of Identity/Alterity: A Structural Approach.* New York: Berghahn Books, 2004.

Bourdieu, Pierre, and Randal Johnson. *The Field of Cultural Production: Essays on Art and Literature.* New York: Columbia University Press, 1993.

Bowden, Brett. *The Empire of Civilization: The Evolution of an Imperial Idea.* Chicago: University of Chicago Press, 2009.

Brody, David. *Visualizing American Empire: Orientalism and Imperialism in the Philippines.* Chicago: University of Chicago Press, 2010.

Browitt, Jeff, and Brian Nelson, eds. *Practicing Theory: Pierre Bourdieu and the Field of Cultural Production.* Newark: University of Delaware Press, 2004.

Bruyneel, Kevin. *The Third Space of Sovereignty: The Postcolonial Politics of U.S.-Indigenous Relations.* Minneapolis: University of Minnesota Press, 2007.

Campbell, David. *Writing Security: United States Foreign Policy and the Politics of Identity.* Minneapolis: University of Minnesota Press, 1998.

Christie, Kenneth, ed. *United States Foreign Policy and National Identity in the 21st Century.* New York: Routledge, 2010.

Cohen, Warren I., Michigan State University, and Asian Studies Center. *Reflections on Orientalism: Edward Said, Roger Besnahan, Surjit Dulai, Edward Graham, and Donald Lammers.* East Lansing: Michigan State University Press, 1983.

Daunton, Martin J., and Rick Halpern. *Empire and Others: British Encounters with Indigenous Peoples, 1600-1850.* Philadelphia: University of Pennsylvania Press, 1999.

Docherty, Thomas. *Alterities: Criticism, History, Representation.* New York: Oxford University Press, 1996.

Dower, John W. *Cultures of War: Pearl Harbor/Hiroshima/9-11/Iraq.* New York: W. W. Norton, 2010.

Fantina, Robert. *Desertion and the American Soldier, 1776-2006.* New York: Algora Publishing, 2006.

Foucault, Michel. *The Archaeology of Knowledge.* London: Routledge, 1989.

Geertz, Clifford. *The Interpretation of Cultures.* London: Fontana, 1993 [1973].

Gerstle, Gary. *American Crucible: Race and Nation in the Twentieth Century.* Princeton: Princeton University Press, 2001.

Halliday, Fred. *Two Hours that Shook the World: September 11, 2001: Causes and Consequences.* London: Saqi Books, 2002.

Hazell, Clive. *Alterity: The Experience of the Other.* Bloomington, IN: Authorhouse, 2009.

Hixson, Walter L. *The Myth of American Diplomacy: National Identity and U.S. Foreign Policy.* New Haven: Yale University Press, 2008.

Hunt, Michael H. *Ideology and U.S. Foreign Policy.* New Haven: Yale University Press, 1987.

Hymans, Jacques E.C. *The Psychology of Nuclear Proliferation Identity, Emotions and Foreign Policy.* Cambridge; New York: Cambridge University Press, 2006.

Jacobson, Matthew Frye. *Barbarian Virtues: The United States Encounters Foreign Peoples at Home and Abroad, 1876-1917.* New York: Hill & Wang, 2000.

Joseph, G.M., Catherine LeGrand, and Ricardo Donato Salvatore. *Close Encounters of Empire: Writing the Cultural History of U.S.-Latin American Relations.* Durham, NC: Duke University Press, 1998.

Kaplan, Amy, and Donald E. Pease, eds. *Cultures of United States Imperialism.* Durham, NC: Duke University Press, 1993.

Kapuściński, Ryszard. *The Other.* New York: Verso, 2008.

King, Desmond S. *Making Americans: Immigration, Race, and the Origins of the Diverse Democracy.* Cambridge, MA: Harvard University Press, 2000.

Knauft, Bruce M. *Critically Modern Alternatives, Alterities, Anthropologies.* Bloomington: Indiana University Press, 2002.

Lepore, Jill. *The Name of War: King Philip's War and the Origins of American Identity.* New York: Vintage, 1999.

Little, Douglas. *American Orientalism: The United States and the Middle East since 1945.* London: I.B. Tauris, 2002.

MacKenzie, John M. *Orientalism: History, Theory, and the Arts.* Manchester: Manchester University Press, 1995.

McAlister, Melani. *Epic Encounters: Culture, Media, and U.S. Interests in the Middle East, 1945-2000.* Berkeley: University of California Press, 2001.

McCoy, Alfred W, and Francisco A Scarano. *The Colonial Crucible Empire in the Making of the Modern American State.* Madison: University of Wisconsin Press, 2009.

Memmi, Albert. *The Colonizer and the Colonized.* Boston: Beacon Press, 1965.

Mohanty, J.N. *The Self and Its Other: Philosophical Essays.* New Delhi; New York: Oxford University Press, 2000.

Nandy, Ashis. *The Intimate Enemy: Loss and Recovery of Self under Colonialism.* New York: Oxford University Press, 1983.

Nealon, Jeffrey T. *Alterity Politics: Ethics and Performative Subjectivity.* Durham, NC: Duke University Press, 1998.

Parmar, Inderjeet, Linda B. Miller, and Mark Ledwidge. *New Directions in US Foreign Policy.* New York: Routledge, 2009.

Rifkin, Mark. *Manifesting America: The Imperial Construction of U.S. National Space.* New York: Oxford University Press, 2009.

Roberts, Kathleen. *Alterity and Narrative Stories and the Negotiation of Western Identities.* Albany: State University of New York Press, 2007.

Ryan, David. *Frustrated Empire: US Foreign Policy, 9/11 to Iraq.* London: Pluto, 2007.

———. *US Foreign Policy in World History.* London: Routledge, 2000.

Rydell, Robert W. *All the World's a Fair: Visions of Empire at American International Expositions, 1876-1916.* Chicago: University of Chicago Press, 1984.

Said, Edward W. *Culture and Imperialism.* New York: Knopf, 1993.

———. *Orientalism.* New York: Vintage Books, 1979.

———. "The Clash of Definitions," in *Reflections on Exile and Other Literary and Cultural Essays.* London: Granta, 2000.

Schroeder, William Ralph. *Sartre and His Predecessors: The Self and the Other.* London: Routledge, 1984.

Schueller, Malini Johar. *U.S. Orientalisms: Race, Nation, and Gender in Literature, 1790-1890.* Ann Arbor: University of Michigan Press, 1998.

Schulten, Susan. *The Geographical Imagination in America, 1880-1950.* Chicago: University of Chicago Press, 2001.

Shannon, Christopher. *A World Made Safe for Differences: Cold War Intellectuals and the Politics of Identity.* Lanham, MD: Rowman and Littlefield, 2001.

Silver, Peter Rhoads. *Our Savage Neighbors: How Indian War Transformed Early America.* New York: W. W. Norton, 2008.

Stephanson, Anders. *Manifest Destiny: American Expansionism and the Empire of Right.* New York: Hill & Wang, 1995.

Telhami, Shibley, and Michael N Barnett. *Identity and Foreign Policy in the Middle East.* Ithaca, NY: Cornell University Press, 2002.

Todorov, Tzvetan. *The Conquest of America: The Question of the Other.* New York: Harper & Row, 1984.

Vaughan, Alden T. *Roots of American Racism: Essays on the Colonial Experience.* New York: Oxford University Press, 1995.

Index

www.ingramcontent.com/pod-product-compliance
Lightning Source LLC
Chambersburg PA
CBHW060034030426

42334CB00019B/2317